Frommer's™

BRITAI

FREE

GREAT DAYS OUT THAT WON'T BREAK THE BANK

BEN AND DINAH HATCH

John Wiley & Sons, Ltd

UK Publisher: Sally Smith
Executive Project Editor: Daniel Mersey
Commissioning Editor: Mark Henshall
Development Editor: Sasha Heseltine
Project Editor: Hannah Clement
Photo Research: Jill Emeny
Cartography: Jeremy Norton
Photos: front cover © Britain on View/Photolibrary; back cover © age footstock/Photolibrary; p. viii © Ronald Weir/TTL; p. 4 © Alan Copson/TTL; p. 58 © Paul Mattock/Fotolibra; p. 88 © Destination Bristol; p. 122 © Mark Burrows/Shutterstock; p. 146 © David Jones/Alamy; p. 166 © Paul Reid/Shutterstock; p. 186 © Darryl Sleath / Shutterstock; p. 210 © David Gowans/Alamy

Wiley also publishes its books in a variety of electronic formats. Some content that appears in print may not be available in electronic books.

British Library Cataloguing in Publication Data

A catalogue record for this book is available from the British Library

ISBN: 978-0-470-68841-0 (pbk), ISBN: 978-0-470-66739-2 (ebk)

Typeset by Wiley Indianapolis Composition Services

Printed and bound in Great Britain by TJ International Ltd

5 4 3 2 1

CONTENTS

About the Authors

Ben Hatch started out as a tea boy in the Royal Bank of Scotland. He became a recruitment consultant, sold advertising space then lawnmowers, worked in a video shop, as a postman and on the McDonald chicken sandwich station before finally becoming a journalist on various local papers. He quit reporting to become a novelist in 1997. He has written two works of Comedy fiction, *The Lawnmower Celebrity* and *The International Gooseberry* and is now on his third. Ben was tempted into travel writing by his wife Dinah who he lives with in Brighton. Together they authored *Frommer's Scotland With Your Family* and *Frommer's England With Your Family*.

Dinah Hatch went into travel journalism after deciding that crime reporting for local papers involved just a few too many evenings talking to dodgy people in dark alleys. Since then she has worked for a variety of national newspapers, magazines, trade publications and websites and writes extensively for the travel industry. Dinah co-authored *Frommer's Scotland With Your Family* and *Frommer's England With Your Family*.

Acknowledgments

To Sasha Heseltine for her edit, Mark Henshall for his helpful steering, Jill Emeny for image help and Charlotte Tomkins and Emma Knott for their contributions.

Dedication

The book is dedicated to my brother Buster, who I once argued with for three solid days about whether there is such a thing as garlic salami, and my sister Penny for the chicken soup she saved me from aged 11.

An Invitation to the Reader

In researching this book, we discovered many wonderful places—hotels, restaurants, shops, and more. We're sure you'll find others. Please tell us about them, so we can share the information with your fellow travellers in upcoming editions. If you were disappointed with a recommendation, we'd love to know that, too. Please e-mail frommers@wiley.com.uk or write to:

Frommer's Britain for Free, 1st Edition
John Wiley & Sons, Ltd, The Atrium, Southern Gate,
Chichester, West Sussex PO19 8SQ

An Additional Note

Please be advised that travel information is subject to change at any time—and this is especially true of prices. We therefore suggest that you write or call ahead for confirmation when making your travel plans. The authors, editors, and publisher cannot be held responsible for the experiences of readers while travelling. Your safety is important to us, however, so we encourage you to stay alert and be aware of your surroundings. Keep a close eye on cameras, purses, and wallets, all favourite targets of thieves and pickpockets.

Britain for Free Icons

We also use a number of icons that point you to the type of attraction you can visit and the amenities available. Throughout the book, look for:

★ Special find – those places only insiders know about

♥ Best bets for kids

☂ Attractions perfect for those less than perfect weather days

☺ Something a bit different!

🌐 Attractions employing responsible tourism policies

⊖ Tube stop

And the amenities:

☕	Café	🛍	Shop
📶	Café with WiFi	🐔	Farm shop
🍴	Restaurant	⛱	Picnic area
🍸	Bar	⋀	Play park
🥤	Pub	👟	Kid's trail
🍦	Snack bar	✿	Garden
🪑	Highchairs	🛠	Garden centre
🧸	Toys	Ⓥ	Visitor centre
P	Car parking	🗺	Maps
£	Car parking (pay & display)	🎧	Free audio guide
P	Park & Ride	ⓘ	Free leaflet
🚲	Cycle hire	BF	Breast Feeding
🛒	Buggy access	🚿	Shower
♿	Wheelchair access		

Frommers.com

Now that you have this guidebook to help you plan a great trip, visit our website at **www.frommers.com** for additional travel information on more than 4,000 destinations. We update features regularly to give you instant access to the most current trip-planning information available. At Frommers. com, you'll find scoops on the best airfares, accommodation rates, and car rental bargains. You can even book your travel online through our reliable travel booking partners. Other popular features include:

- Online updates of our most popular guidebooks
- Holiday sweepstakes and contest giveaways
- Newsletters highlighting the hottest travel trends
- Podcasts, interactive maps, and up-to-the-minute events listings
- Opinionated blog entries by Arthur Frommer himself
- Online travel message boards with featured travel discussions

Ben Nevis.

INTRODUCTION

Before we started to discover what was out there, we had a few sleepless nights panicking about what we could find for free in Britain. We had terrible illusions of dragging the family around dusty museums full of shards of Roman pottery in forgotten glass display cabinets and of having to point out things like, 'Hey look – another sharp stone that might have been a flint thousands of years ago'. We'd be sitting in forlorn parks talking up a dilapidated roundabout and a rusty slide. Or else we'd have to write entirely on the beaches of our coastline, typing endless pages on the quality of the sand for sandcastle building. This worry was, of course, totally needless. It is staggering what there is to do for free in Britain. In London, most of the top museums are free. It is the same in Liverpool, Glasgow and also, surprisingly, Hull. Elsewhere you can go on boat rides and enjoy comedy nights or classical music concerts. Experience steam-train rides, castles, country houses, music festivals, guided walking tours, farms and big-screen movies – all for free. Enrol on fitness courses, see many of the world's most famous paintings, visit the world's only baked-bean museum, see a lock of Nelson's hair, Winston Churchill's dentures and the skeleton of Napoleon's horse. Attend Britain's liveliest pageants. Scale Big Ben, visit the Houses of Parliament or see a record-breaking wind-powered car. Enjoy great views, cycle routes, climbing mountains and rambling across moors.

There are the scores of off-beat British festivals – the Orange Races of Totnes, cheese rolling in Cheltenham or barrel rolling in Westelton. See the World Nettle Eating Championships, the World Gurning Championships and the Stone Skimming Championships. And is there any other country in the world where you can see fleas dressed as Mexican dancers? We doubt it.

And that's not to mention all the museums. We could have filled the entire book with these, not to mention the great parks and scenic beaches. In the end, it was more a question of what to leave out than in. We will, of course, have missed out many attractions, and you might disagree with some of our choices, although we hope you get something out of those we've written about. There are two attractions we have included that have a small fee – one is £1 and another is £2. They were too good to miss out in our opinion. We hope you have as much fun reading and using this book as we had researching it.

The British Museum.

LONDON

There cannot be a city in the world with more free things to do than London. As well as the world-beating Natural History Museum with its enormous blue whale and robot dinosaurs, the interactive Science Museum and the British Museum, home to the world-famous Rosetta Stone, there's plenty of royal pomp. Highlights include Changing the Guard at Buckingham Palace, the Ceremony of the Keys at the Tower of London and Trooping the Colour. The Oxford and Cambridge boat race is staged annually along the Thames, while the colourful Notting Hill Carnival is the biggest of its kind in Europe. There's the celebrity chef endorsed Borough Market that's fantastic for food shopping, while free comedy nights are staged at the Theatre Royal in Stratford, master-classes at the Royal Academy of Music and concerts at the Royal Opera House. There are Jack the Ripper walking tours for the ghoulish, bird walks in Regent's Park and the deer to take in at Richmond Park. You can start a revolution from Speaker's Corner in Hyde Park or plant a foot on each side of the globe on the Greenwich Meridian line at the Royal Observatory. Art highlights include the Turners at Tate Britain, while the National Gallery is home to more than 2,300 paintings. You can catch the evocative Woolwich Ferry on the Thames, climb to the top of Big Ben and enjoy an open-air show at the Scoop arena, while there are a host of lesser known highlights. You can see the remains of Napoleon's horse at the National Army Museum, a whale penis at the Horniman Museum, and the foetus of a cyclops child at the Hunterian Museum.

1 Getting Around London

The easiest way to get around London is by Tube, and Travelcards are the best value for visitors using the underground, plus they are also valid on bus, tram and DLR services. The most useful tickets for visitors are available as one-day or one-week Travelcards. See www.tfl.gov.uk/tickets for all the different combinations available and buy online ahead of time. Otherwise buy Travelcards in Tube stations, where an adult day ticket costs £8.60 for Zones 1–3 (check on the Tube map to see which zones you need to cover), and a seven-day ticket is £30.20.

❶ JOIN A TOUR OF THE NATIONAL GALLERY

Trafalgar Square, London WC2 5DN (ⓒ **020 7747 2885**, www.nationalgallery.org.uk). ⊖ Charing Cross.

Housing one of the greatest collections of western European paintings in the world, there are more than 2,300 masterpieces here by artists ranging from Leonardo Da Vinci and Vincent van Gogh through to Gainsborough, Cezanne, Rembrandt and Michelangelo. You can join free tours to have works of art explained, and there are often hands-on activities in the education centre (check times) for 5–11 year olds as well as workshops for 12–17 year olds. There are roughly four temporary exhibitions a year, usually relating to the permanent collection.

OPEN   Daily 10am–6pm (Fri 10am–9pm).

AMENITIES   ☕ 🍴 🛍 🅿

❷ CHECK OUT PAINTINGS OF SHAKESPEARE & DAVID BECKHAM AT THE NATIONAL PORTRAIT GALLERY

2 St Martin's Place, London WC2H 0HE (✆ **020 7312 2463** or **020 7306 0055**, www. npg.org.uk). ⊖ Charing Cross.

Here you'll find hundreds of portraits of famous Britons ranging all the way from one of William Shakespeare to a study of David Beckham. Among the 120,000 works here about 1,000 are on display including pictures of Samuel Johnson, Judi Dench, the Brontë sisters, the Beatles, Benjamin Disraeli, Lord Nelson and Napoleon. There's also an extensive photography collection featuring a very annoying one of a bare-chested Sting taken by Terry O'Neil; my wife lingered far too long over this.

OPEN   Daily 10am–6pm (Thurs–Fri 10am–9pm)

AMENITIES   ☕ 🍴 🛍 🅿

❸ HEAR TOP MUSICIANS PLAY AT ST-MARTIN-IN-THE-FIELDS

Trafalgar Square, London WC2N 4JJ (✆ **020 7766 1100**, www.smitf.org). ⊖ Charing Cross.

An unbroken 60-year tradition that began to boost civilian morale in World War II sees top classical musicians perform here for free every Monday, Tuesday and Friday lunchtimes. Past performers at this church have included Benjamin Britten, Peter Pears and Myra Hess. The music ranges from Bach and Bartok through to Bernstein and Stravinsky. The concerts last 45 minutes and audiences average around 250, so come early to get a good seat. The church itself is the most famous non-cathedral place of worship in the country and has a history of radicalism. Desmond Tutu regularly preaches here and, as the parish church to the Royal Family, Prince Charles and the Duchess of Cornwall also knee-bend here. Famously designed by James

Gibbs, and much copied in America, the church was where Thomas Chippendale of furniture-making fame, and Nell Gwyn, the actress mistress of Charles II, were buried before all the bodies in the church-yard were exhumed and moved elsewhere.

OPEN   Daily 8am–5pm (depending on services).

AMENITIES ☕ 🛍 🚻

❹ SEE THE GHOST OF LORD NELSON AT SOMERSET HOUSE

The Strand, London WC2R 1LA (☎ **020 7845 4600**, www.somersethouse.org.uk). ⊖ Temple.

On free guided tours you learn how the first perforated stamps were invented here, about the ghost of Lord Nelson, who haunts the court-yard, and also about its role in two contemporary films – Guy Ritchie's *Sherlock Holmes* and *Last Chance Harvey* starring Emma Thompson and Dustin Hoffman. On the 45-minute tour, hear how Lord Nelson visited Somerset House many times to see his brother Maurice, who worked for the Navy Board. His ghost, we were told, moves from King's College through to the courtyard. You'll also see the under-ground Dead House, containing the relocated graves of people bur-ied in the chapel of the Tudor palace formerly on this site. You might, however, also get called Stanley (after stamp giant Stanley Gibbons) by your wife, who feels it's funny to tease you about your stamp-col-lecting past. Also free on Mondays between 10am–2pm is access to the Courtauld Gallery (normally £5), containing a famous Van Gogh self-portrait as well as Manet's celebratory *Bar at the Folies-Bergère* and other Impressionist and Post-Impressionist works. Visiting exhibi-tions have included works by Michelangelo, Renoir, Rubens and Dégas. The Terrace Room is also free to explore and features London-specific exhibitions, which have included photos by Norman Parkin-son and displays on urban regeneration. Attractions within the complex that charge admission include a winter ice-rink, an open-air cinema and the Embankment Gallery (£5).

OPEN   Daily 10am–6pm.

AMENITIES ☕ 🍴 🛍 🚻

❺ VISIT THE OLDEST WINE BAR IN BRITAIN

Gordon's Wine Bar, 47 Villiers Street, London WC2N 6NE (✆ **020 7930 1408**, www. gordonswinebar.com). ⊖ Charing Cross or Embankment.

This famous canoodler's paradise opened in 1890 and was where Lawrence Olivier wooed Vivien Leigh. It was the home of diarist Samuel Pepys in the 17th century and Rudyard Kipling was once a tenant here. With its low vaulted ceilings and semi-dark candlelit cellar, the bar has a timeless feel that made us think that a black-capped highwayman might burst in at any moment, level a smoking pistol at our heads and demand a mouthful of our nibbles before bounding off to rob the night-bus. They serve great bread and cheese and the only problem is getting a table, so get there early.

OPEN   Mon–Sat 8:30am–11pm; Sun midday–10pm.

AMENITIES   ♙♙♙ �️ ▪

❻ LEARN ABOUT DR CRIPPEN & CHARLES DICKENS ON A WALKING TOUR OF COVENT GARDEN

London WC2 (www.coventgardenlondonuk.com/assets/CG-Walking-Guide-DL1.pdf). ⊖ Covent Garden or Leicester Square.

★

One of London's most colourful corners is the vibrant square of Covent Garden, where George Bernard Shaw found his inspiration for *Pygmalion* while watching flower girls selling violets to wealthy opera goers. Although the old fruit-and-veg traders have been replaced with an antiques and crafts market, and the flower girls and prostitutes of Shaw's time have given way to East European acrobats and fey-looking violinists, the area still bustles with activity. To learn how the area once looked, there's a wonderful self-guided walking tour taking in Wellington Street, where Charles Dickens once worked for the magazine *All the Year Round*, and Will's Coffee House on Bow Street, the literary hang-out for writers and poets including Samuel Johnson, Alexander Pope, John Dryden and Jonathan Swift. The tour takes you past the Royal Opera House, where Wagner's *The Ring* was first performed in England, and the empty shell of Bow Street Magistrates Court, which saw the trials of Oscar Wilde and Dr Crippen. On the tour, taking under an hour, you'll see where the artist Turner was born, the area Alfred Hitchcock based his movie *Frenzy* upon, and the lodgings where Jane Austen stayed when visiting from Bath. The self-guided map and commentary, written by the London chronicler Peter Ackroyd, can be obtained from the above web address.

OPEN Times vary.

AMENITIES ☕ 🍴 ♿

❼ TAKE IN A FREE CONCERT AT THE ROYAL OPERA HOUSE

Royal Opera House, Bow Street, London WC2E 9DD (✆ **020 7304 4000**, www.roh. org.uk). ● Covent Garden.

Arriving early for some Bach Variations at one of the Monday lunch-time concerts here, we killed time wandering around the gilded high-ceilinged rooms of the Royal Opera House Collections, containing, among other things, costumes worn by Margot Fonteyn and Rudolf Nureyev. As we strolled, catching snippets of learned conversation about Verdi and *La Traviata*, both my wife and I started walking with our hands clasped behind our backs the way Prince Charles does when he feels awkward. Thankfully the feeling we didn't quite belong here didn't last long. The free concerts in the Paul Hamlyn Hall start at noon and generally last an hour, and were not just full of Hermès-scarf-wearing ladies who lunch but felt welcoming, even to philistines like us. A proportion of tickets can be booked in advance online, the remaining tickets (160 or so) are available at the Royal Opera House Box Office from 10am on the day of recital.

TIME Midday.

AMENITIES 🍴 🍷 ♿

❽ SNOOP AROUND SIR JOHN SOANE'S MUSEUM

13 Lincoln's Inn Fields, London WC2A 3BP (✆ **020 7405 2107**, www.soane.org). ● Holborn.

Famous for designing the façade of the Bank of England, the architect Sir John Soane (1753–1837) hated his son George so much for taking to novel-writing and being 'a general imbecile' that he declined a baronetcy and left his sumptuous home by Act of Parliament to the nation, specifically to stop his son from inheriting either. The house contains some of the finest Canaletto and Hogarth paintings in the world as well as works by Turner and Joshua Reynolds. When it opened in 1937, it effectively became the world's first design museum, containing neoclassical sculpture, Renaissance antiquities, the finest Chinese tile collection in Europe, a clock owned by Sir Christopher Wren and the only fragment of the Acropolis outside Greece. Sir John Soane, who reminded me very much of my own father, ('Ben, you have written an unpublishable novel with a main character who is if anything even more idiotic than you are'), also designed the dining rooms at both 10 and 11 Downing Street as well the Dulwich Picture Gallery, the model for all subsequent galleries. The best time to visit the museum is on the first Tuesday evening of each month, when there are atmospheric candlelit tours by experienced guides. Get there early to avoid queuing.

OPEN   Tues–Sat 10am–5pm (first Tues of each month 6pm–9pm).

AMENITIES   🛍

❾ WITNESS THE POMP OF THE CHANGING OF THE GUARD

Buckingham Palace, London SW1A 1AA (✆ **020 7414 2353**, www.royal.gov.uk). ⊖ St James's Park or Green Park.

The Changing of the Guard is one of the oldest and most popular cere-monies associated with Buckingham Palace and you can gain much kudos with the tourists outside the gates by loudly declaring as my wife did, that its proper name is, of course, the Guard Mounting. The process of changing the guard is as simple as it sounds. The New Guard exchanges duty with the Old Guard, the hand-over accom-panied by a Guards' band. The music played during the ceremony ranges from traditional military

In or Out?

When the Queen is in there are four sentries posted outside Buckingham Palace and the Royal Standard flies from the mast above the façade. Another giveaway, of course, is the loud rap music emanating from her bedroom window.

marches to songs from musical shows. The Foot Guards are in the full-dress uniform of red tunics and bearskins (great coat order in the winter) and it all takes place in the forecourt of Buckingham Palace at 11:30am, lasting about 45 minutes. It's daily from May until the end of July and on alternate days for the rest of the year. There is no Guard Mounting ceremony in very wet weather.

TIME   11:30am.

AMENITIES   ☕ 🍴 ♿

⑩ WAVE TO THE QUEEN AT TROOPING THE COLOUR

Ticket Office, HQ Household Division, Horse Guards, Whitehall, London SW1A 2AX (✆ 020 7414 2353, www.trooping-the-colour.co.uk). ⊖ St James's Park.

Super Troopers

Once upon a time, before the advent of tourism, the custom of Trooping (carrying) the Colour (regimental emblem) had a practical purpose. The regimental colours were used as a rallying point in war, so it was vital that soldiers recognised them in the confusion of a battle. To this end, the colours were trooped in front of the ranks daily. The custom dates back to the time of King Charles II in the 17th century.

To catch sight of the Queen in person, visit the Trooping of the Colour ceremony held once a year to mark the Queen's official birthday (June) on Horse Guards Parade in St James's Park. Involving much pomp, a lot of sweating in bearskins, some pretty cool marching, clanking metal and jostling for position with fellow royal-watchers, the ceremony sees 1,400 officers and men on parade, together with 200 horses and over 400 musicians from seven military bands and corps of drums and 113 issued words of command. The parade extends from Buckingham Palace along The Mall to Horse Guards Parade, Whitehall and back again. Precisely as the clock on the Horse Guards Building strikes 11:00, the Royal Procession arrives and the Queen takes the Royal Salute. The parade then continues with the Inspection; the Queen drives slowly down the ranks of the Guards and the Household Cavalry. After the event, the Royal Family gathers on the balcony of Buckingham Palace to watch an RAF flypast. Tickets to watch the ceremony from a seated stand in Horse Guards Parade are allocated by ballot. Applications, with a stamped addressed envelope, must be sent to the above address between 1 January and the end of February; the winners are picked out in mid-March. Alternatively, the ceremony may be seen from Horse Guards Parade, Whitehall, and the cavalry division's process to Buckingham Palace from a flag-lined Mall.

DATE & TIME June, 11am. Check website for specific dates.

AMENITIES ☕ 🍴 ♿

⑪ SEE THE STATE OPENING OF PARLIAMENT

The House of Lords, London SW1A 0PW (℃ **020 7219 3107**, www.parliament.uk). ⊖ Westminster.

Taking place between late October and mid-November, depending on when MPs slink back to work from their moated castles, this is another opportunity to see Her Majesty up close and personal. Ever since Charles I was beheaded in 1649, British monarchs have been forbidden to enter the House of Commons. Because of this, the Queen opens Parliament in the House of Lords, sitting on a throne and reading an official speech outlining what's going to happen in the following year's business. The Queen rides from Buckingham Palace to Westminster and back again in the Royal Coach with the Duke of Edinburgh, accompanied by the Yeoman of the Guard and the Household Cavalry. The best available points to catch a glimpse of her regal waving hand are from The Mall and in St James's Park.

DATE & TIME Varies; check website.

AMENITIES ♿

⑫ DROP OFF DURING PRIME MINISTER'S QUESTION TIME

House of Commons, Palace of Westminster, London SW1A 0AA (℃ **020 7219 4272**, www.parliament.uk). ⊖ Westminster.

For a front row seat to watch the inner workings of our several-hundred-year-old working democracy, attend this cornerstone of the

British Parliament in the House of Commons. Many years ago I watched former PM John Major strutting his stuff here during a work experience shift shadowing the political editor of *The Sunday Express* and must confess I felt a tremendous thrill about my proximity to this, the seat of power of our nation, until the dullness of the details of the right-to-roam legislation under discussion hit home and lulled me into a career-damaging snooze in the press gallery. PMQs, as Prime Minister's Question Time is known by us insiders, is staged every Wednesday at midday while Parliament is sitting. Book a ticket several weeks in advance from your local MP (if you are a UK citizen) or your embassy in London (if you're not). To contact your MP, call the number given above and you'll be put through to his well-compensated PA, probably his wife, who may well be lying on a chaise longue flinging high-denomination bank notes into the air and wondering what else her husband can claim on expenses.

DATE & TIME   Varies; check website.

AMENITIES

⑬ GO UP BIG BEN

Palace of Westminster, London SW1 0AA (✆ **020 7219 4272**, www.parliament.uk). ⊖ Westminster.

★ ⚐

You can also ask your MP to arrange for you to go on a tour of 96m-high Big Ben, or the Clock Tower as it is officially known here. Tours of this, the most famous clock in the world and Britain's favourite landmark, are at set times of 9:30am, 10:30am, 11:30am and 2:30pm Monday–Friday with a maximum number of 16 people per tour. Preference is given to people with an interest in clocks, watches and bells, although it has to be a proven one; saying, 'bells are great', or even 'I have several clocks myself and have always liked them' when requesting a visit will get you nowhere. Visitors to the Clock Tower, named after the first commissioner of works, Sir Benjamin Hall, are led by a guide who outlines the history of the tower and the bell and explains the works of the most accurate public clock in the world. Children under the age of 11 and overseas visitors are currently not permitted. Meet at Portcullis House (on the corner of Bridge

Big Ben

1. For two years during World War I, the bells were silenced and the clock face darkened at night to prevent attack by German Zeppelins.

2. During the bell's first – and only – major breakdown in 1976, the BBC Radio 4 news had to make do with the pips.

3. The Big Ben chimes (known within ITN as 'The Bongs') are used during the headlines and all ITV News bulletins.

4. The Clock Tower has appeared in many films, most notably in the 1978 version of *The Thirty-Nine Steps*, in which the hero Richard Hannay attempted to halt the clock's progress (to prevent a bomb detonating) by hanging from the minute hand of its western face. It was also used in the filming of *Shanghai Knights* starring Jackie Chan and Owen Wilson, and was depicted as being partially destroyed in the *Doctor Who* episode 'Aliens of London'.

St and Victoria Embankment) 15 minutes before the tour begins. The tour takes about 1 hour 15 minutes and involves clambering up 334 steps to the top of the tower. After your MP has arranged your visit to PMQs and booked you on a Big Ben tour, why don't you ask him or her to make you up a cheese-and-pickle sandwich packed lunch for the day? They have nothing better to do with their time after all.

DATE & TIME   Varies; check website.

AMENITIES   ♟

⑭ SEE THE TURNER CLOUDS AT TATE BRITAIN

Millbank, London SW1P 4RG (✆ **020 7887 8888**, www.tate.org.uk/britain/). ⊖ Pimlico.

We took our children to see this, the most prestigious gallery in Britain, featuring works of art from the 16th to 19th century, expecting them to be nonplussed, bored and rebellious, and although they were all of these at some point, for at least an hour they had fun. The galleries are bright and less busy than its sister gallery, Tate Modern, and the highlight for us was the Clore Gallery collection of JMW Turner pictures, where our daughter in a loud voice made the following wise observation: 'Why does he keep forgetting the ground. He shouldn't only paint clouds, should he Daddy?' Other highlights include works by Old Masters like Gainsborough, Reynolds, Stubbs, Blake and Constable. A regular boat service runs between the two galleries; a single ticket costs £8, or £3.35 with a Travelcard.

OPEN   Daily 10am–5:50pm (first Fri of each month 10am–10pm).

AMENITIES   ☕ 🍴 🛍 £

⑮ BARGE PAST TOURISTS TO PEER AT THE ROTHKOS IN TATE MODERN

Bankside, London SE1 9TG (✆ **020 7887 8888**, www.tate.org.uk/modern/). ⊖ Southwark or Blackfriars.

🚻 ☂

Based in a disused power station designed by Sir Giles Gilbert, who also gave the world Waterloo Bridge and the red telephone box, this gallery, second only in the world to New York's Museum of Modern Art, has upwards of two million visitors a year. It has major works from Fauvism onwards featuring paintings by Picasso and Matisse as well as one of the world's greatest collections of Surrealist works, featuring among others Dalì and Magritte. There are great examples of American Abstract Expressionism with paintings by Pollock and Rothko as well as Pop Art from Warhol. It's a good idea to get here early so you don't have to barge people out of the way to get to the Rothkos, and then to head off somewhere else for lunch as the cafés here are expensive and portions are as minimalist as some of the art. On Level 5 there is a Learning Zone overlooking the turbine hall, with quizzes and games and short films on featured artists and free activity sheets for children to rip to shreds on the Tube home. On level 7 check out the view of St Paul's Cathedral.

OPEN   Sun–Thurs 10am–6pm; Fri–Sat 10am–10pm.

AMENITIES   ☕ 🍴 🛍 ℗

⑯ LISTEN TO LOONIES AT SPEAKERS' CORNER

Hyde Park, London W2 2UH (✆ **020 7298 2100**, www.royalparks.org.uk). ⊖ Marble Arch or Hyde Park Corner.

We spent a couple of hours at this famous spot near Marble Arch, once frequented by famous intellectuals Karl Marx, Vladimir Lenin and George Orwell. We listened to a man on a milk crate trying to convince a crowd of 15 bemused tourists that the human race had been sown and would soon be 'harvested like a crop of barley'. Speakers' Corner, a symbol for free speech around the world, has existed in the north-east corner of Hyde Park since 1872, although contrary to popular belief speakers can still be arrested for blasphemy, obscenity, inciting violence or saying something derogatory about a Stephen Fry tweet. Nevertheless the area still draws large crowds of tourists and hecklers, who tend to allow a new speaker around two-and-a-half minutes to develop their theme before they start shouting, 'Liar'. Our children watched stunned for the first 10 minutes although were soon whispering 'I think he's fibbing, Dad'. Although Speakers' Corner no longer seems to attract the most celebrated minds of the day, it remains London's focal point for free-speech issues. For example, when the British government banned the book *Spycatcher*, about the nation's intelligence operations, the book was read aloud here. Activities in Hyde Park include boat hire, tennis, horse riding, swimming, bowls and a putting green.

OPEN   Daily 5am–midnight.

⑰ WINDOW SHOP AT HARRODS

87–135 Brompton Road, Knightsbridge, London SW1X 7XL (✆ **020 7730 1234**, www.harrods.com). ⊖ Knightsbridge, South Kensington or Sloane Square.

Serving more than 15 million people a year, the largest and most controversial store in Britain isn't somewhere you'll want to open your wallet too wide but it's worth a visit to gawp at people who are prepared to spend £1,000 (yes) on a bedsheet. The store, owned by Mohamed Al Fayed, is the last in Britain to sell real fur, has a dress code barring the wearing of products it sells (bermuda shorts, ripped

Diana & Dodi

Harrods boasts two mawkish memorials to the People's Princess and her lover. The first, unveiled in 1998, consists of photographs of the two lovers behind a pyramid-shaped display that holds a wine glass still smudged with lipstick from Diana's last dinner as well as what is described as an engagement ring Dodi purchased the day before they died in the car accident. The second equally tasteful memorial is located by the Egyptian escalator and is titled 'Innocent Victims'. It's a bronze statue of the two dancing on a beach beneath the wings of an albatross, a bird said to symbolise the 'Holy Spirit'. Prior to the 1997 death of Princess Diana, the store was holder of royal warrants from Queen Elizabeth II for Provisions and Household Goods, the Duke of Edinburgh as Outfitters, the Prince of Wales as Outfitters and Saddlers, as well as the Queen Mother, now deceased, for China and Glass. It is said none of these patrons have spent a penny in the store since the accident, and Mohamed Al Fayed, the store's colourful owner, has removed their coats of arms, once prominently displayed on the façade of the shop.

jeans, sandals, cycling shorts) and it also boasts two shrines to Princess Diana and Dodi Fayed (see box). Some more superlatives from the store with the famous motto Omnia Omnibus Ubique – All Things for All People Everywhere (but especially for those who can afford a £28 Christian Dior baby bib): it has over one million square feet of selling space, more than 300 departments and is lit at night by more than 12,000 (ironically) energy-saving lightbulbs. Its famous customers have included AA Milne, Sigmund Freud, Noel Coward and Kylie Minogue. OK, where is it best to head for first? The chocolate department is fantastic, the food hall makes Fortnum & Mason look like a corner shop, and you must see the pharaohs in the Egypt Room, reputedly modelled on Al Fayed himself, while the swanky loos are worth a snoop. Also, don't come on a Saturday – it's heaving with tourists and foreign shoppers queuing to get their VAT exemptions. If you want extra carrier bags to impress your friends, ask for them – the staff are, as you'd expect, geniality personified.

OPEN   Mon–Sat   10am–8pm;   Sun 11:30am–6pm.

AMENITIES   ¶¶ £

Harrods Hilarity

1. The first moving escalator was used here on Wednesday, 16 November, 1898. The device was a woven leather conveyor belt with a mahogany and silver-plate-glass balustrade. Shoppers were offered brandy at the top to steady their nerves.

2. In 1986 the small town of Otorohanga in New Zealand briefly changed its name to Harrodsville in response to legal threats made by Mohamed Al Fayed against a person with the surname Harrod, who used the name 'Harrods' for his shop. Other town businesses changed their store name to Harrods in support, and the resultant lampooning in the British press led to Al Fayed dropping the legal action.

3. In 2007 Harrods hired a live Egyptian cobra at the shoe counter to guard a pair of haute couture ruby, sapphire and diamond-encrusted sandals launched by designer Rene Caovilla and valued at £62,000.

⓲ SEE NAPOLEON'S HORSE AT THE NATIONAL ARMY MUSEUM

Royal Hospital Road, London SW3 4HT (𝄢 **020 7730 0717**, www.national-army-museum.ac.uk). ⊖ Sloane Square.

Telling the story of the British Army from 1066 to the present day, the highlights here include the skeleton of Napoleon's horse Merengo, trying on medieval chainmail and walking through a mocked-up trench from World War I. The museum's collections are spread over four permanent galleries and allow visitors to compare the lives, weaponry and tactics of red coat-wearing soldiers from the Napoleonic Wars to the khaki-clad squaddies of the 21st century. There are replica tanks and works by war artists such as John Kean, while in the Conflicts of Interest Gallery there's a chance to see a chemical warfare kit and an arms cache found in Northern Ireland, as you listen to oral histories from soldiers fighting in Afghanistan and Iraq. There is a children's zone where youngsters can dress up as red coats, serve/ throw imaginary mess food at each other in a play kitchen area and there are also quizzes.

OPEN   Daily 10am–5:30pm.

AMENITIES   ☕ 🛍 ⋏

⓳ STAND NEXT TO THE WORLD'S LARGEST MAM-MAL AT THE NATURAL HISTORY MUSEUM

Cromwell Road, London SW7 5BD (✆ **020 7942 5011**, www.nhm.ac.uk). ⊖ South Kensington.

I can still remember dropping my chocolate biscuit in shock at the sheer size of the three-double-decker-long Blue Whale exhibit when I visited this museum as a child. Later, for a year between quitting Bristol Poly and starting at Sheffield University, I used to come here moodily with my 'I'm-a-budding-author' notebook and while away whole days annoyingly mugging up about the science of space for use in future counter-arguments for why I had, say, returned my dad's car without petrol. ('Dad, space is infinite and you're worried about £4's worth of Four Star!') The highlight for youngsters is the Dinosaur Gallery with its super-sensing T-Rex, which detects your motion and follows your movements around the room with its scary head. There are other animatronic dinosaurs hanging from the ceiling and a ceiling-height walk-way through giant models of fossil remains. Investigate, meanwhile, is a hands-on science lab for 6–15 year olds, while at the Power Within you can experience an earthquake. There are Discovery Guides (£1) to inspire children (4–16) in their explorations of volcanoes, dinosaur teeth and the source of the earth's energy, while for under sevens, pick up an Explore Backpack (free), which comes with explorer hats, binoculars and drawing materials. Just make sure your toddler doesn't dump it in the Darwin Centre and demand that 'you carry it, Dad'.

OPEN   Daily 10am–5:50pm.

AMENITIES   ☕ 🍴 ♦ 🛍 £

⑳ LISTEN TO PENSIONERS DISCUSSING DOLLY MIXTURES AT THE VICTORIA & ALBERT MUSEUM

Cromwell Road, London SW7 2RL (📞 **020 7942 2000**, www.vam.ac.uk). ⊖ South Kensington.

At the finest decorative arts museum in the world, you'll find exhibits as diverse as Coco Chanel's little black dress, furniture by Charles Rennie Mackintosh, a portrait of Anne of Cleves by Hans Holbein that Henry VIII used when casting about for his next bride, and the wedding suit worn by James II. In addition there's a wonderful photographic collection of some 500,000 images as well as the largest cache of Renaissance sculpture outside Italy, not to mention cartoons by Raphael and (my personal highlight) a pensioner talking into a tape about the thrill of eating her first bag of Dolly Mixtures. The museum has imaginative daily talks, demonstrations, tours and interactive displays – check ahead for times and details.

OPEN   Daily 10am–5:45pm (Fri 10am–10pm in selected galleries).

AMENITIES   ☕ 🛍 £

㉑ DISCOVER YOUR ANCESTRY AT THE SCIENCE MUSEUM

Exhibition Road, London SW7 2DD (📞 **0870 8704868**, www.sciencemuseum.org.uk) ⊖ South Kensington.

Here is where our daughter made a rainbow, our son felt a dinosaur's breath on the back of his neck, and I managed to demean my wife's ancestors. A dauntingly huge museum on five floors, it's a good idea if you have children to head straight for the third floor Launch Pad gallery where there are more than 50 hands-on exhibits. The Imax cinema (adults £8, concessions £6.25) shows 3D films on its double-decker bus-sized screens including, when we visited, one about hunting for dinosaur remains in New Mexico. Elsewhere we learnt how the technologies used in Formula One racing had (a) helped the Beagle 2 space mission to Mars and also (surely more importantly) (b) developed a type of rubber footwear that prevented pet shop workers slipping over in Doncaster. In Who Am I?, trace the roots of your surname, morph your face into a pop star's and find out how your ancestors lived.

OPEN   Daily 10am–6pm.

AMENITIES   ☕ 🍴 🛍 £

㉒ CHECK OUT FAMOUS GRAVESTONES AT BROMPTON CEMETERY

Finborough Road, London SW10 9UG (✆ **020 7352 1201**, www.royalparks.org.uk). ⊖ West Brompton.

Beloved of film directors, this Gothic-looking cemetery has featured in a string of movies including *Johnny English* starring Rowan Atkinson, *GoldenEye* (Pierce Brosnan's first Bond movie) and bitter-sweet Richard E Grant rom-com, *Jack and Sarah*. More interestingly, it's also where an eclectic string of the great and the good are buried including suffragette Emmeline Pankhurst, gruff Yorkshire actor Brian Glover and, my favourite find, Luisa Casati Stampa di Soncino Marchesa di Roma (see box, p. 22). The cemetery opened in 1840 to the design of Benjamin Baud and children's author Beatrix Potter spent time here. There are graves to Mr Nutkin, Peter Rabbit, Jeremiah Fisher, Mr McGregor and Tommy Brock – all names that inspired characters in her children's stories. Amongst the cemetery's shady walks are over 35,000 monuments and 200,000 tombs, which have become, over the years, an unlikely haven for wildlife including birds, butterflies, foxes and squirrels. For the best experience we strongly advise taking a tour, organised by Friends of Brompton Cemetery (check times on ✆ **020 7351 1689**) on every second Sunday of the month, with additional weekly tours during the busier summer months on request. They start at 2pm from the South Lodge, just inside the Fulham Road entrance and last two hours. They're free although there is a suggested £4 donation.

OPEN   Summer 8am–8pm; winter 8am–4pm.

AMENITIES   P

㉓ MOOCH ABOUT PORTOBELLO MARKET

Portobello Road, London W10–11 (www.portobellomarket.org). ⊖ Notting Hill Gate.

The largest antique market in the world takes up most of Portobello Road and you can buy anything from a 100-year-old barometer to the

Mamma Mia

The eccentric wealthy Italian heiress Luisa Casati Stampa di Soncino Marchesa di Roma (1881–1957), who was orphaned at 15, delighted European society for 30 years, captivating artists and literary figures as diverse as novelist and boxing manager Jean Cocteau, photographer Cecil Beaton, Welsh painter Augustus John and beatnik poet Jack Kerouac. She had a long-term affair with fascist author Gabriele D'Annunzio, who Mussolini modelled himself on, and played muse to futurist sculptor FT Marinetti and fashion designer John Galliano. The beautiful and extravagant hostess astonished Venetian society by parading with a pair of leashed cheetahs and wearing live snakes as jewellery. However, by 1930, Casati had amassed a personal debt of $25 million. Unable to satisfy her creditors, her personal possessions were auctioned off. She fled to London, where she lived in poverty and was rumoured to be seen occasionally rummaging in bins searching for feathers to decorate her hair. She died in London on 1 June 1957 and was interred in Brompton Cemetery. The quote 'Age cannot wither her, nor custom stale her infinite variety' from Shakespeare's *Antony and Cleopatra* was inscribed on her tombstone. She was buried wearing not only her black and leopard-skin finery and a pair of false eyelashes, but with one of her beloved stuffed Pekinese dogs. Her tombstone is a small grave marker in the shape of an urn draped in cloth. The inscription misspells her name as Louisa rather than Luisa. It's a hard grave to find and despite her fame, wealth and notoriety is modest compared to the thousands of grand monuments here.

pair of hideous brass candlesticks designed in the shape of hedgehogs that my wife bought to celebrate our fifth wedding anniversary. The market, popular with Sienna Miller and Kate Moss and a location in the movie *Notting Hill* (where Hugh Grant ran a local bookshop), stretches for almost two miles (3km) and has become popular with young fashion designers trying to get their clothes 'out there' as well as established names like Paul Smith, Joseph and Myla. The antique stalls start as Chepstow Villas meets Portobello Road, and continue down to where Elgin Crescent crosses Portobello Road. The main market day is Saturday and it's advisable to get there early, round about 9ish, to catch an elusive bargain. It gets uncomfortably busy by 11:30am.

OPEN   Mon–Wed 8am–6pm; Thurs 9am–1pm; Fri–Sat 8am–7pm.

AMENITIES   ☕ 🍸 🄿

㉔ SCOFF JERK CHICKEN AT THE NOTTING HILL CARNIVAL

Notting Hill, London (✆ **020 7727 0072**, www.thenottinghillcarnival.com). ⊖ Latimer Road, Notting Hill (not on Monday), Bayswater, Queensway, Westbourne Grove or Royal Oak (both exit only).

Bobby Dazzlers

The cult British children's character Paddington Bear, featured in the books written by Michael Bond, often enjoys visiting Portobello Market. His friend Mr Gruber owns an antique shop on the Portobello Road, with whom Paddington has his elevenses every day. Also look out for David 'orange-face' Dickinson, the presenter of the day-time brain fug that is *Bargain Hunt*, which is often filmed here.

An annual event staged since 1964 on the streets of Notting Hill (see box, p. 25) in August, this is the biggest carnival of its kind in Europe, attracting upwards of a million people, and featuring vibrant floats, traditional steel bands, scores of massive thumping sound systems and hundreds of stalls lining the streets selling jerk chicken and curried goat. Usually getting under way on the Saturday before the August Bank Holiday with the steel band competition, Sunday is Kids' Day, when costume prizes are awarded. On Bank Holiday Monday, the main parade begins on Great Western Road, winds its way along Chepstow Road on to Westbourne Grove, and then to Ladbroke Grove. In the evening the floats leave the streets in procession, and most people continue revelling at the many Notting Hill Carnival afterparties. Slightly disappointed Ms Dynamite hadn't shown up as billed last year, but pleased we hadn't been upended in a street riot, we went home early, our ears numbed from all the whistling and stuffed so full with jerk chicken we both had to sleep on our backs.

AMENITIES   🍸

AVOID TORTOISE LIKENESSES AT THE BRITISH MUSEUM

Great Russell Street, London WC1B 3DG (© **020 7323 8299**, www.britishmuseum.org). ⊖ Tottenham Court Road.

The highlights at this enormous museum are the Rosetta Stone in the Egyptian Room, whose discovery led to the deciphering of hieroglyphics, the Elgin Marbles from the Parthenon in Athens in the Duveen Gallery, and the legendary Black Obelisk from Iraq in 860bc. We must confess to being daunted by the scale of the treasures at this museum, and after a frightening episode when my wife was startled by a jade 17th-century tortoise sculpture (she fears the likeness of all tortoises, terrapins and turtles) in Room 34 on the ground floor, we concentrated our attention on the Money Gallery in room 68 tracing the story of cash. There are children's trails available from the Paul Hamlyn Library next to Room 2 and activity packs full of puzzles and games related to artefacts in the museum.

OPEN Sat–Wed 10am–5:30pm; Thurs–Fri 10am–8:30pm.

AMENITIES

STROKE A RABBIT AT CORAM'S FIELDS

93 Guilford Street, London WC1N 1DN (© **020 7837 6138**, www.coramfields.org). ⊖ Russell Square.

This unique seven-acre playground and park is barred to adults not accompanied by a child. Based on the site of the former Foundling Hospital here, the area is named after philanthropist Thomas Coram (see box, p. 27).

Beating the Drum

Notting Hill Carnival began in January 1959 in St Pancras Town Hall as a response to the Notting Hill race riots the previous year. The Carnival, led by members of the Trinidad and Tobago population, has its roots in the Caribbean festivities of the early 19th century, which celebrated the abolition of slavery. Having been forbidden to hold festivals during the period of slavery, the islanders took full advantage of their new freedom. Dressing up in costumes mimicking the European fashions of their former masters, even whitening their faces with flour or wearing white masks, they established a tradition that continues in the flamboyant costume-making of today's Notting Hill Carnival.

Fun Recipe

If you fancy some traditional jerk chicken, why not make your own. Here's the recipe:

2.7 kg (6 lb) roasting chicken

1 tbsp salt

2 tsp garlic powder

1 tsp paprika

1 tsp soya sauce

1 small onion

3 tbsp jerk seasoning

First, rub the whole chicken with salt, then grate the onion and rub it into the chicken. Add paprika and garlic powder to the chicken. Rub the jerk seasoning over the whole chicken and marinate it for at least two hours. Roast it all in the oven at 180°C (350°F) for an hour and a half. Then put on your ostrich-feathered hat and start swinging those hips.

It has a petting zoo with sheep and goats, a paddling pool and a play area with sandpits for under fives, as well as a drop-in centre. There are great picnic lawns plus basketball, netball and football pitches for hire for older children.

OPEN   9am–7pm; winter 9am–dusk.

AMENITIES

❷ LET YOUR CHILDREN DRESS UP IN ARMOUR AT THE WALLACE COLLECTION

Hertford House, Manchester Square, London W1U 3BN (𝄐 **020 7563 9500**, www. wallacecollection.org). ⊖ Bond Street.

Often overlooked, this museum is best known for housing Frans Hals's famous masterpiece, *The Laughing Cavalier*. There are major paintings by Titian, Rembrandt, Rubens, Velázquez, Poussin, Canaletto and Gainsborough. The collection, spread over 25 galleries, displays works collected in the 18th and 19th centuries by the first four marquises of Hertford and Sir Richard Wallace, the son of the fourth marquis. In addition, the museum houses an incredible collection of gold Parisian snuff boxes. Other highlights include a rococo commode delivered by Antoine-Robert Gaudreau for Louis XV's bedchamber at Versailles in April 1739; it's mounted with tasteless swirling, organic gilt-bronzes by Jacques Caffieri. There are sumptuous pieces once owned by Queen Marie-Antoinette, including a desk and a perfume burner from her private apartment at Versailles. A sizeable weapons and armour collection kept our two-year-old son occupied, much of it coming from the early 1870s' collections of Sir Samuel Rush Meyrick and the Comte de Nieuwerkerke, the director of the Louvre under Emperor Napoleon III. Children can dress up in replica armour in the conservation gallery on the lower ground floor.

OPEN   Daily 10am–5pm.

AMENITIES   ¶¶¶ 🛍 ⚟

Thomas Coram

Up to a thousand babies a year were abandoned in early 18th-century London. They were often left by the side of the road in the desperate hope that someone would care for them, but many ended up on rubbish heaps. In 1739, shipwright, merchant and the fairly verbose Thomas Coram (1668–1751) established a 'Hospital for the Maintenance and Education of Exposed and Deserted Children', which looked after more than 27,000 children over three centuries at three sites until its closure in 1953. The painter William Hogarth was among the first governors of the hospital, the world's first incorporated charity. The composer George Frederic Handel allowed a concert performance of Messiah to benefit the Foundation, and donated the manuscript of the Hallelujah Chorus to the hospital.

㉘ DISCOVER YOUR INNER THETAN AT FITZROY HOUSE

37 Fitzroy Street, London W1T 6DX (℅ **020 7255 2422**, www.fitzroyhouse.org). ⊖ Warren Street or Great Portland Street.

🏹 😊

During a free guided tour of the 1950s' former home of L Ron Hubbard, the founder of Scientology, alarm your wife by mumbling under your breath: 'He's right, I am a Thetan who needs to return to my natural clear state'. This 18th-century house, designed in the style of Robert Adam, has a 1950s' time capsule containing exhibits about Hubbard's early life from boy-scout to explorer. It also showcases his career as a top fiction writer in the 1930s and 40s before he began working on his (fairly out there) Scientology ideas (see box, p. 29). The tour of the house included my wife's highlight – seeing a strange instrument that can apparently locate the areas of stress in a person's life (the E-meter) – although mine was hearing some of the grandiose claims made about L Ron Hubbard including (a) 'Mr Hubbard is unquestionably one of the most acclaimed and widely read authors of all time' and (b) 'Mr Hubbard has been described as one of the most prolific and influential writers of the twentieth century. He is the second most widely translated author after William Shakespeare'.

OPEN   11am–5pm (by appointment so ring ahead).

AMENITIES   ♀ ⏚

㉙ GO ON A BIRD WALK IN REGENT'S PARK

North London, NW1 4NR (ℂ 020 7486 7905, www.royalparks.org.uk/parks/regents_park/). ⊖ Regent's Park.

👥 ☂

'I have of late, wherefore I know not, lost all my mirth'. I deliver the *Hamlet* soliloquy Richard E Grant utters at the end of the cult British movie *Withnail and I* to protest at the early hour (4am) we got up (without breakfast) to see a few chaffinches on dawn bird walk here. Grant delivers his speech in this park at the end of the movie in desperation about his failed acting career. I delivered mine outside the Boathouse Café after dirtying my trousers following a pipit into a bush with my binoculars. If you print out the suggested walk and map from the website listed above, the other birds I expected to see in the 410-acre park, originally one of Henry VIII's hunting grounds, include grey herons, tufted and ruddy ducks, pochard, coots, Canada and greylag geese, whooper and mute swans, wagtails, sandpipers, swallows, sand martins, swifts, housemartins, sparrowhawks, hobbies, peregrine falcons, pipits, chiffchaffs, willow warblers, spotted flycatchers, wagtails, finches, cormorants and those chaffinches I mentioned above. Although to be honest if I'm getting up at 4am on a weekend I would expect to spot something on a par with a pterodactyl to make

Scientology

In 1953 L Ron Hubbard (1911–1986) incorporated the Church of Scientology in New Jersey, America. Scientology teaches that people are immortal spiritual beings called Thetans, who have forgotten their true nature. According to Scientologist mythology, Thetans brought the material world into being for their own enjoyment. The material universe – matter, energy, space and time (MEST) – was created by Thetans sometime in a primordial past. It has no independent reality, but derives its apparent reality from the fact that most Thetans agree it exists. It is believed that Thetans became victims of their own involvement with the material universe, becoming entrapped by it. Eventually, this reached a point where Thetans lost their memory of their true nature. The Scientology method of spiritual rehabilitation is a form of counselling called auditing, in which practitioners re-experience traumatic events in their past. Auditing courses are made available to members in return for donations. Scientology is legally recognised as a tax-exempt religion in the US but has often been described as a cult that financially defrauds and abuses its members, charging exorbitant fees for its spiritual services. The Church of Scientology has consistently used litigation against its critics. Further controversy surrounds the church's belief that the practice of psychiatry is destructive and that women must be silent during childbirth. Actors John Travolta, Kirstie Alley, Tom Cruise and Katie Holmes have generated huge publicity for Scientology and some of their claims are highly litigious so we'll say no more if that's OK.

it worthwhile. However, there are great views of Primrose Hill here and Queen Mary's gardens are worth a look. There are more official guided walks with a wildlife officer that start at 8am on Sunday mornings in the spring (Apr–May) and autumn (Aug–Sept) although my wife 'forgot' to tell me about those. They typically last one-and-a-half hours. There's also bike hire and tennis courts in the park.

OPEN   From 5am until dusk.

AMENITIES

Spot the Park in . . .

① An early scene in *Harry Potter and the Philosopher's Stone* (2001) is set at London Zoo within Regent's Park. During a visit to the reptile house, Harry (Daniel Radcliffe) first discovers he has unusual powers when he talks to the snakes and unwittingly frees a boa constrictor.

② Regent's Park boating lake features in the pivotal scene in David Lean's classic British romance, *Brief Encounter* (1945). Alec and Laura, played by Trevor Howard and Celia Johnson, are in a rowing boat when Alec stumbles off the end of the boat near the Long Bridge and ends up knee-deep in water.

③ More recently, in *About a Boy* (2002) the lake in Queen Mary's Garden became a romantic hunting ground for Will, a rich but shallow 30-something played by Hugh Grant. Will courts single mothers in the park because he thinks they are easy targets. There's no conquest but he makes friends with 12-year-old Marcus (Nicholas Hoult) and the two have a heart-to-heart next to the famous penguin pool at the zoo.

④ London Zoo is also where David (David Naughton) wakes up in *An American Werewolf in London* (1981), after attacking tramps near Tower Bridge.

⑳ SWOT IN THE BRITISH LIBRARY

96 Euston Road, London NW1 2DB (✆ **020 7412 7332**, www.bl.uk). ⊖ King's Cross/ St Pancras or Euston.

This, one of the world's great libraries, contains over 14 million books including two of the four surviving copies of the Magna Carta (1215), Lord Nelson's last letter to Lady Hamilton, a Gutenberg bible and the journals of Captain Cook. There are also documents relating to Shakespeare – a copy of his signature on a mortgage certificate and a copy of the First Folio of 1623 – as well as the world's oldest printed item, a Chinese Buddhist text known as the *Diamond Sutra*, and the world's oldest bible, the fourth-century *Sinaiticus Codex*. In the Turning Pages exhibition you can read a complete Leonardo Da Vinci notebook electronically by placing your hand on a computer screen, while elsewhere there is original sheet music by Beethoven, Handel, Stravinsky and by contrast, Lennon and McCartney.

OPEN Mon, Wed–Fri 9:30am–6pm; Tues 9:30am–8pm; Sat 9:30am–5pm; Sun 11am–5pm.

AMENITIES

⑤ HEAR A MASTER-CLASS AT THE ROYAL ACADEMY OF MUSIC

Marylebone Road, London NW1 5HT (📞 **020 7873 7373**, www.ram.ac.uk). ⊖ Baker Street or Regent's Park.

There are several free events daily in term time at this spectacularly grand conservatoire, including regular Friday lunchtime concerts that have seen the world-famous 80-year-old Sir Colin Davis conduct the Academy Orchestra. As well as student singing competitions, jazz, musical theatre and lectures from visiting sopranos, the museum is home to more Stradivarius violins than you can see in any one place in the world. Other highlights include letters written by Mendelssohn, and Yehudi Menuhin's entire archive, featuring among other oddities letters he wrote to Margaret Thatcher and Ghandi. Entertaining master-classes are staged by visiting soloists in the spectacular 400-seat Dukes Hall; these sometimes see students put through their paces on stage in a brutal three-hour lesson. There is no need to book a ticket or even to pretend to be a student musician. Just turn up at the 180-year-old Academy and take up your seat.

OPEN Academy daily 8am–11pm. Museum Mon–Fri 11:30am–5:30pm; Sat–Sun 12pm–4pm.

AMENITIES

⑥ VISIT THE MOVIE LOCATION OF KENWOOD HOUSE

Hampstead, London NW3 7JR (📞 **020 8348 1286**, www.englishheritage.org.uk). ⊖ Archway and Golders Green, then 210 bus.

My wife insisted we visit this 17th-century stately home, based in tranquil parkland containing sculptures by Henry Moore and Barbara Hepworth among others, because it was used during the filming of her favourite British movie, *Notting Hill*. The house, remodelled by Robert Adam in the 18th century, boasts sumptuous interiors and important paintings by artists such as Rembrandt, Turner, Reynolds, Gainsborough and Vermeer. Part of the estate is a Site of Special Scientific Interest (SSI) because its ancient woodlands are home to many birds and insects as well as the largest pipistrelle bat roost in London. Not that my foppish-hair/plumby-voice-loving wife was interested in any of this. She just wanted to stand where her heart-throb Hugh Grant (playing William) stood in the scene where Anna Scott (Julia Roberts playing herself) rebuffs him. There is a good café here in which to remind your wife that Hugh Grant is not a very good actor, and is actually quite short.

OPEN   Daily 11:30am–4pm.

AMENITIES

③③ SEE THE CYCLOPS CHILD AT THE HUNTERIAN MUSEUM

Royal College of Surgeons, 35–43 Lincoln's Inn Fields, London WC2A 3PE (© **020 7869 6560**, www.rcseng.ac.uk/museums). ⊖ Holborn or Temple, both about a 10-minute walk away.

★ ☺

This museum has free 25-minute guided tours every Wednesday at 1pm (limited to 25 places so book ahead) and showcases the fairly gruesome yet strangely alluring collection of 18th-century anatomist, John Hunter. It includes the foetus of a 'cyclops child' with one eye, as well as a set of 200-year-old sextuplets suspended in formaldehyde. The highlight for me, however, was the skeleton of the Irish giant Charles Byrne (1761–1783), who may have been as tall as seven-and-a-half feet (2.3m). Throughout his career touring the country as a circus freak, Byrne was terrified that he would be dissected by curious doctors when he died. He drank himself to an early death at the age of 22, leaving express details for his body to be buried at sea. However, surgeon John Hunter bribed pallbearers to obtain his body for £500 and now his skeleton resides rather freakishly in the Hunterian.

Among other items of interest in the Odontological Collection are some teeth retrieved from soldiers on the battlefield of Waterloo, a necklace of human teeth brought from the Congo by the explorer Henry Morton Stanley and a great entrant into our competition to find the strangest exhibit in Britain behind glass, Sir Winston Churchill's dentures.

OPEN   Tues–Sat 10am–5pm.

AMENITIES   ☕ 🛍 🅿

㉞ HEAR MUSIC AT THE SOUTHBANK CENTRE

Belvedere Road, London SE1 8XX (✆ **0871 663 2500**, www.southbankcentre.co.uk). ⊖ Waterloo, Embankment or Charing Cross.

There are more than 300 free events at Europe's largest and ugliest centre for the arts, which includes the Hayward Gallery, the Royal Festival Hall and the Queen Elizabeth Gallery. They include live music on Friday evenings, featuring anything from jazz and blues to the folk music of Nancy Wallace, as well as lunchtime performances in the Central Bar of the Festival Hall on Fridays and Sundays. Throughout the year there are a whole range of other free shows at the Southbank Centre at all sorts of times on days too numerous to mention. These have included in the past anything from a mass photo call of *Hitchhiker's Guide to the Galaxy* fans to an airing of pop culture videos from Uruguayan artist Martin Sastre. Leave plenty of time to navigate your way around this concrete monolith, so brutal in its design it almost provoked a sensitive nephew of mine to tears when he came here because he felt it looked 'like a horrid, awful car park'. Check the website for current listings.

OPEN   Times vary according to schedule.

AMENITIES   ☕ 🍴 🍷 🅿

㉟ TOUR SHAKESPEARE'S GLOBE THEATRE

Bankside, 21 New Globe Walk, London, SE1 9DT (✆ **020 7902 1400**, www.shakespeares-globe.org). ⊖ Mansion House.

👫 ☂

Building the Globe

In 1949, when American film director Sam Wanamaker visited London for the first time, he searched for the site of the original Globe and was disappointed not to find a more fitting memorial to Shakespeare and his theatre. In 1970 Wanamaker therefore founded what was to become the Shakespeare Globe Trust, and in 1987 building work started on the site. In 1993, the construction of the Globe Theatre began, following the plan of the original. Wanamaker died on 18 December 1993. At that time, 12 of the 15 bays were erected. The plasterwork and thatching started the following year and were finished in 1997.

On or around Shakespeare's birthday each year in April (check ahead for the right day) there's free entry to a stagecraft exhibition here featuring readings of the bard's plays, professional swordsmen revealing the tricks of stage fighting, as well as recitals with 16th-century musical instruments. At this theatre (see box), based on the original Globe where Shakespeare's plays were first performed back in the 1500s, there's the chance to look at and touch some of the costumes used during productions, and, through a series of interactive displays, learn how stage thunder and other Elizabethan special effects were created. The free visit (normally costing £10.50) includes a 30–45 minute guided tour of the building, which takes in the famous open-air yard and other viewing galleries.

OPEN Midday–5pm (free exhibition on bard's birthday).

AMENITIES

⑯ BAG A FREE LUNCH AT BOROUGH MARKET

8 Southwark Street, London SE1 1TL (✆ **020 7407 1002**, www.boroughmarket.org.uk). ⊖ London Bridge.

This, one of the largest food markets in Europe, has grown from a place selling low-rent fruit and veg into a foodie haven regularly eulogised by celebrity chefs as the best place in Britain to buy fresh ingredients. Two hundred and fifty years old, the sights and smells are enough to water the mouth of any self-respecting gastronome. Stalls drawn from across the world offer a huge range of meat, fish, fruit and veg, dairy goods, beers and wines. A lot of the produce is organic and there's a delectable selection of cakes and exotic breads. My wife swears by the German Bavarian rye bread at Artisan de Gustibus. But you don't have to spend a fortune here. In fact, often stall-holders walk around with plates of their goodies hoping a free sample will tempt you into buying their produce. Many of the

Food for Thought

Borough Market has been used in the filming of *Bridget Jones's Diary* (2001), *Lock, Stock and Two Smoking Barrels* (1998) and *Harry Potter and the Prisoner of Azkaban* (2004).

cheese and meat stalls have dishes on the counter offering bite-sized pieces to try. In fact, if you're prepared to look like a skinflint (we are), you can, over the course of a morning, scoff your way through enough calories to constitute lunch for nothing. We are not ashamed to say we have done this a couple of times during harder phases of our life in the 1990s when we worked round the corner from the market. During December, the market takes on a festive air and the air fills with the smell of mulled wine, hot spiced-apple juice, roasting meats and choirs singing carols. Borough Market's Roast restaurant has been voted the Best Breakfast in London and The Rake pub holds the Class Bar Awards 'Best Beer Experience'.

OPEN   Thurs 11am–5pm; Fri 12pm–6pm; Sat 8am–5pm.

③⑦ SEE A SHOW AT THE OPEN-AIR SCOOP

The Scoop at More London, The Queen's Walk, More London, Southwark, London, SE1 2DB (℃ **020 7403 4866**, www.morelondon.com/thescoop). ⊖ London Bridge.

This riverside 1,000-seat sunken amphitheatre in a pedestrianised zone close to London Bridge plays host to an eclectic variety of free theatre, musical and film events over the summer months (June–Oct). The dry weather-dependent shows organised by More London can be anything from a family-orientated theatrical production of *Jason and the Argonauts*, through a 30-voice gospel choir, to the screening of the 30s' classic movie, *The Wizard of Oz*. Seats cannot be booked so it's a good idea to show up early. Most events kick off between 6pm and 8pm. To get there from London Bridge station it's a five-minute walk (15 with children who are insisting they are 'the Tin Man – look, Dad'). Basically, turn right along Tooley Street, then cross the road and after Hay's Galleria cut through More London Place heading towards Tower Bridge.

OPEN   Times vary but roughly between 6pm–8pm.

AMENITIES

⓳ QUIZ YOUR WIFE ON WORLD WAR II COMBATANTS AT THE IMPERIAL WAR MUSEUM

Lambeth Road, London SE1 6HZ (📞 **020 7416 5320**, www.iwm.org.uk). ⊖ Lambeth North.

My wife, annoyingly uninterested in war as evinced by the groans every time she hears the drone of Spitfire engine on TV, was pleasantly surprised here. Expecting it to be a 'Boy's Own' world full of rat-a-tatting machine gun fire, Churchillian speech-making and grown men nodding knowledgeably at the destructive capability of various pieces of large weaponry, it's actually a rather sober place. Yes, Spitfires do hang from the ceiling, and you do see V2 rockets but there are also displays highlighting the human cost of war, most notably in the harrowing Holocaust Exhibition (not recommended for anyone under 14). The main galleries focus on the causes and events of World Wars I and II, while there are further exhibitions on famous war paintings and another about espionage featuring a bottle of invisible ink. 'Not nearly as bad as I thought', was my wife's analysis on the Tube home.

OPEN   Daily 10am–6pm.

AMENITIES

⓴ SEE THE BEDROOM WHERE THE FAMOUS PREACHER DIED AT JOHN WESLEY'S CHAPEL, HOUSE & MUSEUM

49 City Road, London EC1Y 1AU (📞 **020 7253 2262**, www.wesleychapel.org.uk). ⊖ Old Street.

Voted number 50 in a list of 100 greatest Britons, John Wesley was saved from his father's blazing rectory aged five, the escape convincing him he was set apart, as a 'band plucked from the burning'. His religious convictions were further reinforced by being bullied at Charterhouse, Oxford, where he was forced to eat his own underpants and was left thinking, 'if mere children do these things, could not also God do worse?' After an abortive mission to Georgia, where he was sued by a woman who claimed he had promised to marry her, he returned to England and set up the Methodist Church, an evangelical revival of the Anglican Church that saw Wesley ride some 250,000 miles (400,000km) during the course of his life to give more than 40,000 sermons in fields, halls, cottages. More than once, he used his own father's tombstone at Epworth as a pulpit. Wesley, who is buried in the churchyard at the back of the chapel and who is also credited with first writing down the phrase 'agree to disagree', died exclaiming the words: 'the best of all is, God is with us'. Wesley's Georgian house contains his travelling desk, jokingly referred to by the tour guides as 'his laptop', a pair of his shoes, and his coat (and none of his underpants), plus his library and the bedroom where he died. He preached in the next-door chapel, which was blinged up by the Victorians, with only the pulpit he preached from still being original. The Museum of Methodism in the crypt of the chapel has copies of his sermons, miniature copies of the bibles he gave away and other artefacts relating to the movement.

OPEN   Mon–Wed, Sat 10am–4pm; Thurs 10am–12:45pm, 1:30pm–4pm; Sun 12:30pm–1:45pm.

AMENITIES   🛍 £

④ SEE THE LORD MAYOR'S COACH AT THE MUSEUM OF LONDON

150 London Wall, London EC2Y 5HN (℡ **020 7001 9844**, www.museumoflondon.org.uk). ⊖ Barbican, St Paul's or Moorgate.

Recently having undergone a £20 million transformation, this museum houses the death mask of Oliver Cromwell, the cell doors from Newgate Prison and the museum highlight – the fairytale gilded Lord Mayor's Coach built in 1757 and weighing three tons. I almost convinced our daughter that this was the pre-midnight pumpkin from *Cinderella*. There are gallery tours every day at midday and 4pm lasting roughly an hour. One other highlight is the London Before Gallery permanent exhibition, telling the story of our capital from a time 450,000 years ago when its tundra population could be squeezed on to one bendy bus.

OPEN   Daily 10am–6pm.

AMENITIES   ☕ 🛍 ♟

㊶ BRING OUT YOUR INNER SIMON COWELL AT THE COMEDY CAFÉ

66–68 Rivington Street, London EC2A 3AY (℗ **020 7739 5706**, www.comedycafe. co.uk). ⊖ Old Street.

This Shoreditch venue has free open mic comedy nights every Wednesday. You'll either see a cringe-worthy try-out that goes horribly wrong or the next big thing. You can even become one of the judges and help decide which of the eight featured acts gets invited back for a paid gig. Doors open at 7pm and shows start at 9pm. The tables are packed close together, the stage is small and it's normally a goodish atmosphere.

OPEN   Varies, check website.

AMENITIES   🍴 🍸

㊷ SPOOK YOURSELF ON A JACK THE RIPPER WALK

Liverpool Street Station, London EC2M 7QN (londonforfree.net/walks/ripper/ripper. php). ⊖ Liverpool Street.

We well understand it is not enough to give all of you tips on where to see red squirrels for free or where it's best to see great works of art. We're aware that some of you out there, maybe wearing thick black eye liner and possibly turning a kitchen knife over in your hands, are feeling vaguely unsatisfied with our entries suggesting relaxing wild meadows to picnic in, or beaches to take the family to. Well this one is for you guys. The route of this free Ripper three-hour walking tour of the City of London and East End can be printed off from the website above. Starting at Liverpool Street Station, it takes in where the Ripper's victims' mutilated bodies were found at Spitalfields Market and Brick Lane and outlines some salient facts about London at the time. There's even a jaunty Ripper quiz (Which victim of the Ripper was murdered indoors?) for you to complete on your way back home afterwards. Other good walks on the same website for less blood-thirsty readers include the three-hour long Royal Walk, taking in Westminster Abbey, Buckingham Palace, 10 Downing Street and Trafalgar Square, or the Writer's Walk starting at Tottenham Court Road, where you'll learn about locations and stories associated with Charles Dickens, Charles Darwin, Oscar Wilde and the Bloomsbury Group, as well as facts about the Senate House, one-time tallest office building in the capital, which inspired the Ministry of Truth in George Orwell's *1984*.

AMENITIES ⚡

㊽ HEAR ABOUT THE DERANGED NUN AT THE BANK OF ENGLAND MUSEUM

Bartholomew Lane, London EC2R 8AH (✆ **020 7601 5545**, www.bankofengland. co.uk). ⊖ Bank.

This museum is dedicated to the Old Lady of Threadneedle Street and tells the story of the country's central bank from 1694 to the present day. Visitors are encouraged to lift a 13kg gold bar, learn about quantitative easing and stare sadly at some of the old banknotes they didn't cash in before they were withdrawn from legal tender. You'll also hear about some of the quirkier characters associated with the bank, which include a deranged 19th-century nun who stood on the steps of the bank for 25 years awaiting her brother and a former bank teller sentenced to death for forging an acceptance note, as well as the story of a Cockney sewer-man who broke into the gold vaults in 1836. There are activity sheets for children and other exhibits including the bank's bizarrely eclectic and suspiciously extensive collections of photographs, books, silver, coins, paintings, furniture, muskets and pikes, making us wonder whether our august bankers have over recent years been neglecting the fine-tuning of the monetary and fiscal framework of our economy to spend their time on the eBay antique pages? There are steps at the entrance; here helpful staff, if not busy checking their current bid status on collectibles, will assist those with pushchairs and wheelchairs up and down.

OPEN Mon–Fri 10am–5pm.

AMENITIES 🛍 ⓘ ⚡

㊹ SEE THE BELCHING ROBOT AT THE V&A MUSEUM OF CHILDHOOD

Cambridge Heath Road, London E2 9PA (© **020 8983 5200**, www.museumofchildhood. org.uk). ⊖ Bethnal Green.

At this wonderful museum, my wife and I got to sit around in deck-chairs reading the Sunday papers playing a game called 'Imagine it's 2003 and we haven't had children yet', while our daughter and son amused themselves for ages on a mocked-up beach. The museum explores all aspects of childhood from play to the history of children's clothing and has among its highlights 8,000 dolls, a model Hogwarts Express train, a child-sized Rolls-Royce, a Robosapien robot that belches on command and loads of interactive exhibits. There are adult- and child-sized Punch and Judy booths for visitors to put on their own shows and a dressing up and dance area with a free juke-box. Our daughter's favourite aspect of the museum after the Creative Gallery, where she got the chance to record her thoughts about Catty the Cat, her imaginary friend ('he has pink ears'), was the *High School Musical 3* Got the Moves Dance Mat.

OPEN   Daily 10am–5:45pm (first Thurs of month 6pm–9pm).

AMENITIES   ☕ 🛍 🅿

㊺ LOAD UP AT THE COLUMBIA ROAD FLOWER MARKET

Columbia Road Flower Market, Columbia Road, London E2 7RG (www.columbia-flower-market.freewebspace.com/). ⊖ Old Street.

We visited this market a few days after our son was born looking to buy a 'couple of plants' to finish off the flat we'd just decorated. There are more than 52 stalls here and 30 garden-and-craft themed shops selling anything from sunflower seeds to huge tree ferns and exotic cut flowers. The atmosphere, a thousand times better than the musak-atmosphere of a garden centre, is funny, bantering and so relaxed we left the market laden with so many large exotic house plants that I was pulled over on the M25 by a policeman who thought I'd 'been over-taken by a hedge, sir'. We had a boot full of hanging baskets and three ferns hanging out of the passenger window. In the driver's seat I was peering through the fronds of a Yucca plant while in the back my wife, wedged between my son and daughter, was in the tuck position because of the amount of decorative vases we'd bought. Amazingly we made it back home, where many of these plants are still alive.

OPEN   Sun 8am–2pm.

AMENITIES

⑥ ATTEND THE CEREMONY OF THE KEYS

Tower of London, London EC3N 4AB (📞 **020 3166 6278**, www.hrp.org.uk/TowerOfLondon). ⊖ Tower Hill.

The Ceremony of the Keys is the traditional locking up of the Tower of London that has taken place without fail every night for over 700 years. You can witness this spectacle by writing in person to the Ceremony of the Keys Office at the above address. You must include two possible dates that you can attend that are at least two months in advance (three months in advance if you wish to attend in July or August) as well as a stamped addressed envelope. The ceremony starts at exactly 9:53pm when Chief Yeoman Warder of the Tower emerges from the Byward Tower in his long red coat. He carries a candle lantern and the Queen's Keys. With what is deemed 'solemn tread', he moves along Water Lane to Traitor's Gate, where his

Where it Stems From

Columbia Market was built on an area known as Nova Scotia Gardens, once the stomping ground of a notorious gang called the Resurrection Men who stole freshly buried bodies for sale to anatomists. On 7th November 1831 the suspiciously fresh corpse of a 14-year-old boy was delivered by the gang to the King's College School of Anatomy. It led to the arrest of the gang. By an extraordinary arrangement, the police then opened up the gang's base for public viewing, charging five shillings. The public immediately carried away the dwelling, piece by piece, as grisly souvenirs. By 1840, the area had degenerated into a slum. It is for this reason that philanthropist Angela Burdett-Coutts purchased the land and established the Columbia Market in 1869. The market quickly began to specialise in flowers and caged birds but suffered in World War II and went into a long decline not fully arrested until a resurgence in the popularity of gardening was sparked by programmes featuring Alan Titchmarsh.

escort, provided by one of the duty regiments of Foot Guards, awaits him. Some saluting ensues, after which you hear the following dialogue.

'Halt, who comes there?'

'The Keys!' answers the Chief Yeoman Warder.

'Whose Keys?' says the sentry, who after 600 years should really have known by now.

'Queen Elizabeth's Keys.'

'Oh, those keys,' replies the sentry, after which there is some saluting, some God preserve Queen Elizabeth-ing, a bit of drumming and 'The Last Post' is played, before you go home to lock up your own house with considerably less fanfare.

TIME   Daily 9:53pm.

AMENITIES

Key Fact

The Ceremony of the Keys was interrupted only once during World War II when, during an air raid, a number of incendiary bombs fell on the old Victorian guardroom just as the Chief Yeoman Warder and the escort were coming through the Bloody Tower archway. The shockwave blew the escort and the Chief Yeoman Warder over, but they stood up, dusted themselves down and carried on. The Tower holds a letter from the Officer of the Guard to King George VI apologising for the ceremony being late. The King's reply states that the Officer is not to be punished as the delay was due to enemy action. If you're British doesn't it make you proud?

❼ SEE HOW MIDDLE-CLASS FASHIONS HAVE CHANGED AT THE GEFFRYE: MUSEUM OF THE HOME

Kingsland Road, London E2 8EA (© **020 7739 9893**, www.geffrye-museum.org. uk). ⊖ Liverpool Street then 149 or 242 bus from Bishopsgate.

From harpsichord to widescreen TV and lacy doilies to designer coffee tables, this museum charts how the domestic tastes of the middle class have evolved over the last 400 years. In 11 period living rooms from the 1630s right up to a recreated loft warehouse with laminated floors from Wapping in the 1990s, visitors can see how styles of furniture, carpeting and curtains have changed over time. There are occasional visiting exhibitions including a Christmas event that sees the rooms garlanded with era-specific festive decorations, while outside between April and October you can see a series of five town gardens planted according to how they'd look going back to Tudor times as well as a walled garden containing 170 varieties of herb. There is also an alms-house to look round (guided tours on Wednesday and Saturday £2).

OPEN   Tues–Sat 10am–5pm; Sun 12pm–5pm.

AMENITIES   ¶¶ 🛍 ☼ ♟

④⑧ CUDDLE BUNNY RABBITS AT HACKNEY CITY FARM

1a Goldsmiths Row, London E2 8QA (✆ **020 7729 6381**, www.hackneycityfarm.co.uk). ⊖ Bethnal Green is a 20-minute walk away.

♙ ◑

Based at an old brewery, this urban farm – with its pigs, sheep, goats and chickens – brings a welcome whiff of the countryside to Hackney. Founded more than 20 years ago, it's strong on cuddly furry friends like chinchillas and Guinea pigs. The rabbits were our children's favourites. The farm is also home to an Italian café while the events programme includes pottery (for children £5 on Tuesday, Wednesday and Sunday), art, craft and upholstery (book this one) workshops, plus one-day courses in low-impact, green living – although most of these are charge-able. The best time to come is around 4:30pm when it's feeding time.

OPEN   Tues–Sun 10am–4.30pm.

AMENITIES   ¶¶ ☼ ♟

④⑨ TAKE PART IN A VICTORIAN LESSON AT THE RAGGED SCHOOL MUSEUM

46–50 Copperfield Road, London E3 4RR (✆ **020 8980 6405**, www.raggedschoolmuseum.co.uk). ⊖ Mile End.

★ ♙ ☂

This ragged (free, but so-called because the pupils were poor and often dressed in rags) school was once the largest in London. It was open for 31 years before closing in 1908. Visitors take part in a Victorian lesson on the 3 Rs (reading, writing and 'rithmetic) at this former Dr Barnardo

Barnardo Boy

Thomas John Barnardo (1845–1905) was an Irish philanthropist born in Dublin. His medical work in the East End of London during the cholera epidemic of 1866 first drew his attention to the numbers of destitute children in the cities of England. Encouraged by the support of the seventh Earl of Shaftsbury and the first Earl Cairns, he gave up his ambition to be a foreign missionary and began his life's work. The first 'Dr Barnardo's Home' was opened in 1870 at 18 Stepney Causeway, London. By the time of his death, nearly 60,000 children had been rescued and educated. The work of Thomas Barnardo continues today by the British charity, Barnardo's.

school, although be warned – the mistress carries a cane and there'll be trouble if you've got dirty hands. The lessons, conducted by an actress dressed as a schoolmistress from the turn of the century, take place at 2:15pm and 3:30pm on the first Sunday of every month and there are only 34 seats at the lift-up desks so turn up early. The lessons, as they would have done 100 years ago, include a religious element to reflect Barnado's wish for children to have respect for the Bible. There is an old-fashioned East End kitchen and displays about the area's melting-pot history and, of course, on Barnardo himself. Pre-booked group talks are also available.

OPEN   Wed–Thurs 10am–5pm (first Sun each month 2pm–5pm).

AMENITIES   ☕ 🚻 ⛱ £

⑤⓪ WATCH LAMBS FROLIC IN FRONT OF CANARY WHARF AT MUDCHUTE PARK & FARM

Pier Street, Isle of Dogs, London E14 3HP (✆ **020 7515 5901**, www.mudchute.org). Docklands Light Railway: Mudchute. Cross East Ferry Road and immediately left is the entrance to Mudchute Park and Farm.

The largest city farm in Europe had a strange and really quite pleasant post-apocalyptic feel to it when we visited, which had something to do with the odd urban–rural juxtaposition of watching lambs gambolling in fields against the backdrop of Canary Wharf Tower. And also something to do with the city trader that we discovered here near the pig pen 'clearly in the early stages of a mental meltdown' according to my wife, who surmised this because (a) he was still in his suit and

(b) he had no family with him. The farm is home to more than 200 animals, including many rare breeds of goats, donkeys, ducks, llamas, geese and turkeys. There's a Pet's Corner, an equestrian centre for riding lessons (chargeable), regular animal-encounter sessions, and, if you're peckish, the Mudchute Kitchen serves farm-fresh eggs and fairy cakes, which our children loved so much they have since entered family folklore. The farm is set in 31 acres and there are bags of pellets available for 50p to feed the animals and indeed glassy-eyed traders with.

OPEN   Farm: Tues–Sun 9am–5pm. Park: open all the time.

AMENITIES   ☕ ⛩ ♇

⑤ SEE FREE COMEDY AT THE THEATRE ROYAL STRATFORD EAST

Gerry Raffles Square, Stratford, London E15 1BN (✆ **020 8534 0310**, www.stratford east.com). ⊖ Stratford.

★

Every Monday at 8pm (doors open half an hour earlier) there are free comedy nights in the bar; in July and August these gigs include many Edinburgh preview shows. Our hopes weren't overly high for this free gig in Stratford when we visited, but the grand setting of the bar with its blood-red walls attracted an appreciative and discerning comedy crowd and we saw a pretty good turn by Jim Grant, currently big on the circuit. The acts tend to be up and coming, so it's pot luck what you see, but the bar is nearly always full so come early or you'll find yourself standing.

OPEN   Mon–Sat 10am–7pm (8.30pm if a show is on).

AMENITIES   ¶¶ ♉

⑤ FIRE A CANNON AT THE NATIONAL MARITIME MUSEUM

Romney Road, Greenwich, London SE10 9NF (✆ **020 8858 4422**, www.nmm.ac.uk). Dockland Light Railway: Cutty Sark.

At this family-friendly museum you can fire a cannon, have a go at sailing a ship into port and see the fatal hole in the coat Lord Nelson died in at the Battle of Trafalgar in 1805. The museum is dedicated to the glory that was once Britain at sea, and also features replica ships and a children's trail, which saw our daughter so enthused by Lord Nelson's heroics she cast herself a seafaring medal on a disk of cardboard cut from an All Bran cereal box. There are also interesting exhibitions on the quest to find the North Passage and the slave trade.

OPEN   Daily 10am–5pm.

AMENITIES   ☕ 🛍 £

❸ STAND EITHER SIDE OF THE EARTH AT THE ROYAL OBSERVATORY

Blackheath Avenue, Greenwich, London SE10 8XJ (✆ **020 8858 4422**, www.nmm. ac.uk). Dockland Light Railway: Cutty Sark, a 15-minute walk away.

Founded by King Charles II in 1675 to solve the problem of finding longitude at sea, here you can stand on the famous meridian line with a foot on each side of the Earth's globe, guide a space mission and touch a 4.5 billion-year-old meteorite. There are photos of Saturn taken from the *Cassini* spacecraft, a chance to learn how the universe was formed, and on certain Sundays (check ahead) visitors can view sunspots through a Hydrogen Alpha 28-inch telescope, once the largest in the world. While you're here, check out the bright red Time Ball on top of Flamsteed House, first used in 1833. It was one of the world's earliest public time signals, alerting ships on the Thames, and it still operates each day at 12:55pm when the ball rises half way up its mast. The Time and Longitude Gallery is also worth a visit for its collection of marine clocks. The planetarium is chargeable. The best time to come is before 11:30am, the busiest is 1pm on Saturday and Sunday afternoons.

OPEN   Daily 10am–5pm.

AMENITIES   ☕ 🛍 P

❺❹ SEE THE WHITE LADY GHOST AT QUEEN'S HOUSE

Greenwich, London SE10 9NE (✆ **020 8858 4422**, www.nmm.ac.uk). Dockland Light Railway: Cutty Sark.

Designed by Inigo Jones, Queen's House was the first Palladian villa in England. It was commissioned by King James I, possibly to apologise to his wife Anne for losing his temper after she accidentally shot his pet hound during a deer hunt. The house showcases the National Maritime Museum's fine-art collection, including paintings by Gainsborough, Hogarth and Reynolds and is also renowned for its elegant Tulip Staircase, the first geometric self-supporting spiral stair in Britain. The staircase is also the location of the Rev RW Hardy's famous 'ghost' photograph taken on 19 June 1966, which revealed what appeared to be two or three shrouded figures on the staircase (see box). This was the main excuse my fretful wife used to refuse to enter the building, meaning I was forced to go in alone with the children. I had to carry them up a flight of the Tulip Staircase, one under each arm like surf boards because they were tired from pelting up and down the Maritime Museum (see p. 45). Don't miss the Great Hall, with its impressive geometric black-and-white floor tiling and wooden balcony running around the walls, where musicians played during King James's times.

OPEN   Daily 10am–5pm.

AMENITIES

55 SEE GREAT VIEWS OF LONDON FROM THE WOOLWICH FERRY

New Ferry Approach, Woolwich SE18 6DX (✆ **020 8853 9400**, www.greenwich. gov.uk). ⊖ North Greenwich.

The best way to see the iconic Canary Wharf tower and the O2

A Bridge Room too Far

In 2002 the gallery assistant at the Queen's House, Tony Anderson, had an unsettling experience. Here it is in his own chilling words: 'On Monday 20 May 2002 at 9:45am, myself and two colleagues were talking about which breaks we were on, when something caught my eye. One of the double doors from the Bridge Room closed and I thought at first it was the girl who does the talks at weekends, then realised the woman just glided across the balcony and went through the wall on the west side. I could not believe what I saw. I went very cold and the hairs on my arms and neck were on end. We went into the Queen's Presence Room and looked down towards the old Queen's Bedroom, and something passed through the ante-room and out through the wall. My two colleagues also felt cold at that time. The lady was dressed in a white-grey colour, old fashioned, something like a crinoline-type dress'.

Arena (the Millennium Dome in a previous incarnation) is from the river Thames on a 10-minute crossing on the Woolwich ferry. The free commuter service has been running since 1889, although there's been a ferry on this site from the 1300s. It's a workmanlike crossing handling one million vehicles and two-and-a-half million foot passengers a year; it's busiest at rush-hours in the morning, evening and at lunchtime, especially if the Blackwall Tunnel closes, although it's this overcrowding that gives the experience its rich atmosphere. If you're crossing from the south side of the river at the address given above and heading for Pier Road in North Woolwich on the opposite bank, set yourselves up on the left-hand side of the ferry for views that include the Thames Barrier. If you're a foot passenger or cyclist expect to get straight on the ferry, which leaves every 20 minutes from both sides of the river; if in a car you'll queue for about 20 minutes.

TIMETABLE   Mon–Sat 6:10am–8pm; Sun 11:30am–7:30pm. Journey lasts 10 minutes.

⑤⑥ SEE A WHALE PENIS AT THE HORNIMAN MUSEUM

100 London Road, Forest Hill, London SE23 3PQ (℃ **020 8699 1872**, www.horniman. ac.uk). Railway station: Forest Hill.

★

The highlights at this collection of over 800,000 exhibits, amassed by Victorian tea trader Frederick John Horniman (1835–1906), include a whale penis, a torture chair supposedly used during the Spanish Inquisition, an overstuffed walrus and some rare artwork plundered from King Oba's Benin palace. What is it with these Victorian businessmen? Can you imagine Sir Alan Sugar filling his home with whale penises or bonnets made by North American plains Indians? Why did they do it then and they don't do it now? Or maybe they do in secret. Is Richard Branson clandestinely filling his living room with Inuit seal-skin clothing and masks from the Tyrol region of Europe? And the sheer number of exhibits! If Horniman collected these items over a 50-year span, to get to 800,000 items and allowing for a short sleep each night, he'd have to be acquiring a new exhibit roughly every 22 minutes for that entire period. There is also an aquarium and gardens containing a nature trail and children's farmyard. Incidentally the walrus exhibit is overstuffed because the taxidermist had never seen a walrus before and didn't realise they had loose skin.

OPEN   Daily 10:30am–5:30pm.

AMENITIES   ☕ 🛍 🏕 🚹

57 SHOUT OUT RUDE NICKNAMES FOR OXBRIDGE CREW MEMBERS DURING THE OXFORD & CAMBRIDGE BOAT RACE

Thames Rowing Club, Putney Embankment, London SW15 9AA (www.theboat race.org). ⊖ Putney Bridge.

If the Walsall College of Arts and Technology took on Aberdeen University in a tug of war competition do you think 250,000 spectators would turn up to watch the spectacle and a further seven million tune in to watch it on the box? Yet every year these are the numbers who line the Thames or sit at home to view the Oxford–Cambridge Boat Race. You can watch the race at any point along the river from Putney to Mortlake, although the most popular hangouts are Putney Bridge, Putney Embankment and Bishops Park (at the start), Hammersmith and Barnes (mid-course) and Dukes Meadows and Chiswick Bridge (at the finish). The race is four-and-a-quarter miles (6.8km) long so you won't catch more than a glimpse of the boats. Better to see the whole event on free big screens at Bishops Park in Fulham or Furnival Gardens in

The Boat Race

The idea for a rowing race between the universities came from two friends – Charles Merivale, a student at Cambridge, and his Harrow school-friend Charles Wordsworth (nephew of poet William Wordsworth), who was at Oxford. On 12 March 1829, Cambridge sent a challenge to Oxford and thus the tradition was born, continued to the present day, where the loser of the previous year's race challenges the opposition to a rematch. The first Boat Race took place at Henley-on-Thames in Oxfordshire, the event eventually morphing into the Henley Royal Regatta. After the first year, the Boat Race took place at Westminster in London, but by 1845, when Westminster had become too crowded, it was moved six miles (10km) upstream to the then-country village of Putney.

You're Going to Like This, but Not a Lot

Former alumni of the Royal Ballet School include yachtswoman Clare Francis, Darcy Bussell, Wayne (no surprise) Sleep, ex-Blue Peter presenter Lesley (remember her straight back) Judd, and 'the lovely' Debbie McGee, wife and assistant of TV magician Paul Daniels.

Hammersmith. Of course you could pretend to be from Oxford or Cambridge University yourself and bellow made-up nicknames for the rowers along with general encouragement. 'Come on Bosher' or 'Flatdick – get stuck in'. Famous names who have rowed in this race include comic actor Hugh Laurie, Lord Snowdon, Geoffrey Archer and Matthew Pinsent.

TIME   Apr 4:30pm.

⑤⑧ TIPTOE AROUND THE WHITE LODGE MUSEUM & BALLET RESOURCE CENTRE

The Royal Ballet School, White Lodge, Richmond Park, Richmond, Surrey TW10 5HR (℃ **020 8392 8440**, www.royalballetschool.co.uk). ⊖ Richmond.

★

Based at an offshoot of the Royal Ballet School that Billy Elliott tried so desperately to get into, this, the only purpose-built ballet museum in Britain, has among its highlight exhibits a pair of Margot Fonteyn's autographed pointe shoes, the death mask of Anna Pavlova and letters typed by economist John Maynard Keynes about costumes for his Russian ballerina wife, Lydia Lopokova. The 80-year-old ballet school here is one of the most famous in the world and hothouses boys and girls aged 11–16. It is based in a Grade I-listed Palladian mansion that was once residence of royals including Queen Caroline, George III and Queen Victoria. It was also the honeymoon home of the Queen Mother and the future George VI and is a place that's very hard to walk around, without rising to your tip-toes and pirouetting as you hum The Nutcracker Suite.

OPEN   Tues and Thurs, during term-time 1:30pm–3:30pm (by appointment only).

AMENITIES

⑤⑨ LOOK FOR DICK TURPIN'S GHOST AT HEATHROW AIRPORT

Heathrow Airport, Hounslow, Middlesex TW6 2GW (ℂ **0844 335 1801**, www.heathrow airport.com). ⊖ Heathrow.

The ghost of the famous 18th-century highwayman apparently stalks passengers and staff at the world's busiest airport. Heathrow Airport is based on the site of Hounslow Heath, stalked by Turpin in life; it is rumoured that there was an unofficial exorcism in the 1990s to rid the airport of his ghost. Dick Turpin, popular with the poor because he focused his cruelty on the rich, stole livestock while robbing and murdering his way round England in the 1730s before being hanged in 1739. Sightings of him, most commonly in Terminal 4 and the long-stay car parks, have him wearing a jacket with blood-red sleeves, a black tri-cornered hat, black cape, high boots and riding a black stallion although lately (possibly because of stricter security restrictions) he's experienced as an unnerving hot breath on the back of the neck or an unworldly howling, not to be confused with exasperated groans coming from beneath flight information boards. The highwayman is not the only ghost at Heathrow. In 1948 a DC3 Dakota from Belgian Airlines crashed on approach during a foggy night. No one survived the accident, although rescue crews saw a gentleman in a hat appear from the wreckage asking for his briefcase. He faded away as he was approached and was later found dead in the carnage, but is often seen along the runway, still searching for his valise.

AMENITIES ☕ 🍴 🍷

⑥⓪ LEARN HOW BEETLES SUMMONED LIGHTNING ON A GUIDED WALK IN RICHMOND PARK

Richmond Park, London TW10 5HS (ℂ **020 8948 3209**, www.royalparks.org.uk). ⊖ Richmond, then 65 or 371 bus.

During a guided stroll through London's largest royal park, learn about the 600 deer that live here, the protected view from Henry's Mount to St Paul's Cathedral 10 miles (16km) away and why the park's famous stag beetles were blamed for summoning thunder and lightning – medieval folklore claimed they buzzed around with burning coals in

61–67 Go Star-Spotting

The best places to bother celebrities are usually associated with pricey food and drink. London is therefore not surprisingly where you'll find most home-grown celebrities, although the stars have been increasingly migrating further away from the prying eyes of the paparazzi to places such as Edinburgh and Brighton and Hove. Below is a top seven list of where to hang out with your mobile phone poised for that off-guard shot to flog on to the 3am Girls at *The Mirror*.

The Groucho Club

45 Dean Street, Soho, London W1D 4QB, (℗ **020 7439 4685**, www. thegrouchoclub.com). ⊖ Leicester Square.

Who: Kate Moss, Lily Allen, Courtney Love.

Top tip: Membership to the Groucho Club is more exclusive than the SAS and nearly as tough to get into – you'll need a friend with a membership just to get near the bar. Although if you do know any members of the SAS you could storm the building with stun grenades.

The Ivy

1–5 West Street, Covent Garden, London WC2H 9NQ (℗ **020 7836 4751**, www.the-ivy.co.uk). ⊖ Covent Garden.

Who: Everyone who's anyone – regulars here include Tom Cruise, Victoria and David Beckham, Elton John and George Michael.

Top tip: We're assuming your vigil takes place outside the building but if you do intend to eat here, be warned: the waiting list is several months long and it's very expensive.

Leicester Square

Soho, London WC2H. ⊖ Leicester Square.

Who: Most big London movie premieres happen in Leicester Square, so if you're around at the right time, you might spot Tom Cruise, Johnny Depp, Keira Knightley, Katie Holmes, Kirsten Dunst, George Lucas and more.

Top tip: If you want to catch a glimpse of your favourite star, make sure you turn up early – fans camp overnight outside cinemas.

Primrose Hill

North London NW2. Tube: Chalk Farm, Camden Town or Regent's Park.

Who: Kate Moss, Jude Law, Sadie Frost and Sienna Miller are all part of the famous Primrose Hill set.

Top tip: As well as being a great place to spot your favourite celebs, the view of London from the top of Primrose Hill is breathtaking. Stuck for something interesting to say after bumping into one of them in the street, we suggest you mention that the final Martian encampment from HG Wells's sci-fi classic novel *War of the Worlds* was based on Primrose Hill. They may think your fun-fact is erudite and invite you for a coffee to hear more of your bookish insights. Alternatively they will call the police or spray you with mace.

The Hawley Arms

2 Castlehaven Road, Camden, London, NW1 8QU (© **020 7428 5979**, www.thehawleyarms.co.uk). ⊖ Camden Town or Chalk Farm.

Who: Amy Winehouse, Kelly Osbourne, Liam Gallagher, The Mighty Boosh's Noel Fielding, Johnny Borrell from Razorlight and Kirsten Dunst have all been seen falling out of this local celebrity haunt.

Top tip: Wear tight rock-star jeans and a washed out T-shirt and don't mention the other Noel.

The Golden Heart

110 Commercial Street, Shoreditch, London E1 6LZ (© **020 7247 2158**). ⊖ Shoreditch.

Who: Amongst local shopkeepers and workers, artists (Gilbert and George, Tracey Emin, Chapman Brothers), fashion students, and the occasional alcoholic celeb (Pete Doherty).

Top tip: Don't get too out of control – it is said the ghost of the famous 18th-century Christian philanthropist Elizabeth Fry (the face on the back of the £5 note) lives in the basement and turns the beer taps off if things get too rowdy. A good jukebox keeps it buzzing inside and open fires soon warm even the most miserable drinker.

St Margaret's Tavern

107 St Margaret's Road, Twickenham, Middlesex, TW1 2LJ (© **020 8439 4685**). ⊖ Richmond. Station: St Margaret's.

Who: Based opposite Twickenham Studios, the pub serves many off-duty stars of the silver screen during a quiet lunchtime – Jude Law, Guy Ritchie and Colin Firth have been spied here.

Top tip: Don't mention the adoption of African children.

their jaws, dropping them and setting fire to thatched roofs and wooden stables. Designated an SSI, the 2,500-acre park also boasts 144 species of birds and Pembroke Lodge, the former home to Prime Minister Lord John Russell and subsequently his grandson, the famous philosopher Bertrand Russell. Walks led by Friends of Richmond Park last a couple of hours and take place on the first Saturday of every month, usually at 10am and most starting from Pembroke Lodge, but check online for individual details. If you haven't got a car, get to Richmond Station and then catch the 371 or 65 bus to the pedestrian gate at Petersham. Warning: many of the deer in the park are infected with a bacterium called Borrelia burgdorferi, which can be transmitted to humans through a tick bite causing Lyme Disease. The symptoms are as follows: a bull's eye-patterned rash, facial palsy, back pain, psychosis and bladder problems. Park attractions include horse riding, cycling, golf and fishing.

OPEN   Summer 7am until dusk; winter 7:30am until dusk.

AMENITIES   ☕ 🍴 ♀ 🅿

2 And to do Online . . .

❻⑧ CHANGE THE WORLD WITH THE CLICK OF A MOUSE

www.petitions.pm.gov.uk

☺

OK, we have just discovered the best thing to do in Britain on a rainy day. Signing online petitions to Number 10 Downing Street. While this is not strictly speaking a touristy type of activity we have never felt better about ourselves than we do right now after an exhilarating morning putting the world to rights. Not only have we been doing good but we were able to drink a cup of tea and eat a packet of custard creams while we did this. These are the petitions we have so far signed – a petition by Anita Jackson to change the law to stop the inbreeding of pedigree dogs. We signed a petition to rethink import duty on mobility scooters and, incensed, like 2,609 others, we have also petitioned to apologise for the chemical castration of Alan Turing, the gay scientist who helped break the Nazi enigma code. Other issues we are now involved with include banning lash inserts used in mascara ads (we are *not* really sure about this), knighting the Pythons and banning dog washing machines in the UK. The advantage of signing these petitions is that the confirmation email bears the title 10 Downing Street, making you feel like you have been involved in a productive exchange of views with the Prime Minster himself.

⑥⑨ MAKE FACES BEHIND SIMON COWELL ON THE X FACTOR

www.applausestore.com

What better way could there be to spend your Saturday night than to be sat a few rows back from pop svengali Simon Cowell baying with your wife 'off, off, off' at a talentless upstart from Solihull trying to make his dream come true while murdering a Whitney Houston song. My wife cannot think of one, which is why to mark her birthday, we are on the reserve waiting list for a seat in the Wembley Fountain Studio audience for this very show. I can barely find the words to sum up how much I am looking forward to this milestone in my life as a music lover. Apply to be part of this (un)edifying pantomime at the Applause Store on the web address above. Alternatively, if this show is not your idea of entertainment and you'd rather tear your ears from your head and boil them than be there, the website has free seats in the studio audience up for grabs for a string of other shows including *Celebrity Big Brother*, *QI*, *Nevermind the Buzzcocks*, *Britain's Got Talent*, *Dancing On Ice*, or Channel 4's *Big Food Fight*. If you can't find anything here, try Hat Trick (www.hattrick.co.uk), BBC Tickets (www.bbc.co.uk/tickets) and ITV tickets (www.itv.com/beontv/tickets). Apply online for free tickets that are available normally on a first-come-first-served basis after supplying a few details about yourself. Then wait to hear whether you've been selected. For most shows you can claim up to four tickets, although there are often restrictions on the ages of children.

⑦⓪ SEE LATEST FILM RELEASES BEFORE ANYBODY ELSE

www.seefilmfirst.com

British cinemas hold pre-release screenings of movies in an attempt to gauge public reaction and generate a word-of-mouth buzz. All you have to do to get free tickets, normally costing upwards of £12 a head, is register at the above web address. After this you're sent an email alert when a film is due to be released along with a screen code. Use this screen code on the web link provided to access the list of cinemas showing the pre-screening. Select the cinema you want to go to, how many tickets you want and book them online. Print off the tickets, turn up, hand over the ticket and you're in. Simple as that. The first time we went we felt sure someone would jump out from behind the purple curtain to try and sell us a timeshare in Alicante, but actually the experience was better than a normal visit to the cinema. Even watching a bad movie (and we're talking *Wolverine*) you can't help feeling slightly more favourable towards it when you've watched it for free.

ⓩ DO SQUAT THRUSTS WITH A SQUADDIE

Military Fitness Limited (℡ **020 7751 9742**, www.britmilfit.com).

Yes Sir, Sergeant Major Sir! Have a free outdoor army work-out pretty much anywhere in the UK by registering at the above web address. After registering and filling out a health questionnaire, you are invited to attend one of 80 venues nationwide to be put through your paces by an ex-member of the armed forces. The training sessions last an hour, with a 15-minute warm up and 10-minute warm down sandwiched around a gruelling series of squat thrusts, burpees, press-ups and paired exercises designed to simulate the rigours of a military fitness regime. The participant-to-instructor ratio is about 15 to 1, all levels of fitness are catered for and the company has about 15,000 members. If you liked it, or at least felt the benefits of the workout (because face it, you're not going to like it), join up for courses costing between £20 to £46 a month. There are around four sessions a week in your area if you're up for them. No Sir, Sergeant Major Sir!

Helter-Skelter, Brighton.

SOUTH-EAST

In the south-east free highlights include activities as varied as looking for Kate Moss on West Wittering beach, entering the British and World Marble Championships in Crawley and marvelling at real fleas dressed as Mexicans in the Natural History Museum at Tring. There are three great piers worth visiting including the buzzy one at Brighton, the posh one in Southwold and the pier in Worthing where every year fancy-dressed lunatics jump off the end of it in the name of entertainment. For culture lovers there are the imps at Lincoln Cathedral to check out, the constable paintings at Bridge Cottage in Suffolk and the world famous Christmas Eve Carol Service at King's College Cambridge. Other recommendations include the museum dedicated to the TV series *Dad's Army* in Thetford, the earthship in Brighton, a building made from only recycled materials and the Lord Nelson pub where Britain's famous sea admiral came to drink between naval commands. The Fitzwillian Museum in Cambridge is full of art treasures while other fun things to do include attempting to bump into the Queen walking her corgis on Holkham Bay in Norfolk and getting yourself blessed at the Shrine of Our Lady of Walsingham. Outdoors there's Derek Jarman's famous driftwood garden near Dungeness to visit, the chance to play Pooh-sticks at the bridge in the Ashdown Forest that inspired AA Milne and the wonderful woodland of Burnham Beeches in Farnham that has been an inspiration for film directors. Finally walking the white cliffs of Dover is an experience to savour and it's a real eye opener visiting Bethlem Royal Hospital Museum, where they used to poke lunatics in less enlightened times.

⑫ STAND ON AMERICAN SOIL IN RUNNYMEDE

Runnymede, North Lodge, Windsor Road, Old Windsor, Berkshire SL4 2JL (✆ **01784 432891**, www.nationaltrust.org.uk\runnymede).

☺

The John F Kennedy Memorial at the same site where the Magna Carta was signed in 1215, is officially part of American soil. When you've pondered the significance of the birth of constitutional law and the passing of the US's most charismatic president, you can send text messages to your friends saying, 'In US for next 20 minutes but around for cup of tea later this afternoon if M25's clear'. There are guided group tours available off the National Trust site (pre-booking essential), bat walks in the evenings (£2 – again call ahead), as well as free self-guided way-marked walks, although the best thing to do after you've soaked up the history is to have a lazy picnic in the meadows of Long Mede or on the banks of the Thames. The JFK memorial was unveiled in 1965 by Queen Elizabeth II and Jacqueline Kennedy, is accessed via 50 granite steps and bears the legend: 'Died by an assassin's hand 22nd November, 1963'. The other memorials on Cooper's Hill are to the Commonwealth airmen of World War II (download a guide to your MP3 player or iPod from www.cwgc.org) and also to the Magna Carta itself, which was paid for in acknowledgement of the document's importance to the drafting of the US constitution by members of the American Bar Association. Across the river is the revered Ankerwycke Yew, which may mark the site where the Magna Carta was signed and under which Henry VIII had a tryst with Anne Boleyn in the 1530s.

OPEN All year around.

AMENITIES

⓭ DRESS UP AS A VILLAGE IDIOT AT THE MUSEUM OF ENGLISH RURAL LIFE

Redlands Road, Reading, Berkshire RG1 5EX (*C* **0118 378 8660**, www.reading.ac.uk/merl/).

At this nationally important collection, watch the film about barrel-making, check out the blazer worn by David Jason in his role as Pop Larkin during the *Darling Buds of May* TV series or dress up as an old-fashioned farmer/village idiot in the straw hat, clogs and smock. Housed in the former home of the Palmer family, of Huntley & Palmer biscuit fame, there are also tractors, old horse-drawn wagons and an example of everyone's O-level history bête noire, Jethro Tull's seed drill. Guided tours lasting 45 minutes give access to archives that contain other agrarian treasures and one of the world's largest teapots (holding six gallons). These are free and regular visiting lecturers talk here on subjects as varied as the plight of child evacuees during World War II through to tips on growing shallots.

OPEN Tues–Fri 9am–5pm; Sat–Sun 2pm–4:30pm.

AMENITIES

⓮ ENJOY QUIET CONTEMPLATION WHERE THOMAS GRAY PENNED HIS FAMOUS ELEGY

Monument to Thomas Gray, Church Lane, Stoke Poges, Buckinghamshire SL2 4NZ. No phone or website but some info on www.stoke-poges.com.

One of the most famous verses in the English language was composed among the gravestones in this ancient graveyard. *Elegy Written in a Country Churchyard* was written a couple of miles south of Stoke Poges by Thomas Gray (1716–1781). He was one of the foremost poets of the Romantic movement and wrote his memorial to his parents in Gray's Field next to the Church of St Giles off the B416, where he is buried. There is a grandiose monument marking the spot, erected in 1788, although Gray's actual tomb lies curiously hidden opposite a small plaque on the church wall and sheltered behind a straggle of rose plants.

OPEN　All year round.

AMENITIES　

⑦ PRETEND TO BE AN OUTLAW IN BURNHAM BEECHES

East Burnham Common, Lord Mayor's Drive, Farnham, Buckinghamshire (✆ **01753 647358**, www.cityoflondon.gov.uk/burnham).

This is the setting for the outlaw scenes in Kevin Costner's *Robin Hood: Prince of Thieves* movie and is the perfect place to climb an 800-year-old beech tree and shout to your wife through the branches, 'Milady, a woman of your beauty has no need for such decoration' before jumping down to rip the accessories off her wrists. The 540 acres of Burnham Beeches is designated an SSI because of the high number of old, pollarded oak and beech trees as well as the 60 rare species (mainly beetle-y type creatures but also scarce dragonflies) which live in the rotting wood of the ancient trees. A riot of browns, golds and yellows in autumn, it's a great picnic spot, the haunt of many an amateur photographer and a good place to stumble into a film crew. Other movies shot here have included *King Arthur*, *The Wind in the Willows* and parts of two Harry Potters as well as four Carry On movies. Close to Pinewood Studios, you can pretty much bet that any British film with a rural setting has been filmed here at some point. Owned by the City of London, which bought the woodland in the 19th century in a farsighted greenbelt policy against the sprawl of the city, wildlife attractions include buzzards, red kites, tawny owls, sparrowhawks, roe and muntjac deer. There are self-guided walks to download as well as a map on the website above showing you the sites of the two oldest trees – the Cage Pollard and Druid's Oak.

OPEN　All year round.

AMENITIES　

⑦ MAKE SURE YOU TIE YOUR SHOELACES UP AT THE FITZWILLIAM MUSEUM

Trumpington Street, Cambridge CB2 1RB (📞 **01223 332900**, www.fitzwilliam.cam. ac.uk).

I was almost wrestled to the floor by security at this famous museum, not for attempting to deface a priceless Titian painting, pinching a sublime Japanese print or for attempting to steal an archaic 500BC coin from Knossos. It happened because I walked into the Antiquities Gallery with (drum roll) my shoelaces untied. The Fitzwilliam Museum, which highlights masterpieces from, among others, Veronese, Rubens, Van Dyck, Canaletto, Hogarth, Gainsborough, Constable, Monet, Dégas, Renoir, Cézanne and Picasso, is particularly safety conscious because in January 2006 a man tripped over his untied shoelaces and fell into a priceless 17th-century Qing dynasty vase, smashing it into hundreds of pieces. Not knowing this story at the time, in among all the Roman and Romano-Egyptian art I felt like a five-year-old boy who was told off by a teacher and barred from the De Wit Collection of Anglo

Shades of Gray

Thomas Gray, born in Cornhill, London, was the son of an exchange broker and a milliner. The fifth of 12 children and the only one to survive infancy, he was educated at Eton College and Cambridge. A delicate, scholarly boy, Gray spent his time reading great literature, avoiding athletics and playing the harpsichord for relaxation. He made friends at school with Horace Walpole, son of Prime Minister Robert Walpole, at whose insistence his greatest work, *Elegy Written in a Country Churchyard*, was published in 1751. Although one of the least productive poets to have lived (only 13 verses were published in his lifetime), Gray is regarded as the predominant Romantic poetic figure of the mid-18th century and his elegy was an instant sensation. It's reflective, calm yet stoic tone was hugely admired, and it is still one of the most frequently quoted poems in the English language. It contains several phrases that have passed into the common English lexicon, including 'far from the Madding crowd' and 'kindred spirit'. Less successful, however, was another poem of Gray's, entitled *Ode on the Death of a Favourite Cat*.

Saxon coins when they found out I'd not eaten my ploughman's lunch. Guided tours available.

OPEN   Tues–Sat 10am–5pm; Sun midday–5pm.

AMENITIES   ☕ ♿ 🛍 🅿

⑦ ANNOUNCE A MOMENTOUS BREAKTHROUGH IN THE EAGLE PUB

8 Benet Street, Cambridge CB2 3QN (✆ **01223 505020**).

Coincidentally in this pub, where scientists James Watson and Francis Crick announced to regulars they'd cracked the secret of life by discovering the structure of DNA, we cracked our own equally unfathomable code – how to turn off our daughter's talking Piglet, which had been annoying us since Norwich. Crick and Watson used to work at the Cavendish Laboratory, a part of Cambridge University around the corner from here, and there is a blue plaque at the entrance commemorating the historic day they burst in on 28 February 1953 to announce their breakthrough. Other highlights include the back RAF room, whose ceiling is covered in the signatures of Cambridge-stationed American pilots from World War II (including that of the crew of the *Memphis Belle*, inspiration for the movie of the same name). The beer and food are slightly more pricey (and frankly not that fantastic) than neighbouring pubs but worth it to revel in that bit of history.

OPEN   Mon–Sat 11am–11pm; Sun midday–10:30pm.

⑦ HEAR THE FAMOUS CHRISTMAS EVE CAROL SERVICE AT KING'S COLLEGE

King's College, King's Parade, Cambridge CB2 1ST (✆ **01223 331215**, www.kings.cam.ac.uk).

This carol service, representing Christmas for millions of people across the globe, is played annually on the BBC World Service, where it's been broadcast on Radio 4 nearly every year since 1928, even during World War II, when ancient glass was removed from King's College Chapel windows and the heating switched off. To experience this symbol of archetypal Britishness, and revel in the history of the chapel (see box), attend the Festival of Nine Lessons and Carols – as it's officially called – in person. The festival was first staged in 1918 by Eric Milner-White, the Dean of King's College, after his experience as an army chaplain convinced him that the Church of England needed more imaginative worship. Traditionally starting with *Once in Royal David's City*, the carols are sung by the choir of King's College, Cambridge with the congregation only allowed to join in with the hymns.

As you'd expect this is a very popular service, so start queuing in the college quad before 7am on the morning of the service to be guaranteed a seat, although some enthusiasts camp out in survival sleeping bags on King's Parade up to three days beforehand. The chapel seats 1,000 and it only opens up to the public after it has filled up with students and fellows of the college. The service begins at 3pm and lasts an hour and a half. It's a good idea to wrap up warm and get the person ahead of you to save your place in the queue so you can visit the college coffee shop once in a while for a warming drink. Bags and packages cannot be taken into the chapel and must be left with the porters in designated areas. A limited number of advance tickets are available for people unable to queue because of disability or illness. If you cannot face any of this hullabaloo, come along to the college for Evensong at 5:30pm (Monday through to Saturday) or at 10:30am and 3:30pm on Sundays to hear the choir. Arrive 20 minutes before the service and queue at the same point in the college quad.

King's College Chapel

The first stone of King's College was laid by Henry VI in 1446, who envisaged it as the university of scholars from Eton College. However this fine late Gothic masterpiece was not completed until 100 years later in the reign of Henry VIII. The chapel and ornate choir are open to explore; its delicate fan-vaulted ceiling is one of the largest in the world and there are 12 massive stained-glass windows modelled by Flemish craftsmen through which shafts of light sparkle on a sunny day. The chapel's famous choir has 16 young choristers, all educated at the college's choir school. The youngsters travel the world giving recitals and concerts for much of the year.

⑲ PLAY POOH-STICKS AT WINNIE THE POOH'S FAVOURITE SPOT

Ashdown Forest Centre, Forest Row, East Sussex RH18 5JP (✆ **01342 823583**, www.ashdownforest.org).

We played 34 games of Pooh-sticks in the rain at Pooh's famous wooden bridge amid loud cries of 'you're cheating' and 'stop *throwing* it', before our daughter finally won one game and we were allowed to squelch back to the car. The game of Pooh-sticks featured in *The House at Pooh Corner* and was inspired by AA Milne's own games with his son Christopher Robin, himself a character in the stories – the animals featured in the books were all based on his toys. For more Pooh-related fun, download walks in the Ashdown Forest (the model for 100 Aker Wood) from the web address above. They take in locations from the books including the Heffalump Trap, the Enchanted Place, the North Pole and Eeyore's Sad and Gloomy Place, renamed Dinah's Sad and Gloomy Place by us after my wife fell in a puddle and ruined her overcoat. To get to Pooh-sticks Bridge, drive for a mile south on the B2026 from Hartfield and turn right down the small lane at the tiny village of Chuck Hatch. Twenty yards in there's a car park. Follow the well-beaten path of the bridleway for 10 minutes before emerging at a public highway and some gates. Past the gates on the right is another bridleway. The bridge is a 10-minute walk along here.

OPEN   All year round.

AMENITIES   Sticks

A Stickler for the Rules

In the traditional version of Pooh-sticks, participants drop sticks simultaneously on the upstream side of a bridge and then run to the other side where the winner is the player whose stick is first to appear on the other side of the bridge. The stick must be made of organic materials, preferably willow, and must be dropped, not thrown, into the water. Any player deemed to have thrown their stick is disqualified, or in our son's case barred from the next chocolate treat hand-out.

80 WATCH STREET PERFORMERS AT THE BRIGHTON FESTIVAL

Brighton, East Sussex BN1/BN2 (© **01273 700747**, www.brightonfestival.org).

Britain's largest arts festival kicks off its three-week knees-up with the world's cutest parade – more than 4,000 dressed-up local school children parading through city streets. Attracting 10,000 visitors, it's the curtain-raiser for a string of city events bringing in internationally known actors, authors, musicians and other performers. As well as many paid-for events, there are dozens of free shows, which have included madcap eco-fables performed in the Trafalgar Street Arches or Queen's Park being given a night-time makeover involving molten-glass sculptures and creepy sound effects. Local artists' work is showcased via a variety of open houses, and there's also a fringe festival with over 600 events running alongside the main festival, including acts based from insect circuses to escapology. The festival culminates in the Brighton International Buskers Festival, on the final weekend of May, which concludes with a firework display at the marina.

OPEN   May. Check website for dates.

AMENITIES

81 BEAM DOWN TO ENGLAND'S FIRST EARTHSHIP

Stanmer Organics, Stanmer Park, Brighton, East Sussex BN1 9PZ (© **01273 206306**, www.lowcarbon.co.uk).

Earthships are cutting-edge 'green' buildings, constructed using old car tyres and recycled materials like discarded glass bottles. They use the planet's natural systems to provide all utilities – the sun's energy and rain for heat, power and water. This Earthship was built by the Low Carbon Trust and is now a community centre that looks like a cross between a Mexican adobe, a children's Wendy House and a recycling skip. On a wander around, learn all about terms like photovoltaic panels, grey-water recycling and low-impact materials and use them later to impress your right-on friends at dinner parties. The

Earthship was featured on *Grand Designs* and evolved from the pioneering work of radical sustainable-living architect Michael Reynolds in New Mexico. Try not to arrive at the Earthship by car, as you may well be tarred and feathered, albeit with low-impact materials. Take the bus from Brighton, alighting at the Stanmer Park stop. The area is served by buses 25, 25c and 78. If arriving at Falmer Railway Station, take the underpass towards Sussex University. Tours of the Earthship are normally £5 but free during the Brighton's Regency Open House festival in September and on various other open days in the summer. Check dates and book tours on the website above.

OPEN　Tours start at 10:30am daily.

❽❷ LEARN ABOUT THE MODS & ROCKERS' SCRAPS AT THE BRIGHTON MUSEUM & ART GALLERY

Royal Pavilion Gardens, Brighton, East Sussex BN1 1EE (✆ **03000 290900**, www. brighton-hove-rpml.org.uk).

This museum tells the bohemian tale of Brighton's history, covering its days as roustabout hang-out for the Prince Regent in the mid-18th century, through to its setting for the famous seafront scraps between the Mods and Rockers of the 1960s, all the way up to its present-day status as the gay capital of Britain. Highlight exhibits include a 1963 Lambretta, a pair of George IV's outsize 19th-century breeches and a Goldstone Ground turnstile from Brighton and Hove Albion's former football stadium. The museum houses the largest Art Nouveau and Art Deco collections outside London, as well as Surrealist artwork including the famous Mae West's Lips Sofa designed by Salvador Dalí. Its fine art galleries contain works by Dutch master painter Jan Lievens and Victorian domestic artist GD Leslie. Our children loved Renegade Clothes, featuring some of the whackier outfits worn by locals going back to the teddy boys of the 1950s.

OPEN　Tues–Sun 10am–5pm.

AMENITIES　

⑧ GO ON A RIDE AT BRIGHTON PIER

Madeira Drive, Brighton, East Sussex BN2 1TW (℡ **01273 609361**, www.brighton pier.co.uk).

Scoffing candy floss or an ice-cream, wander on to Brighton's iconic pier, widely regarded as the finest built in Victorian England and with fantastic views of Brighton's Regency seafront. A great place to lounge about on a breezy deckchair, the 111-year-old pier is crammed with sheepish-looking adults, many of whom look a bit blue around the gills and might have just experienced 3.6gs at 120 feet (36.5m) above the sea in a revolving pod on the Booster ride (£5). There are plenty of other less intense rides for children and arcades to lose change in, plus cafés to fill up in, although mostly the pier is simply a fun place to people-watch on.

OPEN   Daily 10am–11pm; some attractions close earlier.

AMENITIES

⑧ STAR SPOTTING AT THE CHILDREN'S PLAY-PARK

West Pier, Brighton, East Sussex BN1 2FL.

The play-park with a play-pool for children in the summer just off the beach has a great café next door.

Who: Patsy Palmer, Marcus Brigstock and Samantha Janus bring their offspring here.

Top tip: get your own children to play with their children to give you a fantastic opportunity to sidle up in the sandpit and introduce yourself.

⑧ DEBATE THE FANCY DRESS FLEAS AT THE NATURAL HISTORY MUSEUM AT TRING

Walter Rothschild Building, Akeman Street, Tring, Hertfordshire HP23 6AP (℡ **020 7942 6171**, www.nhm.ac.uk/tring).

The collection of stuffed animals here was assembled by the eccentric Walter Rothschild (1868–1937) of the celebrated banking dynasty, whose home Tring Park was once thronged with kangaroos, a tame wolf and the zebras to draw his carriage. Notable displays at this museum include the South African quagga (a bit like a zebra, now extinct), an enormous stuffed infant elephant and a couple of fleas dressed somehow by someone perhaps slightly insane (we really are not making this up) in Mexican dancer outfits. There are hands-on exhibits for children in the Discovery Room as well as activity sheets and a café to debate the fancy dress fleas in.

'Why Mexican outfits?'

'I don't know'

'Was the person who did it Mexican?'

'It didn't say'

'Imagine whoever did it, doing it. Bent over the fleas, measuring the cloth ...'

'I can't'

'Did she tailor them for individual fleas or find the fleas that fitted the outfits? Did she have to kill the fleas? Think about the fleas. What were the chances that they'd end up dressed in Mexican clothes being stared at in a museum?'

OPEN   Mon–Sat 10am–5pm; Sun 2pm–5pm.

AMENITIES

⑧⑥ SEE WHERE THEY ONCE POKED 'LUNATICS' WITH STICKS AT THE BETHLEM

Royal Hospital Museum, Monks Orchard Road, Beckenham, Kent BR3 3BX (*C* **020 3228 4227**, www.bethlemheritage.org.uk).

★

At this notorious hospital for mental patients, which gave the world the word 'bedlam', it was once possible, for a penny, to visit 'lunatics in their cells' and poke them with long sticks to enrage them. Originally a priory for treating the sick in 1247, the hospital grew into a symbol in the 18th century for the brutal treatment of the mentally ill, whose inherent moral weakness was considered to blame for their plight. The hospital name was corrupted to Bedlam (meaning 'uproar and confusion') and it has been home to, among others, Charlie Chaplin's mother Hannah and several would-be assassins including James Hadfield, who attempted to shoot George III, Edward Oxford who fired a pistol at Queen Victoria and Prince Albert as well as

Daniel M'Naghten, who mistakenly killed a civil servant while believing him to be Prime Minister Robert Peel. The hospital is now a world leader in psychiatry and although the museum based here doesn't shy away from telling its brutal story, it focuses mainly on progress in the treatment of the mentally ill and also showcases some of the work of two of its most famous inmates (see box, below).

OPEN   Mon–Fri 9:30am–4:30pm.

AMENITIES

⑧ VISIT DEREK JARMAN'S GARDEN

Prospect Cottage, Dungeness Road, Dungeness, Kent TN29 9NE (www.dungeness.org.uk).

★

Standing in the shadow of the Dungeness Nuclear Power Station, the famous driftwood garden of the legendary film-maker and painter Derek Jarman isn't strictly speaking an attraction. However, the lack of any fence separating it from the shingle beach means it's easy to see from the path without being intrusive to the owner, Jarman's partner (Jarman died in 1994). The garden is full of interesting wooden sculptures, and the colourful (somehow) sea-spray resistant wild flowers seem out of keeping with the barren, darkly black-and-white lunar-like landscape thrumming with an audible buzz

Dadd's Dad

As well as being able to see inhuman restraints used in the past at Bethlem, the work of its celebrated artist inmates – Richard Dadd and Louis Wain – are also showcased. Thought now to be a paranoid-schizophrenic, Dadd was brought to Bedlam after killing his father in 1843, believing him to be the devil. Before his incarceration he was a major Victorian painter. His work, in particular his intricate masterpiece *The Fairy Feller's Masterstroke*, went on to influence British composers and artists as diverse as sci-fi writer Sir Terry Pratchett and the pop group Queen. Painting from the early 1900s onwards, Wain may have suffered from schizophrenia and was famous for painting cats; it is even possible that his illness was triggered by toxoplasmosis caught from the animals he loved.

of electricity from the power station. The old clapboard fisherman's cottage, where Jarman came for solace after being diagnosed with AIDS, is captivating in itself. It has the first stanzas and last five lines of John Donne's poem, *The Sun Rising*, down one wall and stands out

More Bedlam

① The hospital is mentioned by William Shakespeare.

② The lunatics were first called 'patients' in the 1600s – perhaps taken from the French for patience.

③ Eighteenth-century Bethlem was most notably portrayed in a scene from William Hogarth's *A Rake's Progress* (1735), the story of a rich merchant's son whose immoral living causes him to end up in a ward at Bethlem.

④ At one time it was believed that patients discharged from Bethlem Hospital were licensed to beg. They wore a tin plate on their arm as a badge and were also known as Bedlamers, Bedlamites or Bedlam Beggars. In William Shakespeare's *King Lear*, the Earl of Gloucester's son Edgar takes the role of a Bedlam Beggar in order to remain in England unnoticed after his banishment.

with its bright-yellow window frames. Jarman, who on top of highbrow films like *Jubilee*, *Caravaggio* and *The Tempest*, made pop videos for The Smiths, Marianne Faithfull, Suede, the Sex Pistols and the Pet Shop Boys, created the garden by retrieving washed-up jetsam on walks along the beach. The entire area in fact has a sinister allure and has been used in pop videos by The Thrills and Turin Brakes. To find the cottage, take the Dungeness Road south-east out of Lydd. Past the coastguards' cottages, the road narrows to a single-track lane and Prospect Cottage is about 350 metres on the right. The sculptured driftwood at the front is the giveaway; don't blame us if you glow in the dark on your way home.

OPEN   All year round.

⑧ WALK THE WHITE CLIFFS OF DOVER

White Cliffs of Dover Visitor Centre, Langdon Cliffs, Upper Road, Dover, Kent CT16 1HJ (✆ **01304 202756**, www.nationaltrust.org.uk/main/w-thewhitecliffsofdover).

With stunning 20-mile (32km) views to France along a chalk downland path rich in rare butterflies and Exmoor ponies, even our effort-shy children enjoyed this walk, popular for its staggeringly beautiful scenery and easy access. The route starts from the Visitor Centre, a former Victorian prison that has displays on the conservation in the area and also about the prison, which provided the labour that built the port of Dover. From here it covers a three-mile (5km) slice of the Saxon Shoreway path from Gravesend to Hastings, ending in beautiful St Margaret's Bay. Along the way you might catch sight of peregrine falcons and ravens nesting in the 250ft (76m) high cliff-tops; if you're here between May and August you'll see endangered Silver Spotted Skipper and Small Blue butterflies – this is their only habitat in the world – while Exmoor ponies graze the slopes identified as an SSI. To get children on board, borrow one of the 15 tracker packs available at the visitor centre. They contain magnifying glasses, binoculars, compasses, a map and checklist of wildlife to look out for. We stopped for our picnic two miles (3km) into the walk at Foreland Lighthouse, which was decommissioned in 1987 (guided tours to the top: £4) and it was here that our daughter identified a bloody-nosed beetle from the checklist that squirted a hand-off-me red secretion onto our son's finger after she encouraged him to pick it up and play with it. At the end of the walk, St Margaret's Bay is great for rock-pooling. Activity packs and guided walks available.

OPEN   Daily: summer 10am–5pm; winter 11am–4pm (visitor centre).

AMENITIES

⑧⁹ SEE THE IMPS AT LINCOLN CATHEDRAL

Minster Yard, Lincoln, LN2 1PX (✆ **01522 561600**, www.lincolncathedral.com).

Visible more than 25 miles (40km) away, the cathedral is 525 feet (160m) tall and for a quarter of a millennia it was the tallest building in the world. Indeed, if part of it had not collapsed in 1549, sending the tower back down to 271 feet (83m), it would have remained the highest building in Britain until the 1967 Post Office (now Telecom) Tower. The chief tourist draw here is the famous gargoyle, the Lincoln Imp (see box, p. 74), in the Angel Choir, which our children had a lot of fun trying to find. Also worth a peek is the Christopher Wren-designed library and the cloisters which were used during the filming of *The Da Vinci Code*. The cathedral is the third to have stood

Ooh, I Could Stand on a Stone Column

During medieval times Satan sent two wicked imps to Earth to cause chaos. They ran wild in northern England before alighting on Lincoln Cathedral, where they caused havoc smashing furniture and tormenting the bishop. Eventually God lost his patience and sent an angel to put a stop to the imps' rampage. It appeared in the choir and demanded that they behave or get sent back to Hell. One of the imps threw rocks at the angel and was turned to stone. He can still be found sitting on top of his stone column in the Angel Choir. The other imp escaped and years later became the Wee Jimmy half of the Crankies. He was last seen doing panto work at the Wolverhampton Grand Theatre, starring alongside Paul Nicholas in *Captain Hook*.

on this site. The other two were both destroyed in the 12th century – the first by fire, the second by an earthquake on Palm Sunday. To get in it normally costs £5 (adults) but on Sundays between 1pm and 3pm, admission is free.

OPEN   Summer Mon–Fri 7:15am–8pm, Sat–Sun 7:15am–6pm; winter Mon–Sat 7:15am–6pm, Sun 7:15am–5pm.

AMENITIES

⑨ LEARN ABOUT SIR ISAAC NEWTON AT THE GRANTHAM MUSEUM

St Peter's Hill, Grantham, Lincolnshire NG31 6PY (✆ **01476 568783**, www.lincolnshire.gov.uk/granthammuseum).

An intelligent local history museum concentrating on its town's two chief claims to fame – that it was home to both Sir Isaac Newton and Lady Thatcher. You can see some of Thatcher's old dresses and the museum has a few good low-level interactive exhibits on Newtonian experiments for children. There are some bits and pieces of Anglo-Saxon pottery and an eclectic collection of African shields, Buddhas and carved ivory pieces from India as well as military mementos and objects representing Grantham's industrial heritage.

OPEN   Mon–Sat 10am–4pm.

AMENITIES

❶ LEARN ABOUT THE USES OF A BOXED SPIDER AT THE FENSCAPE: THE FENS DISCOVERY CENTRE

Fenscape, Springfields, Camelgate, Spalding, Lincolnshire PE12 6EU (℡ **01775 764800**, www.fenscape.org).

We hope that you share our fascination with the fens. Speaking for ourselves we confess our hearts very often miss a beat when we hear about them. In fact upon mention of any lowland area prone to flooding and surrounded by chalk limestone elevations, we start to feel giddy with excitement. Imagine then what a wonderful time we had at this museum, the only one in Britain dedicated solely to the fens. That's right – just the fens. The museum tells the story of the fens, their evolution, natural habitat and wildlife, through a series of interactive games and a mocked-up courtroom debate in which you can vote to decide if draining the land to create the fens was a good idea or not. There is even a fenland apothecary where you can find out what a boxed spider was used as a cure for in less enlightened fenland times. To recover from the shot of pure adrenalin to the heart that a visit to this museum of the fens constitutes, take a wander in next door's Springfield Festival Gardens (also free, www.springfieldsgardens. co.uk), sections of which have been designed by green-fingered TV celebrities Kim Wilde and Charlie Dimmock.

OPEN   Mon–Sat 10am–5pm; Sun 10am–4pm.

AMENITIES

❷ LEARN HOW ALCHEMY RUINED A GREAT FAMILY AT BACONSTHORPE CASTLE

Baconsthorpe, Holt, Norfolk NR25 6LG (no phone, www.english-heritage.org.uk/server/show/nav.17825).

About one mile (1.5km) north of the village of Baconsthorpe, this castle tracks the 200-year-old fortunes of the Heydon family from their great wealth in the 15th century to such poverty and ruin that by the turn of the 17th century they were forced to demolish and sell off half their home for building materials. On the free guided tour (download from the above web address to your MP3 or iPod) of the now abandoned stronghold, you can also learn how the deterioration of the estate coincided with wool merchant Sir Christopher Heydon's preoccupation with alchemy in the 16th century. The castle was finally abandoned in the 1920s. The tour comes in five parts and is on the whole fairly lively apart from one interlude about East Anglian-dressed flint-work. The site itself is very pretty with a bridge over the moat that opens out into a broad swan-filled lake. Walk around the dilapidated castle walls and the gatehouse or play a great game of hide-and-seek among the ruins.

OPEN   Daily during daylight hours.

AMENITIES

❽ HEAR ABOUT A LIFEBOAT HERO AT THE RNLI HENRY BLOGG MUSEUM

The Rocket House, The Gangway, Cromer, Norfolk NR27 9ET (✆ **01263 511294**, www.rnli.org.uk/henryblogg).

★

Coxswain Henry Blogg (1876–1954) was the RNLI's most decorated lifeboat-man, who helped to save 837 lives during his 53 years of service, and his Bronze Bust sits on the cliff-top in North Lodge Park, Cromer. He skippered the lifeboat *HF Bailey* between 1935–1945, which has pride of place in the museum along with his medals and wreckage from some of the ships he plucked survivors from. Blogg was awarded three Gold and four Silver RNLI medals for gallantry, as well as the George Cross and British Empire Medal, and continued to risk his life putting to sea 11 years after the normal retirement age. Succeeding his own step-father into the lifeboat service, Blogg was in turn succeeded as coxswain by his nephew Henry 'Shrimp' Davies, whose own brave years of service were recognised in 1976 when Eamonn Andrews surprised him with his 'Big Red Book', making him the subject of the ITV show *This is Your Life* on the night before he retired. Interactive displays enable visitors to try on old-fashioned waterproofs, buoyancy aids and other RNLI outfits as well as have a go at Morse code and make emergency calls from a boat in distress. Children are guided round the museum by images of Monte, an Italian dog adopted by Blogg in 1932 after rescuing him from the sinking *Monte Nevoso* along with 29 of the ship's crew.

OPEN   Feb–Mar Tues–Sun 10am–4pm; Apr–Sept 10am–5pm; Oct–Nov 10am–4pm; Dec Sat–Sun 10am–4pm.

AMENITIES

⑨ PRETEND TO BE A VIETNAM VET ON HOLKHAM BAY

Holkham, Norfolk NR23 1AB (✆ **01328 710227**, www.holkham.co.uk).

The Queen has been known to walk her corgis on seven-mile (11km) long Holkham Beach when staying at nearby Sandringham, while other famous visitors have included Gwyneth Paltrow, who walked across the sands at low tide during the closing scenes of the film *Shakespeare in Love*, and also the girl band All Saints, who shot one of their videos here. Even if you don't catch Her Majesty flinging drift-wood for her dogs to retrieve, or see Nicole Appleton sunbathing in a bikini, the beach, part of the country's largest nature reserve, is worth a visit for the wonderful pine woods and dunes that back it. A mile wide at low tide in the summer, the beach Lord Nelson enjoyed combing as a boy was packed with families when we visited, who were all flying kites, making sandcastles and quoting lines (OK, just me) from the Vietnam film *Full Metal Jacket,* part of which was filmed here – the beach being used to represent Da Nang. This idyllic pic-nicking beach does, however, have a very fast tide, according to my wife, whose parents once got into difficulties here on what she described as 'a romantic cockling expedition'. Access to the beach is via Lady Anne's Drive at Holkham village, just off the A149, opposite The Victoria Hotel. It is approximately a mile to Holkham Bay.

OPEN   All year round.

AMENITIES

⑨ SHOUT: 'DON'T TELL HIM YOUR NAME, PIKE', AT THE DAD'S ARMY MUSEUM

The Old Fire Station, Cage Lane, Thetford, Norfolk IP24 2DS (Thetford Tourist Infor-mation Centre: ✆ **01842 751975**, www.dadsarmythetford.org.uk).

For nine years from 1968 onwards, Thetford became Walmington-on-Sea, the home of *Dad's Army* in the popular TV sitcom. At this museum, based at the rear of the Guildhall (the old town hall in the series), you can sit in Captain Mainwaring's chair, put on Warden Hodges's hard hat, learn why this seaside town was chosen to be the location of the programme and read about Thanet's real Home Guard.

The Barmy Army

The much-loved BBC sitcom *Dad's Army* – written by Jimmy Perry and David Croft – featured the exploits of the Walmington-on-Sea Home Guard led by the pompous Captain Mainwaring and supported by the debonair, indecisive Sergeant Wilson. Set during World War II, the series boasted some memorable comedy catchphrases including Corporal Jones's 'Don't panic!' as well as Fraser's laconically fatalistic 'We're doomed!'. Each week the platoon would attempt to protect England from German invasion and the original idea came from Perry's own experiences in the Home Guard. He was only 15 when he joined the Hertfordshire Battalion and he based Private Pike and his mother Mavis on himself and his mother. While serving in the platoon he also came across a veteran of Kitchener's campaigns who talked about the 'Fuzzy Wuzzies' – the inspiration for Corporal Jones. Much of the humour came from the fact that all the leading characters had 'day jobs' in Walmington-on-Sea. Mainwaring, Wilson and Pike all worked in Swallow's Bank, while Jones was the butcher, Hodges the greengrocer, Fraser the undertaker and Walker the local black marketer.

There are a few other props, some signed memorabilia and afterwards you can pick up a free self-guided Dad's Army walking tour from the Thetford Tourist Information Centre (2 Market Place). It starts at the Bell Hotel, where the cast used to stay and takes in Mill Lane, a location famous for the 'Don't tell him your name, Pike' episode when a captured U-Boat crew turned the tables on the hapless platoon. The tour passes the Anchor Hotel, where the cast used to drink in the evenings, and various other sites before finishing up back at the museum. There are also tours costing £7.50 a head with guides. The gift shop sells copies of Private Pike's West Ham United scarf.

OPEN   Sat 10am–2pm; also Tues in Aug 10am–2pm (check for additional times).

AMENITIES   🛍 🅿

❾❻ DRINK AT LORD NELSON'S LOCAL

Walsingham Road, Burnham Thorpe, Kings Lynn, Norfolk PE31 8HN (✆ 01328 738241, www.nelsonslocal.co.uk).

What you must do here immediately on arrival is sit yourself in Nelson's favourite drinking spot, the high-backed settle by the door, assume a haughty naval mien, push one arm up inside your jacket and say, before toppling gently sideways in your most convincing death swoon, 'Thank God I did my duty'. Once this crucial re-enactment of the Battle of Trafalgar is complete, retire to the pub garden, where there is a children's adventure playground. This atmospheric pub has no bar. Instead you order drinks and pub grub direct from the tap room. Several hours later, after you have been warned by your wife not to buy any more Nelson's Blood (a unique rum-based concoction I liked a lot) you can hand her your car keys, and on the way back to your hotel, slumped in the passenger seat you can then tell her all about the political significance of the English defeat of the French at the Battle of Trafalgar; facts that you just read about in documents on the pub wall and will remember nothing about in the morning.

OPEN   Mon midday–2:30pm; Tues–Sun midday–2:30pm, 6pm–9pm.

AMENITIES

➒ SEE THE WORLD'S FASTEST WIND-POWERED CAR

EcoTech Centre, Turbine Way, Swaffham, Norfolk PE37 7HT (✆ **01760 726100**, www. ecotech.org.uk).

A witty take on *Bluebird*, the famous Donald Campbell record-breaking car, the *Greenbird* is on display here, which clocked up 126.2mph on Nevada's Lake Ivanpah in March 2009 to become the fastest vehicle powered by wind. Looking fairly clunky with its massive sail, this part-boat, part-plane, part-Formula One racing car looks if anything more like a massive but broken children's toy. Made of carbon fibre and driven at the time by Richard Jenkins, it weighs just 600kg and topped the previous record of 116mph set 10 years earlier on the same site by Iron Duke. Other highlights here include an organic garden, a supervised children's craft table (summer months 11am–3pm) and, when we visited, the thought-provoking Hard Rain exhibition featuring images about climate change, poverty, habitat loss and human rights set to the lyrics of Bob Dylan's single of the same name. If you have a spare fiver, climb the 300 steps (not for the claustrophobic) to the top of the UK's first megawatt wind turbine. It is the only place in the world where you can do this. In the fabulous viewing gallery, there are fantastic views of the Norfolk countryside all the way to Ely Cathedral on a clear day. The café serves tasty sandwiches.

OPEN   Mon–Fri 10am–4pm, plus last Sun of month May–Aug.

AMENITIES   ☕ 🛍 ⚙ 🅿

➒ BE BLESSED AT THE SHRINE OF OUR LADY OF WALSINGHAM

Holt Road, Little Walsingham, Norfolk NR22 6BP (✆ **01328 820255**, www.walsingham. org.uk)

☺

The Walsingham story goes back to 1061, when Saxon noblewoman Richeldis de Faverches had a vision in which she was taken by the Virgin Mary to the house in Nazareth where the Angel Gabriel proclaimed the birth of Christ. Mary then asked Richeldis to make a replica of the house in Walsingham. The story of 'England's Nazareth' grew into legend and a priory was eventually built, with pilgrims in their thousands, including between 1226 and 1511 every king and queen of England, visiting the spot. During the Reformation Henry VIII had the priory destroyed, although in the 19th century renewed fascination with the Walsingham story led to the restoration of the 14th-century Slipper Chapel, so named because pilgrims traditionally removed their shoes to make the last mile or so of the journey to the priory. For Anglicans, there's also now the 20th-century Shrine Church, which contains a modern version of the holy house in Nazareth and a new statue of Our Lady of Walsingham. At this church there are blessings every day at 2:30pm (not between November and March) with hundreds of excited pilgrims arriving to have holy water sprinkled on their heads. After your blessing, why not wander into the small village to buy a carving of The Last Supper from the Shrine Shop at £200 a pop? The churches are at opposite ends of the village. The Roman Catholic Shrine is 1.3 miles south of Walsingham in a hamlet just outside the village of Houghton St Giles.

OPEN   7:30am–6pm (depending on services).

AMENITIES    ☕ 🛍 £

⑨ SEE THE CONSTABLES AT BRIDGE COTTAGE

Flatford, East Bergholt, Suffolk C07 6UL (© **01206 298260**, www.nationaltrust.org.uk/flatford).

This beautiful 16th-century thatched cottage inspired the work of England landscape master John Constable and is now home to an exhibition of his paintings, including his most famous work, *The Haywain*, painted in 1821. Other works Constable painted of this area include *View of the Stour Near Dedham and Flatford Mill, Scene on a Navigable River*. Helpful staff members are on hand to explain Constable's work and why his paintings are seen as epitomising the English countryside. There are walking tours available, starting from the shop and leaving three times a day (£3 a head) in which you're able to stand, or paint, in the exact spot Constable positioned himself to complete some of his famous 19th-century works. If you cross the bridge by the cottage, there is a field where cows bathe in the river Stour on sunny days that makes an idyllic spot for a picnic. On leaving, if you've come by car, the one-way road passes East Bergholt Church, where Constable's father is buried along with Willy Lott, who owned the house featured in *The Haywain*. Bridge Cottage is accessed via a short walk from the private car park. Just follow the crowds.

OPEN   2 Jan–28 Feb Sat–Sun 11am–3:30pm; 3–31 Mar Wed–Sun 11am–4pm; Apr daily 11am–5pm; May–Sept daily 10:30am–5:30pm; Oct daily 11am–4:30pm; 3 Nov–23 Dec 11am–3:30pm.

AMENITIES   ☕ 🍷 🛍 £

⑩ PICNIC ON ALDEBURGH BEACH

Aldeburgh, Suffolk IP15 (Aldeburgh Tourist Information Centre © **01728 453 637**, www.suffolkcoastal.gov.uk/tourism).

This quaintly unspoilt Suffolk seaside town, once a medieval fishing village, has a wonderfully tranquil pebble beach, which, like the town itself, is synonymous with the nation's greatest composer, Benjamin Britten, honoured here by a 13-ft (4m) high steel scallop by Maggi Hambling. Backing on to the beach are rustic fishermen's huts selling that day's catch and a lifeboat station, while the town itself is full of delis, boutiques and tea shops. A stone's throw further along the coast is Thorpeness. Built in the 1900s, this quirky seaside village was created by local landowner Glencairn Stuart Ogilvie as a fashionable resort 'for people who want to experience life as it was when England was Merrie England'. The charming resort, complete with predominantly Tudor-style architecture and the 64-acre, one-metre-deep Meare boating lake in the shadow of the remarkable House in the Clouds (a converted water tower that from a distance looks like a house built at the top of a tree, available for rent at www.houseinthe clouds.co.uk) is the perfect spot for a picnic.

OPEN   All year round.

AMENITIES   ⓟ

⑩ SOUTHWOLD PIER – THAT'S THE WAY TO DO IT

Southwold Pier, North Parade, Southwold, Suffolk IP18 6BN (**℗ 01502 722105**, www.southwoldpier.co.uk).

This has to be the only pier in England where you can buy a crayfish and artichoke salad, attend an organic Farmers' Market and watch a Punch and Judy show sitting beside *Truly Madly Deeply* actress, Juliet Stephenson. The pier has a fantastically unique Under the Pier Show arcade, the brainchild of Cambridge-educated engineer Tim Hunkin. Games here involve submitting a strand of hair to the gene forecaster, a trip underwater in a virtual submarine and an auto-frisk robot. Set against the pleasing thread of multi-coloured beach huts along the refined seafront, Southwold is Britain's most fashionable pier as evinced by its celebrity regulars, who include rom-com movie director and writer, Richard Curtis and artist Lucien Freud. Check out the marvellously idiosyncratic plaques on the pier railings, some of which tell poignant, sad, but also occasionally funny personal stories about visits here down the years.

OPEN   Summer May–Sept 9am until late; winter Oct–May 10am–4pm.

AMENITIES   ☕ 🍴 🛍 ⓟ

⑩ WATCH THE SILLIEST SPORT IN BRITAIN AT THE WESTELTON BARREL FAIR

Westleton, Suffolk IP17 (Aldeburgh Tourist Information Centre ✆ **01728 453637**, www.westletonbarrelfair.com).

☺

My wife and I came away from watching this event realising it really wasn't a natural eye for games that saw us British come up with football, cricket, rugby, and other popular home-grown past-times now enjoyed the world over. We just must have tried thousands of different games until one or two of them were bound to be quite good. Started in 1951, and revived after a lull in 1995, this very daft but hugely endearing example obviously never got out of Westleton. To go with the bog snorkelling, orange racing, cheese rolling, stone skimming and nettle eating, how about this one for inclusion in the 2012 Olympics – prodding a metal beer barrel as fast as you can up and down a village green using a six-foot oak stick. The spectacle has taken place for nearly 60 years, and the onus is on dexterity. Ideally, the barrel must maintain a straight trajectory, although this is virtually impossible since the slightest skewed touch sends it careering towards the spectators like a wonky shopping trolley. Events lick off with a team race between two rival pubs, then it's down to individual competitions, leading to the nail-biting finals. There are even miniature barrel races for children.

OPEN   August. Check website for dates.

⑩ COMPETE IN THE BRITISH OPEN CRABBING CHAMPIONSHIP

Walberswick, Suffolk IP17 (✆ **01502 722359**, www.walberswick.ws).

☺

Around 1,000 entrants compete annually in this pretty coastal village, using a single line and often a top-secret bait to try and land the heaviest crab in a 90-minute period. Although a fee of £1 is payable to enter the competition, you receive a free pot of crab paste and it is no charge to watch. We loved the atmosphere but caught absolutely nothing (probably something to do with our bait). Did we choose a hunk of fish? No. Bacon, like some others? No. We used a jelly baby. Crabbing takes place in the harbour and quayside area. The winner receives an engraved silver salver, a medal and £50. You can purchase buckets and bait on the day if you forget your own.

OPEN   August.

AMENITIES   ᵀ⬧ ⚲

104 LOOK OUT FOR KATE MOSS AT WEST WITTERING BEACH

West Wittering, Chichester, West Sussex PO20 8AJ (✆ **01243 514143**, www.west witteringbeach.co.uk).

Existing in its own benign microclimate sandwiched between the Isle of Wight and the Downs, West Wittering beach has tidal pools in which our children love to search (in vain) for fish from *Finding Nemo*. This sandy enclave along the normally pebbly shores of Sussex is a Blue Flag beach and the perfect spot for a summer barbecue. It has among its fans Rolling Stone Keith Richards and supermodel Kate Moss, who we are still yet to see here in swimwear. The beach has great views of Chichester harbour and the Downs and it doesn't take much ferreting to pick up pearl-lined slipper limpet shells and clams. By car the beach is sign-posted 200 metres past the West Wittering village shops.

OPEN   All year round.

AMENITIES   ☕ £

105 WATCH CRAZY FLYING MACHINES AT WORTHING INTERNATIONAL BIRDMAN

Worthing Pier, West Sussex BN11 3PX (✆ **01903 221017**, www.worthingbirdman. co.uk).

Join 20,000 other spectators to watch magnificent men in their flying machines (well, not exactly – some may be dressed as cows or Dr Who's tardis) compete for a £30,000 prize attempting to fly for 100 metres off the end of Worthing Pier. The event, staged on a variety of south-coast piers since 1971, attracts Wacky-Races style entrants utilising

Losing your Marbles

Tolley: the larger marble used for hitting the 49 others used in the game. The contest tolleys off when the captains of the team drop the tolley from nose height into the six-feet ring. The thrower of the tolley that finishes up closest to the edge of the ring begins the game.

Fudging: any forward or other advantageous movement of a player's shooting hand while he's shooting is deemed a foul known as a fudge.

Cabbaging: any attempt by a player shooting from within the ring to shoot from any point other than that detailed in Rule 6(b) of the marble code of law constitutes a foul known as cabbaging.

insane helium balloons attached to their heads or malfunctioning dragon wings and there's often a stalling flying carpet as well. Staged for most of its history in Bognor, the festival was moved to Worthing for safety reasons in 2008 after Bognor pier was shortened during repair work. Held over a weekend in August, the first day sees the staging of the Leonard and Condor classes for serious competitors, mainly hang-gliding enthusiasts having a pop at the main prize. The Kingfisher class on the second day brings out the truly crazy contraptions and points are awarded for the eccentricity of the costumes.

OPEN   14-15 August for 2010. Check times.

AMENITIES

⑩ LOSE YOUR MARBLES AT THE BRITISH & WORLD MARBLE CHAMPIONSHIPS

Greyhound Pub, Tinsley Green, Crawley, West Sussex RH10 3NS (✆ **01403 730602**, www.britishmarbles.org.uk).

☺

Playing marbles is one of the country's oldest games, and if you come along here you can find out what a tolley is and learn more about the technical terms of cabbaging and fudging (see box, above). This annual event is organised and overseen by the British Marbles Board of Control (BMBC) and draws large crowds of enthusiasts. In West

Sussex the marble season, now some 300 years old, traditionally takes place between Ash Wednesday and Good Friday, with this competition marking its climax. The tournament is played in a knock-out format between around 20 teams, with group and individual titles up for grabs. An over-50s competition has also been recently introduced. It is free to watch and £5 to participate, for which it is advisable to book in advance.

OPEN   Around Easter annually.

AMENITIES   **P**

The Arnolfini.

SOUTH-WEST

The south-west is probably the country's battiest region. Here, for free, you can commune with a fairy king at the top of Glastonbury Tor, see in the summer solstice at Stonehenge and take part in the World Nettle-Eating Championships. You can roll down a hill chasing cheese near Gloucester, re-enact the persecution of the Earl of Rone in Combe Martin and see part of the actual stake that Bishop Hooper was burnt at in 1555. And we haven't even mentioned casting your own sorcerer's spells in Merlin's Cave in Tintagel. More conventionally you can pat sad looking eeyores at the Devon Donkey Sanctuary, letterbox around Dartmoor in your waterproofs and make your own assessment of recent Turner prize winners at Southampton City Art Gallery. Elsewhere you can go on a pirate walking tour of Bristol and a Jane Austen ramble through Bath. There are sand dunes to surf at Saunton Sands beach in North Devon and the romantic Keynance Cove in Cornwall. Laurie Lee's local in Stroud is worth stopping at for a drink, while the Ashmoleon Museum and Art Gallery in Oxford is packed with treasures.

⑩⑦ LEARN ABOUT BRISTOL'S PIRATE PAST

Merchant Venturers' Almshouses, King Street, Bristol BS1 4ED (✆ **0333 3210101**, www.visitbristol.co.uk/site/visitor-information/multimedia/mp3-audio-tours/).

★

A free VisitBristol tour is available at the above website to download to your iPod or MP3 player and will guide you through the city's famous association with Robert Louis Stevenson's classic buccaneering tale, *Treasure Island*. The two-hour tour (called the Bristol Quayside Adventure) stops at places and buildings said to have inspired the 19th-century novelist and begins at the Merchant Venturers' Almshouses at the bottom of King Street. Other points of interest include the Theatre Royal on King Street, the Hole in the Wall pub, eerily reminiscent of the Spy Glass Inn where wicked pirate-landlord Long John Silver ran his dockside pub, plus the legendary Llandoger Trow pub and the Redcliffe caves. There are other themed tours on the slave trade and the heritage of Bristol available at the same web address.

TOURS   All year round.

AMENITIES

⑩⑧ SEE THE JUMPER-WEARING GORILLA AT BRISTOL'S CITY MUSEUM & ART GALLERY

Queen's Road, Clifton, Bristol BS8 1RL (✆ **0117 922 3571**, www.bristol.gov.uk).

The highlight at this museum is Alfred, the stuffed gorilla, one of the first to be kept successfully in captivity. He won Bristolian hearts in the 1930s by throwing snowballs at visitors in the winter while walking around in woolly jumpers. As he became a city icon, American

Shiver me Timbers

① Bristol's most famous pirate, Blackbeard, was also known as Edward Teach. He carried multiple swords, knives and pistols in his belt and placed lit cannon fuses in his enormous black beard during battle to intimidate his enemies. Blackbeard, who according to the legend had 14 wives, is regarded as the archetypal image of the seafaring pirate and terrorised the Caribbean in the late 17th and early 18th centuries plundering trade ships.

② Fictional pirates have also been inspired in Bristol. Marooned castaway Alexander Selkirk spent five years on Juan Fernandez Island before being rescued and taken back to Bristol where he allegedly met author Daniel Defoe in the Llandoger Trow pub. Selkirk later became the inspiration for Defoe's eponymous character in *Robinson Crusoe* and also Ben Gunn in Robert Louis Stevenson's *Treasure Island*.

GIs sent postcards of him back home during World War II. Alfred, who hated double-decker buses, planes and bearded men, died in 1948 and was the subject of a short prize-winning film for the 2008 Wildscreen Festival, which envisaged the gorilla as a polymath *au fait* with calculus, who'd read all the classics and was murdered and stuffed because he rose too high in Bristol local politics. Apart from the Alfred memorabilia, there are Egyptian galleries here, natural history exhibitions featuring an aquarium of freshwater fish indigenous to the region and a mini-museum called Curiosity, specifically aimed at the under sevens to complement the children's trails. Other family-friendly activities include drawing dinosaur fossils and recognising animal noises. Exhibitions have included the work of local-born world-famous guerrilla artist Banksy (see box, p. 93), who took over the gallery in 2009 with more than 100 pieces of artwork.

 Daily 10am–5pm.

⑩ CATCH UP-&-COMING ART TALENT AT ARNOLFINI

16 Narrow Quay, Harbourside, Bristol BS1 4QA (℗ **0117 917 2300**, www.arnolfini. org.uk).

Based in an old Victorian sugar warehouse, this Grade II listed building attracts over 500,000 visitors a year to its contemporary visual, dance and performing arts programme that showcases up-and-coming talent. Founded in 1961, artists who have exhibited here in the past include Banksy, Patrick Caulfièld, Michael Nyman, Bridget Riley and Rachel Whiteread. Events include talks, free gallery tours and Mash Up activity days (midday–4pm on Saturdays – check ahead) aimed at parents fed up with *Gigglebiz* on CBeebies who want to explore art and ideas with their children. There are five gallery spaces, a reading room and a 200-seat theatre/cinema, which stages some free events.

OPEN   Tues–Sun 10am–6pm.

AMENITIES

⑩ CHECK OUT TORTURE IMPLEMENTS AT BLAISE CASTLE HOUSE MUSEUM & ESTATE

Henbury Road, Henbury, Bristol BS10 7QS (℗ **0117 903 9818**, www.bristol.gov.uk).

★ ᴦᴦ

The highlight of this museum, recounting the social history of Bristol, is a cabinet of curiosities that includes a glass bottle melted during the atomic blast at Hiroshima, the carved arm bone of a Bristol participant in the 1831 rotten-borough riot and an 18th-century scold's bridle, a torture implement worn to punish female gossips. Set in the old mansion home of wealthy 18th-century banker John Harford, among 400 acres of landscaped grounds, there are also displays of old-fashioned toys (our son loved the trains and lead soldiers) as well as a pre-flush Victorian toilet we couldn't get our daughter to stop talking to strangers about. There are Georgian costumes, a gallery highlighting the landscape work of the Bristol school of artists, who painted between 1810–1840 and included William Muller, while from the folly at the back of the house there are great views of the Severn Bridge and Welsh hills. There is a large adventure playground for children and summer activities for families (ring ahead for details).

OPEN Sat–Wed 10am–5pm.

AMENITIES 🛍 🅿

⑪ RIDE THE BRISTOL & BATH RAILWAY PATH

St Philips Road, Bristol BS2 (✆ **0117 922 4325**, www.bristolbathrailwaypath. org.uk).

Crossing the river Avon through ancient woodland, you'll be treated to some great views of the Cotswold Hills on this 13-mile (21km), flat, traffic-free, tarmacked cycle route along the track bed of the old Midland Railway between Bristol and Bath. Alive with birdsong and butterflies and passing beautifully colourful wild flower meadows, the route, dotted with sculptures by local artists, is also popular with walkers and you can expect to see blackberry pickers as well as other families foraging for the apples and plums that grow close to the path. The trail is part of National Cycle Network Route 4 and begins at St Philips Road in the centre of Bristol (follow the signs from Temple Meads Station); it ends near Bath Spa railway station. It's ideal for buggy pushers and wheelchair users, with only a quarter of a mile of its length forming a gentle gradient.

OPEN All year round.

Banksy

The notorious Bristol-born artist and darling of the chattering classes has never revealed his true identity and even his own parents still believe he is a painter and decorator. He was involved in freehand graffiti as a member of Bristol's DryBreadZ Crew in the late 1990s and produces work charged with a caustic, political sense of humour. He has gathered an enormous following over the years, rising above the hip-hop underground scene to become an iconic figure among the artistic community and even the celebs of Beverley Hills. Many of his most famous pieces of graffiti have become landmarks in Bristol, from the distinctive *Mild, Mild West* mural in Stokes Croft to the naked adulterer apparently hanging from a window on the wall of a sexual-health clinic in Park Street. In the early 2000s he climbed into the penguin enclosure at London Zoo and painted 'We're bored of fish' in seven-feet-high letters on the wall; in the elephant enclosure at Bristol Zoo he left the message, 'I want out. This place is too cold. Keeper smells. Boring, boring, boring'.

⑫ BUILD SANDCASTLES ON WATERGATE BAY

Two miles (3.2km) north of Newquay, B3276 Newquay to Padstow near Tregurrian, Cornwall TR8.

This two-mile (3.2km) sandy beach has great rolling waves, which saw it play host to the English National Surfing Championships in 2007 and its photogenic bay was used during filming of Kate Winslet's 2003 surf movie, *Plunge*. Watergate's distance from Newquay and its sheer size ensures it's always relatively peaceful, although visitor numbers have shot up since celebrity chef Jamie Oliver opened his restaurant, Fifteen. Set between the cliffs of Trevelgue Head to the south and Stem Point, we spent a fantastic day here building complex irrigation works from the rivulets of water running from the rocks at the top of the beach to keep a small fish alive that our son found in a rock-pool. It eventually died during a doomed bid to take it back to our hotel in a cheese-and-onion crisp packet.

OPEN   All year round.

AMENITIES   ☕ 🛍 £

⑬ PROPOSE TO YOUR PARTNER AT KYNANCE COVE

The Lizard, Cornwall TR12 7PJ (✆ **01326 561407**, www.nationaltrust.org.uk).

At the end of the hillside path on the Lizard Peninsula, Kynance is without doubt one of the country's most romantic beaches and has been popular with poets, painters, royalty and lovers for centuries. Lord Tennyson came here for inspiration, as did Pre-Raphaelite master William Holman Hunt, but it was Prince Albert's visit with his two sons in 1846 that put the beach, an SSI for its preponderance of rare wild flowers (twin-headed clover and spring sandwort), on the tourist map. You'd expect to find a black-hearted *Famous Five*-type smuggler in the fabulous caves and rock-pools, but it's the serpentine rocks, the spectacular sunsets, beautiful white sand and turquoise waters that have inspired all those marriage proposals down the years.

OPEN   All year round.

AMENITIES   ☕ £

⑭ LEARN ABOUT A MERMAID IMPERSONATOR AT BOSCASTLE VISITOR CENTRE

The Harbour, Boscastle, Cornwall PL35 OHD (℃ **01840 250010**, www.visitboscastle andtintagel.com).

The Visitor Centre in this pretty, touristy little town has displays on the horrific freak flood in August 2004, which saw two million tons of water pour off the Dartmoor hills and almost wipe the town out. The centre is based within a stone's throw of the now peaceful river Valency (widened by 6.5 feet (2m), which also burst its banks after unprecedented rainfall during Hurricane Lili in 1996, sweeping cars down the high street like toy boats. Also featured in the exhibitions are memorabilia of 19th-century writer Thomas Hardy and local mermaid impersonator Reverend Stephen Hawker, the vicar of Morwenstow from 1834 and the very essence of the English eccentric. He won the Newdigate Prize for Poetry at Oxford but is most famous for penning *The Song of the Western Men*, the unofficial Cornish anthem, and most infamous for impersonating a mermaid on Bude Bay. Hardy's association with the area is down to the fact that he was once a practising architect and was charged with restoring the local St Juliot church. While doing so he fell in love with the vicar's daughter Emma, who, despite enduring an unhappy marriage (she didn't understand him), inspired many of his poems. Boscastle itself was the setting for many passages in Hardy's favourite book, *A Pair of Blue Eyes*, published in 1872. To entertain the children, there's brass-rubbing at the Visitor Centre.

OPEN   Daily Mar–Oct 10am–5pm; Nov–Feb 10:30am–4pm.

⑮ WATCH COWS BEING MILKED AT ROSKILLY'S ICE-CREAM & ORGANIC FARM

Tregellast Barton, St Keverne, Helston, Cornwall TR12 6NX (℃ **01326 280479**, www. roskillys.co.uk).

Roskilly's is the second largest organic ice-cream producer in the country, and on a family day out here, children can watch cows being milked and ice-cream-making demonstrations held daily in the kitchen annexe, showing how their 80 flavours of ice-cream are made; visitors are actively encouraged to sample products and ask questions. The cows in the dairy herd used for ice-cream production are milked every day in the summer at 4:30pm. There is a barn full of calves and donkeys to coo over as well as wandering cats and mongrel dogs to pat. For adults, there's a scenic two-mile (3.2km) walk across the 180-acre farm to the secluded beach of Rosenithon, leading past a pond full of geese and ducks that can slow the walk down considerably if you have children eager to part with small segments of their least favourite type of lunchtime sandwich filling (ham).

OPEN   Daily, summer 8am–9pm; winter 11am–5pm.

AMENITIES   ♦♦♦ ↳ ♿

⑪ CAST SPELLS IN MERLIN'S CAVE

Tintagel, Cornwall PL34 0HE (℅ **01840 770328**, www.english-heritage.org.uk).

Beneath the rocky outcrop on which Tintagel Castle sits, lies the cave where Merlin the sorcerer from the legends of King Arthur is reputed to have lived. The atmospheric cave, where it is fun to wave a knobbly stick around while shouting echoing and wild-eyed incantations to your frightened children, does beg one question: if you really were the finest wizard in the land, wouldn't you at least live somewhere a little less dank and cold than a cavern full of seagull droppings? To get here is an Arthurian quest in itself. Park in the town's pay & display, walk past all the King Arthur-dominated retail outlets to get to a spot behind Wootons Country Hotel, where Land Rover taxis operate (adults £1.50, children 75p, under threes free) from Easter to October until 6pm daily. If you choose to walk down to the cave, it will take 30 minutes – follow the steep path and the stream of people. The cave is accessed via the beach and fills with water at high tide, it is only explorable at low tide.

Boil & Bubble, Toil & Trouble

In the 12th century Arthurian chronicler Geoffrey of Monmouth claimed that Tintagel Castle was the site of the wizard Merlin's seduction of Queen Igraine of Cornwall, while disguised as her husband Gorlois. The result of this illicit liaison was King Arthur; it was not until the 19th century that Alfred, Lord Tennyson made the castle Arthur's birthplace in his epic poem *Morte d'Arthur*. Merlin supposedly lived in a cave below the fortress of Tintagel as Arthur was growing up, so he could be his tutor.

There is a free Visitor Centre here telling you and the strange people with dyed hair who like this kind of thing the Arthurian legend connected with the area. The 13th-century Tintagel Castle (£4.90 for adults) is in ruins but there are some great views of the rugged North Cornwall coastline from its spot on the cliffside.

OPEN   Cave open all year round.

AMENITIES

⓫⃝ WATCH THE UK NATIONAL SANDCASTLE COMPETITION

Woolacombe, Devon (✆ **01271 344248**, www.northdevonhospice.org.uk).

This 16-year-old competition draws crowds of up to a couple of thousand people to a two-mile (3.2km) stretch of sand on a Blue Flag beach in the heart of Woolacombe. Effigies that have been produced in the sand here include daleks, the Simpson family, dragons and turtles. The contest is open to teams of six, who each get three hours and seven square metres of sand to work with. Anybody can take part, with entry fees (£75 per team last year) going to the North Devon Hospice. The event takes place either June or July depending on tides and is free to watch.

OPEN   June or July. Check website.

AMENITIES

⓫⃝ QUESTION HUMAN NATURE AT THE DONKEY SANCTUARY

Sidmouth, Devon EX10 0NU (✆ **01395 578222**, www.thedonkeysanctuary.org.uk).

There must be more donkeys at this sanctuary than in any one place anywhere in the world. The whole of donkeydom is here, in all its richest hues (brown and grey mostly). There are mentally scarred donkeys, happy donkeys, sad donkeys and worried donkeys. Donkeys with damaged tails, donkeys that have seen too much, donkeys that have led sheltered lives. In the barn there are photos of each resident, giving their names and a summary of their lives including a few facts about whether they prefer carrots or polo mints. The Hayloft Restaurant is a good place afterwards for a quick dinner and a lively debate about the mindset of the benefactors who leave everything to donkeys they don't know. There are lots listed on boards here. Are they mad? I think not. There is something unerringly piquant about a donkey, something hangdog and worthy of sympathy. Many of the animals at this sanctuary have been horrifically maltreated and no animal is ever turned away; once here they have a home for life. This is why old people disinherit their relatives and leave their cash to Eeyores. The sanctuary receives no public funding so relies on visitors donating. It's also very easy to donate to the sanctuary by post or online, or you can adopt certain donkeys – look at the website for details.

OPEN   Daily 9am–dusk.

AMENITIES   ¶¶ ● ₽

⑪⑨ TAKE UP LETTERBOXING ON DARTMOOR

Dartmoor (℡ **01392 832768**, www.dartmoorletterboxing.org).

◯

Letterboxing is a way of making walking through the windswept, rainy and often freezing British countryside seem slightly more exciting. This outdoor hobby combines the rigours of orienteering with the nerdiness of stamp collecting and involves walkers searching for weatherproof boxes hidden all over Dartmoor. These boxes might be found under rocks or hidden in the roots of a tree and contain inky stamps plus a visitors' book. Once you find a letterbox, record the stamp for your records as proof that you found it, then use your stamp (you must make one – see box, p. 99) to make a print in the visitors' books. Although it sounds a bit like a busy morning of mindless bureaucracy dealing with the DVLC, this pastime is increasingly popular and there are thousands of letterboxes dotted all over the moor.

   The aim is, of course, to find as many boxes as possible and this is subject to some strange customs. For instance, it is up to you to find your first 100 boxes, either by word of mouth or by following the 'forum' link at the above web address, where you can wheedle

Boxing Clever

The origin of letterboxing is traced to Dartmoor in 1854 when James Perrott placed a bottle for visitors' cards at Cranmere Pool on the high moor. Following this, hikers began to leave letters or postcards inside boxes along the trail (hence the name 'letterboxing'). The next person to discover the site collected the postcards and mailed them. The first Dartmoor letterboxes were so remote that only determined walkers could find them, allowing weeks to pass before the letter made its way home. Until the 1970s there were no more than a dozen such sites but since then letterboxes have been located in relatively accessible sites and today there are thousands within easy walking distance of the road. As a result, the tradition of leaving a letter or postcard in the box has been forgotten. Make your Stamp . . .

1. Choose a simple black-and-white picture.
2. Place a photocopy of the image face down on an eraser. Iron over the paper to transfer the image.
3. Use a sharp scalpel to carve the picture. Angle your cuts away from the design to avoid undercutting the image and use a pale ink to check your carving progress.

information from veteran letterboxers who'll point you in the direction of areas such as Feather Tor or Arms Tor (if they are kind they will give you map references), where there are supposedly high concentrations of letterboxes. In fact we found nothing but thistles, a dead bird and a soggy black sock at Hay Tor. After you have found 100 boxes and have the stamps to prove it, contact the 100 Club (www.letterboxingondartmoor.co.uk) and ask the elusive Sylvia Moore to post you a copy of The 100 Catalogue (postage £7.30). This catalogue has attained mystical status amongst letterboxers and contains clues to find your next 100 boxes. To be successful, get a map of Dartmoor – the Explorer OL28 is most widely used – and a compass. It is cheating to use a GPS navigator.

⓬⓪ ATTEND THE TOTNES ORANGE RACES

Totnes, Devon TQ9 (✆ **01803 863168**, www.totnesinformation.co.uk).

The ennobled seaman Sir Francis Drake is best known for rolling bowls along Plymouth Hoe as the Spanish Armada advanced, but apparently he accidentally sent a young boy's orange scooting down the steep high street of Totnes in the 1580s. The infamous incident (yes, they're very touchy about fruit in Devon) is remembered every August when locals relive the travesty by chasing their own fruit down the hill for prizes. The winner is the person to reach the bottom first with their orange, with one sticky race rule: competitors must boot or throw the orange ahead as they run. Any holding of the orange results in disqualification, although what makes the event interesting is that you don't have to be holding your own orange at the end. Inevitably this leads to some wonderful fights. Entry is free and all ages from babies to pensioners (competing on a flatter section of the hill) are welcomed. Trophies are awarded to category winners and the races are organised by the Totnes Elizabethan Society.

OPEN   August 11am. Check website for date.

AMENITIES   ☕ 🍴 🥡 🛍

⓬① GO BACK TO VICTORIAN TIMES AT MORWELL-HAM QUAY

Near Tavistock, Devon PL19 8JL (✆ **01822 832766**, www.morwellham-quay.co.uk).

Growing up to support the largest and richest copper deposits ever found, Morwellham became the largest quay in England in Victorian times before falling into decline. Now it forms part of a UNESCO World Heritage Site, with costumed staff wandering around the restored port and transporting visitors back to the bustling 1860s, when heaps of copper ore filled the quays and a forest of ships' masts lined the river. Wander around the miner's cottage and visit pigs, shire horses and sheep at the village farm as well as exploring an old Victorian ketch. However, there is a charge of £9.50 to go down the copper mine and attend a lesson in the Victorian school, so be gone quickly before you're tempted, skinflints.

OPEN   May–end Oct 10am–5pm (for winter times ring ahead).

AMENITIES   ☕ 🛍 £

122 ENTER THE WORLD NETTLE-EATING CHAMPIONSHIPS

Bottle Inn, Marshwood, Dorset DT6 5OJ (☏ **01297 678254**, www.thebottleinn.co.uk).

Hundreds of nettle-guzzlers compete to become King of the Stingers at Dorset's strangest annual event in mid-June. The rules are as simple as they are harsh. Entrants from as far as New York, Poland, Australia, Northern Ireland and Belgium attempt to consume the toxic leaves from as many two-feet (60cm) long nettle stalks at they can within an hour. To enter just turn up early (there are only 65 places available) but don't even think about coating your tongue in Bonjela beforehand – numbing medicines are not allowed. That said, the unpalatable leaves and their sting are just two of the problems. The third? Nettles act as a powerful laxative and visiting the lavatory before the end of the competition

The Sting

The nettle plant (*urtica docia*) is a nutritional powerhouse rich in iron, potassium, calcium and abundant vitamins, and the leaves have been used in traditional English stews, teas and beers for centuries. Italians sometimes use them for making *pesto* and the Scandinavians cherish a nettle soup called *nasselsoppa*. The complications come from eating them raw. *Urtica* leaves are covered in thousands of microscopic hypodermic needles, each filled with boric acid. On contact the needles break, causing the acid to flood out and burn your mouth.

results in immediate disqualification. The contest, staged on the Saturday before summer solstice, began more than 20 years ago when two customers at Marshwood's 16th-century Bottle Inn argued over who had the worst infestation of stinging nettles. One of them said, 'I'll eat any nettle of yours that's longer than mine' and so it began. The record chomp is an impressive 76 feet (23m) of nettles. There's also live music and a hog roast on the day.

OPEN   Check website for dates.

AMENITIES

⑫ RELIVE O-LEVEL HISTORY AT THE TOLPUDDLE MARTYRS MUSEUM

Tolpuddle, near Dorchester, Dorset DT2 7EH (℃ **01305 848237**, www.tolpuddle martyrs.org.uk).

The Tolpuddle Martyrs were a group of 19th-century agricultural labourers convicted of being members of a fledgling trade union in 1834. The case provoked a national outcry because three days before their arrest, the punishment for this crime had been increased from a small fine to transportation to Australia for seven years. The martyrs were all eventually pardoned by the King (although not by me as I had to study their incredibly dull story for history O-level); they have since become part of trade-union folklore and a source of inspiration for, among others, lefty-protest songsmith Billy Bragg. In the museum telling the martyrs' story, there are court records relating to the convictions. After you have taken these in, walk down to the sycamore tree in the village where the martyrs took their oath. Here there is a covered bench commemorating the historical act. Further along the main street you'll find Martyr's Cottage, where oath-taker Thomas Stanfield lived, while the village graveyard contains the body of James Hammett, another of the martyrs.

OPEN   Summer Tues–Sun 10am–5pm; winter Thurs–Sun 10am–4pm.

AMENITIES

⑫ PRETEND TO BE A HARDY HEROINE ON A TOUR OF MAIDEN CASTLE

Off the A354, two miles (3.2km) south of Dorchester, Dorset DT2 (℃ **0870 3331181**, www.english-heritage.org.uk/server/show/nav.17836).

Download a free audio tour of the largest and best-preserved iron-age hill fort in Britain from the web address above. The castle, which inspired the writings of Thomas Hardy in the 19th century, was laid out in 600BC over the remains of a Neolithic settlement. Its impressive ramparts enclose an area equivalent in size to 50 football pitches and were once home to hundreds of people. The fort was conquered in AD43 by the Romans, forcing the inhabitants to move to the new town of Durnovaria (Dorchester) – after centuries of abandonment it was excavated in the 1930s. There are information panels at the site, which is accessed via a steep slope to the right of the car park, although the best way to learn about this amazing place is through the informative audio tours.

OPEN   All year round.

AMENITIES   P

⑫⑤ SWIM NEAR THE DURDLE DOOR

West Lulworth, Dorset BH20 (📞 **0845 450 1054**, www.lulworth.com).

☺

This towering limestone arch gets around a bit. It's been used as a backdrop in several music videos, including the Tears for Fears' classic single *Shout,* Cliff Richard's not-quite-so-classic Christmas number one from 1990 and Billy Ocean's disco favourite, *Loverboy*. Images of Durdle Door feature in the movies *Nanny McPhee* and *Wilde*. It even crops up in the computer game *Grand Theft Auto III*. In fact so beautiful is the arch and its setting that Durdle Door was recently used to promote the coastline of the United Arab Emirates when an advertising agency appropriated the landmark and placed its image in a hotel brochure from Ras Al Khaimah. In geological terms, the arch was formed because the 394-ft (120m) isthmus (the door) adjoining the Purbeck limestone is made of a 164-ft (50m) band of rock sediment, shells and pebbles and hundreds and thousands . . . OK we admit we are not really sure about the actual geology of the Durdle Door. What we do know is that if you park in the Lulworth Cove car park – this leads down to the lovely secluded Lulworth Cove – and scramble west some 2.5 miles (4km) up and down a steep hill, along a ridge and descend about 150 steps to Durdle Door beach, you will completely destroy the suspension of your buggy. The journey takes about one hour and will leave you too exhausted to swim through Durdle Door, which is just as well as there are strong currents here. A better option is to park in the Durdle Door caravan-site car park above the beach and walk down from here, which only takes about 20 minutes.

OPEN   All year round.

AMENITIES

ⓘ CHECK OUT THE TALENT AT THE STUDLAND BEACH & NATURE RESERVE

Studland, Swanage, Dorset BH19 3AX (☏ **01929 450259**, www.nationaltrust.org.uk).

There are three miles (5km) of sandy beach at Studland, stretching from South Haven Point to the chalk cliffs of Handfast Point, including a designated naturist area. The fittingly named Studland Beach (see box, p. 105) is at the north end and has become popular with body-building gay nudists, who have taken to posing atop the dunes like Greek statues. We know this because we accidentally stumbled into this area when staying at a hotel nearby and admit we felt out of place carrying the family picnic hamper with blow-up Rory the Racing Car floats tucked under our arms. It didn't help that I was wearing, after a regrettable packing mix-up, a pair of red, white and blue Speedos. Once you have retraced your steps and found a good picnic spot, surrounded by other tubby fathers in ill-judged swimwear, sit back and enjoy the beach, which is voted the fourth best in the country by *Which?* magazine. While your wife pretends to look out for razorbills, you can imagine the beach on 8 April 1944, when King George VI, General Sir Bernard Montgomery and General Dwight D Eisenhower visited to observe the troops training for the D-Day landings. The heathland behind the sand dunes is popular with rare birds, a designated National Nature Reserve and the richest area for wild flowers in Britain.

OPEN   All year round.

AMENITIES

ⓘ ROLL AFTER CHEESE IN GLOUCESTERSHIRE

Cooper's Hill, near Brockworth, Gloucester GL3 (www.cheese-rolling.co.uk).

The Cooper's Hill Cheese-Rolling and Wake is an annual event going back almost 200 years and held on the last bank holiday in May at Cooper's Hill. Originally the competition was only for the people of nearby Brockworth but nowadays it's open to anyone. Now, my favourite food is cheese, but did I like it enough to risk spinal injury chasing an eight-pound wheel of double Gloucester down a vertical

Now for Something Completely Different

1. Studland Beach, with Bournemouth in the background, was the setting of the opening scene from the first episode of *Monty Python's Flying Circus*, when Michael Palin staggered out of the shallow sea and collapsed on the beach, saying 'It's . . .' before the scene cuts to the opening credits.

2. Egdon Heath, which figures prominently in Thomas Hardy's classic novel *The Return of the Native*, is a fictionalised version of Studland Heath.

3. The video for the Coldplay single *Yellow* was filmed on the beach.

slope in the Cotswolds? Rolling down a hill, what could be hard about that? On the way to the Cross Hands pub, where the cheese-chasers traditionally meet for Dutch courage, I pictured myself winning the cheese and imagined how proud I would be with my prize chuck of Double Gloucester under my arm. The race starts at noon and before I knew it I was perched at the top of Cooper's Hill staring down the 1-in-2 gradient as the master of ceremonies, clad in a top hat, prepared for the first cheese roll. I'd like to say I plunged down the hill after the cheese, which reaches speeds of up to 70mph, and won the race, but at this point I started mulling stories overheard in the pub (dislocated shoulders, spinal boards, concussions). I stared down at the rugby players lined up along the hay bales at the bottom of the hill ready to catch people and noticed I'd begun to slide back down the incline on my bottom. Instead we had a picnic and watched 11 other people carted off to

Hard Cheese

Nobody is really sure where this tradition, dating back to the 1800s, at least, comes from. During World War II, rationing was introduced, preventing the use of a cheese in the event. Consequently, from 1941 to 1954, a wooden 'cheese' was used instead, with a piece of cheese in a hollow space inside the wooden replica.

hospital after one race. In all there were 58 injuries that day, including one spectator who fell out of a tree. There are five downhill cheese races (one is for ladies) and four uphill.

OPEN Last bank holiday in May.

AMENITIES

ⓒ RE-ENACT THE EXECUTION OF BISHOP HOOPER AT THE GLOUCESTER FOLK MUSEUM

99–103 Westgate Street, Gloucester GL1 2PG (© **01452 396868**, www.gloucester. gov.uk/folkmuseum).

This beautiful museum houses the bishop's seal of Protestant Bishop John Hooper (b.1495) plus a two-feet (60cm) section of the charred stake on which he was burned to death during the reign of Bloody Queen Mary in 1555. Hooper spent his last night in this building, then a merchant's house, and was executed in front of his home church, Gloucester Cathedral, for refusing to convert to Catholicism. Other less macabre highlights include helmets and cannon balls unearthed from the Gloucester Siege during the English Civil War, when 4,500 townspeople held out against the Royalists. There's also a stuffed Gloucestershire Old Spot, a display on making Double Gloucester cheese and an exhibit about the pin factory once based here. The toy cupboard includes a puppet theatre where, with the aid of a 2B pencil, we staged a short history play re-enacting the execution of Bishop Hooper.

OPEN Tues–Sat 10am–5pm.

AMENITIES

ⓒ DRINK A PINT OF CIDER IN LAURIE LEE'S LOCAL

Woolpack Inn, Slad, Stroud, Gloucestershire GL6 7QA (© **01452 813429**, www. thewoolpackinn-slad.com).

Laurie Lee's local pub was famously, in the writer's words, 'six stumbling paces' from his home at Rosebank Cottage, where he penned his classic autobiographical work about growing up in the rural idyll of Slad, *Cider with Rosie*. There is a display case of memorabilia devoted to Lee, who died in 1977, containing several of his books, a collection of old beer bottles donated to the pub after his death plus portraits and photos of the author on the walls. The pub serves, according to my wife, a revolting 'Cider with Rosie' cocktail made up of cider with rosé wine. Safer is the Old Rosie cider, although to get the real Laurie Lee experience drink whisky, his tipple of choice. Lee, who famously fought in the Spanish Civil War, went to a school around the corner that is described vividly in his famous novel, a book my wife confessed (after her second cocktail) that she couldn't actually stand.

OPEN   Daily midday–midnight.

AMENITIES

⑬⓪ SURF THE SEVEN BORE

Minsterworth, Gloucester GL2 (www.seven-bore.co.uk).

☺

Ok, it's not exactly catching a fat tube at Bondi Beach, but this freak wave gets up in Sharpness and rolls unbroken for miles along the river Severn and sometimes reaches six feet (1.8m) in height before crashing down in Avonmouth. When the Romans first witnessed this natural phenomenon, they thought it presaged the end of the world, but it is caused by wax and wane of the moon. The first person to ride the bore was former commando Colonel Churchill in 1955, and since then the sport of bore-riding has gradually grown so that today the web buzzes with online bloggers boasting about wave rides. The record, disputed by some, is claimed by Steve King, who rode the wave for an hour-and-a-quarter along a seven-mile (11.2km) surf in 2006. The best bet is to catch the wave, formed by a tidal surge squeezing the river into an increasingly narrow channel, between Minsterworth and Lower Parting in Gloucester. The wave is small enough to demand a heavy long-board with trick short-boards struggling to pick it up; it's not huge enough to wipe you out although you'll struggle to get very far on it if you're not a decent surfer. The website above has bore times within half an hour of accuracy and gives a rating on the likely strength of the wave. There is generally one bore per month, following a full moon. Times are given for five locations to pick up the wave – Newnham, the Severn Bore Inn, Minsterworth Church, Stonebench and Over Bridge.

⑬ SEE THE GRAVE OF THE 'REAL' ALICE FROM ALICE IN WONDERLAND

New Forest Centre, Lyndhurst, New Forest, Hampshire SO43 7NY ((℗ **0203 8028 3444**, www.newforestnpa.gov.uk/visiting).

'Curiouser and curiouser!'
Download an audio tour and map (follow the link at the above web address) that takes you to the last resting of Alice Liddell (1852–1934), the eponymous model in the children's storybook *Alice in Wonderland*. The short tour starts at the New Forest Centre, off the High Street in Lyndhurst, and concludes at St Michael's and St Agnes Church graveyard, where Alice lies buried; it's fairly pedestrian in tone (at one point it involves a local man discussing carpeting his home when he first moved to the New Forest) although it does tell the story of Lyndhurst's most famous resident pretty well. The name on the gravestone in the churchyard is, however, Mrs Reginald Hargreaves, after Alice's husband, so don't miss it. Alice, who by all accounts died in her 80s, was heartily sick of being known as the lead character in *Alice in Wonderland* and fell out with the author in 1863 aged 11; because of missing pages in Dodgson's diaries from around this time speculation in many biographies has often focused on the less seemly possibilities of their relationship. Not that Alice Liddell isn't new to controversial linkages – one biographer has even

Alice's Story

The story goes like this: Charles Dodgson (who wrote under the pseudonym Lewis Carroll) was a friend of the Liddell family and it was on 4 July 1862, in a rowing boat travelling on the river Isis from Folly Bridge, Oxford, to Godstow for a picnic outing, that 10-year-old Alice Liddell asked Dodgson to entertain her and her sisters, Edith (8) and Lorina (13), with a story. The result was the adventures of a girl named Alice, who fell into a rabbit-hole. Alice Liddell liked her name-checked story so much she asked Dodgson to write it down for her. He eventually presented her with the manuscript of *Alice's Adventures Under Ground* in November 1864. Dodgson rewrote the story as *Alice's Adventures in Wonderland* and it was published in 1865. A second book featuring Alice, *Through the Looking-Glass*, followed in 1871.

speculated that as a young woman during her Grand Tour, she had an affair with Prince Leopold, who was the youngest son of Queen Victoria. She named her first child Leopold and the prince was godfather to him; Leopold in turn named his daughter Alice.

'Oh my ears and whiskers, how late it's getting.'

OPEN New Forest Centre daily 10am–5pm.

AMENITIES

PICNIC IN FRONT OF HMS VICTORY AT THE ROYAL NAVY HISTORIC DOCKYARDS

Victory Gate, HM Naval Base, Portsmouth, Hampshire PO1 (**℃ 023 928 39766**, www. historicdockyard.co.uk).

Eat a picnic in front of HMS Victory, Lord Nelson's flagship and the oldest still-commissioned warship in the world, wander around the 300-year-old naval site and visit the dockyard's Apprentice Exhibition. Although you have to pay to actually board Victory and the 19th-century HMS Warrior, once the fastest ship in Queen Victoria's fleet, there's still plenty to do for free. The Dockyard Exhibition tells the story of shipwrights once based here using interactive gizmos that include allowing your children to communicate 'I want another sandwich' in semaphore. Elsewhere there's a soft-play area.

OPEN Apr–Oct 10am–6pm; Nov–Mar 10am–5:40pm.

AMENITIES

SEE THE TURNER PRIZE WINNERS AT SOUTHAMPTON CITY ART GALLERY

Civic Centre, Commercial Road, Southampton, Hampshire SO14 7LP (**℃ 023 8083 2277**, www.southampton.gov.uk/lesiure/arts/sotongallery).

The most prestigious art gallery in southern England has paintings from the 14th century to the present day, including works by Monet, Lucien Freud and Lowry as well as sculpture by Antony Gormley. Housed in the 1930s Neo-Classical civic centre, the gallery has a permanent collection of more than 2,500 works majoring strongly in contemporary British art, and especially on Turner Prize winners from the 1970s onwards. Its strengths include the Impressionists, with most leading names from Pissarro to Renoir, although my favourite painting was L.S. Lowry's 'matchstick men and matchstick cats and dogs', Lowry's painting of Southampton's famous old floating bridge. The gallery has visiting exhibitions, some of which charge, and in 2010 will feature a new work by Bridget Riley, who'll also be curating a gallery here. There are children's activity trails and family-related activities themed around exhibits during school holidays.

OPEN   Summer Mon–Fri 10am–6pm, Sat–Sun 11am–6pm; winter Mon–Fri 10am–4pm, Sat–Sun 11am–4pm.

AMENITIES

⑬ HEAR THE SADDAM SUPERGUN STORY AT THE ROYAL ARMOURIES MUSEUM

Fort Nelson, Portsdown Hill Road, Fareham, Hampshire PO17 6AN ((01329 233 734, www.royalarmouries.org/visit-us/fort-nelson).

The stand-out displays here include various parts of Saddam Hussein's intended British-made 'supergun', disguised as oil-refinery parts and confiscated at customs prior to the first Gulf War, as well as three cannons used by Napoleon's army at the Battle of Waterloo. There are regular performances by costumed actors throughout the day telling, amongst other stories, that of the 1836 sinking of the Nantucket whaler that inspired Herman Melville's lengthy novel *Moby Dick*, and the capture of the German Enigma code machine in World War II. During the summer a 25-pounder field gun is fired twice a day at midday and 3pm (winter just once at 1pm) on the parade ground. Another display features the Mallet Mortar, made for use in the 19th-century Crimean War and mentioned in *The Guinness Book of Records* for having, at three feet (1m), the biggest bore of any gun in the world. The museum is based at Fort Nelson, which was built in the 1860s to protect Portsmouth from French invasion, and is spread across 19 acres with impressive views of the Solent and Meon Valley. This arm of the Royal Armouries, which has further sites in London and Leeds, also boasts among its 350-strong collection, the Great Turkish Bombard, the bronze gun cast for the Sultan of Turkey in the

15th century, which you can fire for £1 a time at passing ships in the Solent (not really).

 Daily Apr–Oct 10am–5pm (Wed 11am–5pm); Nov–Mar 10:30am–4pm (Wed 11:30am–4pm).

⓭⑤ WITNESS THE PERSECUTION OF THE EARL OF RONE

Combe Martin, North Devon EX34 (✆ **01271 882366**, www.earl-of-rone.org.uk).

This annual festival involves 600 villagers from in or around Combe Martin and re-enacts their persecution of the Earl of Tyrone in 1607. It does make you wonder slightly about the hospitality of Devonians. During the last bank holiday weekend in May, the climax of the event sees locals dressed as grenadiers and hunting for the (now abbreviated) Earl of Rone (according to legend shipwrecked in Rararee Cove and hiding in Lady's Wood) on the evening of the bank holiday Monday. When the Earl is caught, he's mounted back-to-front on a donkey and paraded through the village while being shot at by the grenadiers. After falling from the donkey, he is revived by individuals playing the hobby-horse and fool. The procession, accompanied by drummers and dancers, continues until it reaches the sea, whereupon the Earl is launched as far as possible into the water. The participants in the event, revived in 1974 after it was banned in the 19th century, are only allowed to hail from Combe Martin or the surrounding parishes of Berrynarbor, Trentishoe and Kentisbury, although visitors are welcome to watch.

 Last bank holiday weekend in May.

 £

⓭⑥ SAND SURF AT SAUNTON SANDS BEACH

Braunton, North Devon EX33 (✆ **01271 816400**, www.northdevon.com/site/things-to-do).

Our children spent a wonderful day at this wide, three-mile (4.8km) long beach rolling down the largest sand dunes in Britain, leaving my wife free to languish in the sun dreaming about Robbie Williams, who dipped his toe in the Atlantic here making the video to *Angels*. While long-board surfers muster near the hamlet of Saunton at one end of the beach, which consists of a few pretty private beach houses and the white-washed Saunton Sands Hotel, the other end is a designated military training area. Cordoned off occasionally, this stretch is converted into an air strip for military transport planes to practise beach landings. The dunes behind the beach, known as the Braunton Burrows, have recently been voted a – wait for the clunky title – UNESCO Biosphere Reserve, due to the diversity and abundance of their rare flora (500 species of flowering plant), meaning it ranks in importance alongside Mount Vesuvius in Italy. Its surreal other-worldliness was noted by the director of *A Matter of Life and Death*, the 1946 David Niven film, who used the location for the scene where Niven wakes up on the beach and thinks he's in heaven. Graphic designer Storm Thorgerson set up the shot for the 1987 Pink Floyd album here, hauling 700 wrought-iron hospital beds onto the sands for the shoot.

OPEN   All year round.

AMENITIES   ☕ 🎒 ✈ P

⓭ HUNT FOR THE FAIRY KING AT GLASTONBURY TOR

Off the A361 to Shepton Mallet, near Glastonbury, Somerset BA6 (✆ **01934 844518**, www.nationaltrust.org.uk or www.glastonburytor.org for the more insane stuff).

☺

If you enjoy nutter-spotting, and my wife and I do very much indeed, there's no better place in England to go than Glastonbury. Bulging with mystic bookshops and adults in floaty white robes, it's a perfectly ordinary day when the streets suddenly throng with bell-ringing Hari Krishnas. Not even pensioners are immune – here the elderly have grey pony-tails and carry spell-books. If Glastonbury is the nation's church of weirdness, then Glastonbury Tor is its high altar. This millennia-old holy hill is one of Somerset's most famous landmarks with the remains of St Michael's Church standing at the top of the 158-ft (48m) mound. It was destroyed by an earthquake in 1275 and is believed to be the opening to a fairy kingdom, the confluence of the many ley-lines and the possible birthplace of King Arthur. Once you get to the top of the tor (it's a five-minute climb) there are views across the counties of Somerset, Wiltshire and Devon as well as the chance to hear excitable chatter about the famous balls of bright light that witnesses claim to have seen here. However, all that happened to us is that we realised we'd left our lunch sandwiches in the car.

OPEN   All year round.

AMENITIES

TREAD CAREFULLY AT THE ASHMOLEAN MUSEUM OF ART & ARCHAEOLOGY

Beaumont Street, Oxford OX1 2PH (☎ **01865 278000**, www.ashmolean.org).

> ### Getting There
>
> You can catch a shuttle bus for £2.50 from the car park at the front of Glastonbury Abbey to the Tor, although many walk for free (don't even think about using your car because, never mind the ley-lines, it's the yellow lines, the double ones that the police are very hot on ticketing, that you need to be careful about). To walk there park in the free car park at the Somerset Rural Life Museum at Abbey Farm, Glastonbury. The Tor, seen from all directions, is approximately a quarter of a mile from here along windy roads.

The world's first public museum, reopened in December 2009 after a £60 million facelift, has among its prize exhibits a lantern carried by gunpowder plotter Guy Fawkes, and a collection of posie (finger) rings said to have inspired JRR Tolkien's 'One Ring' in his novel *The Lord of the Rings*. Established in the 17th century to house the collection of art and archaeological finds of Elias Ashmole, it now features a journey through time spiralling upwards from the ground floor, showcasing artefacts and artworks from prehistory to date, from Egyptian mummies through Roman coinage in the Heberden Coin Room to Uccello's sublime exercise in perspective, Hunt in the Forest. Other highlights of this beautifully presented collection include the Alfred Jewel, a mint-condition Stradivarius called 'The Messiah' and work by Michelangelo, plus an activity trolley for children and study

Staff & Nonsense

According to legend, the boy Jesus built Glastonbury's first wattle-and-daub church on a visit to Britain together with his uncle, Joseph of Arimathea. Following Jesus's crucifixion years later, Joseph fled Palestine to Glastonbury with the Holy Grail, used by Christ at the Last Supper. When Joseph pitched up on the mythical island of Avalon (people could still sail to Glastonbury up until the late Middle Ages), below Wearyall Hill and Glastonbury Tor, he dug his staff into the ground overnight. By morning, it had taken root and bloomed into a thorn tree, which was later moved to Glastonbury Abbey and where it flowers to this day. Joseph then buried the Holy Grail just below the Tor, a spring of red blood flowed forth from the spot, which is known as Chalice Well and believed to bring eternal youth to those supping from it. Years later, locating the Holy Grail was the challenge behind the quests of King Arthur, who was mortally injured in battle and is reputedly buried in Glastonbury Abbey. To confuse legend and fact further, fire destroyed the abbey in 1184; it was at this point, with no money in the coffers, that the resident monks cannily discovered the tombs of Arthur and Guinevere in the abbey grounds. The money raised from the thousands of pilgrims to the graves more than paid for the repairs.

centres where visitors are allowed hands-on contact with examples from the collections.

OPEN   Tues–Sun 10am–6pm.

AMENITIES   ☕ 🍴 🏪 £

⓭⁹ WALK IN THE FOOTSTEPS OF JANE AUSTEN

www.visitbath.co.uk/janeausten/audio-tour.

★

It is a truth universally acknowledged that you can download a self-guided walking tour of Bath, conducted by what sounds like a prim, dapper gentlemen in linen trousers, to your MP3 player or iPod from the website above. The 90-minute tour of this UNESCO World

Heritage Site city starts at the Abbey Church Yard and takes in the Roman Baths (very expensive, and a bit of a bunfight getting around), the Royal Crescent, the famous (for having shops on it) Pulteney Bridge, as well as some of the addresses Jane Austen wrote about in her satirical novels. The tour includes salient extracts from Austen's books and comes with a downloadable map.

OPEN   All year round.

AMENITIES   ☕ 🍴 🍸 🛍

⑭ SEE GLASTONBURY & THE BEST SUMMER MUSIC FESTIVALS WITH OXFAM

(℃ **0300 2001300**, www.Oxfam.org.uk).

Get into the festivals for free? OK, you probably guessed there's a catch. It's this: if you want to hear the best music of the summer for free you'll have to work for the festivals wearing a highly visible Oxfam tabard, either as a steward or as a campaigner with your face painted blue in protest about climate change. That said, this is a great way to enjoy some of the best festivals, and, as a bonus, you feel great about yourself at the same time. Volunteers over 18 years of age are needed for all the top venues: Isle of Wight, Camp Bestival, V, Womad, Latitude, Leeds, Glastonbury, Beautiful Days, Summer Sundae, Rockness, Glade, Shambala, Cream Fields and Reading. The deal is as follows: you have to work three shifts during the festival, each lasting eight hours and 15 minutes. One shift is early morning, one in the afternoon or evening, and the last an overnighter. You get to camp in the Oxfam area (they have their own showers) and sometimes you can bring in children under 13 for free. If you have friends also working for Oxfam, arrange to share the same shifts by giving their details when you apply online on the Oxfam website. Stewarding involves checking tickets, staffing gates or patrolling camp sites, while campaigning is tougher to be accepted for and is more smiley-salesy – your role will be to get petitions signed, talk about Oxfam projects and to encourage revellers out of the bar tent and into the Oxfam marquee for a fair-trade coffee and a chat about third-world debt. The £175 deposit is refunded within a month of completing your shifts. Applications are considered from March onwards for that year's festivals and competition is fierce. For extra tips on getting accepted, go to the stewards' and campaigners' forum on the website above.

⓵ SEE THE WORLD'S OLDEST WORKING CLOCK AT SALISBURY CATHEDRAL

33 The Close, Salisbury, Wiltshire SP1 2EJ (*℗* **01722 555120**, www.salisbury cathedral.org.uk).

Elegant Salisbury's 13th-century cathedral has the tallest spire in Britain at 404 feet (123m), and is also home to Europe's oldest working clock and the world's best-preserved copy of the *Magna Carta* from 1215. The subject of a famous series of paintings by John Constable in 1823, the cathedral took just 38 years to build and its spire leans almost 28 inches (70cm) to the south, something that alarmed Sir Christopher Wren back in 1668 and my two-year-old son in 2009, 'It's falling over, Daddy. Crash'. The world's oldest working mechanical clock was made in 1386; it's found in the nave and despite having no hands or clock face, still chimes every hour, calling bishops to services. The *Magna Carta* is displayed in the Chapter House and was brought to the city by William Longpre, Earl of Salisbury and half-brother to Royal signatory, King John. There are regular art exhibitions in the cloisters, the cathedral itself and sometimes the cathedral close, plus you can hear the famous choir (girls and boys) gallantly perform evensong at 5:30pm daily. The tower has 332 steps to its summit and great views across the surrounding countryside although the admission fee is almost as steep as the spire (£8). To book a tour, call *℗* **01722 555156.**

OPEN   7 June–28 Aug 7:15am–7:15pm (Chapter House 9:30am–5:30pm), rest of year 7:15am–6:15pm (Chapter House 10am–4:30pm).

AMENITIES

⓶ GET MYSTICAL AT THE AVEBURY STONE CIRCLES

Avebury Ring, near Marlborough, Wiltshire SN8 1RF (*℗* **01672 539250**, www.national trust.org.uk).

Voted one of the UK's five most spiritual places, this 5,000-year-old Neolithic arc of stones is said to lie at the confluence of ley-lines, and thus swarms with druids, pagans and New Age hippies, particularly

when it's close to the summer solstice around 21 June. The two circles of 30 to 40 stones are up to 12-ft (3.7m) high and arranged across
a mile-wide area bisected by the A4361, which crosses the site. The
stones were rediscovered during the reign of Charles II after they had
been buried by Christians and then partly broken up to help make the
once-cobbled streets of nearby Swindon, only to be forgotten again
and subsequently excavated by playboy millionaire and archaeolo-
gist Alexander Keiller in the 1920s and 30s. Ever since they have been
an important pilgrimage for various bell-ringing elements who
believe, despite evidence to the contrary (no job, money, clean
clothes or sexual partners), that they draw great power from the
stones. It's a great people-watching site – when we visited, a pagan
wedding was taking place, with the participants in full robes while a
clutch of hippies burned incense and pattered a few bongo drums
near the car park. The Alexander Keiller Museum contains archaeological relics from the site but costs £4.70 to enter.

OPEN   All year round.

AMENITIES   ☕ 🛍 £

❶❹❸ SEE THE GRAVE OF THE FIRST BRITON KILLED BY A TIGER AT MALMESBURY ABBEY

Malmesbury, Wiltshire, SN16 9BA (✆ **01666 826666**, www.malmesburyabbey.com).

☺

This former 7th-century Benedictine Abbey, now a parish church, has
an unlikely claim to fame – the first woman in Britain to be eaten by a
tiger, Hannah Twynnoy, is buried in the churchyard here. An 18th-
century barmaid at the White Lion pub, she was killed aged 33 on 23
October 1703, when she tried to cuddle a tiger from a travelling circus. There is a (slightly too jaunty?) poem on her gravestone reading:

In bloom of life
She's snatched from hence
She had no room
To make defence
For tyger fierce
Took life away
And here she lies in a bed of clay
Until the Resurrection Day.

Hannah was believed to be pregnant at the time of the mauling (hence 'bloom of life') and on the 300th anniversary of her death in 2003, every girl called Hannah in the town under the age of 11 placed a flower on her grave. This is not the only quirky tale worth bearing in mind on your visit to the abbey. In 1010 a monk called Elmer became so obsessed with the jackdaws circling above that he constructed a pair of homemade wings and leapt from the abbey tower in a mis-guided attempt to emulate the birds. He flew a laudable 200 yards up the high street before he crashed to the ground, breaking both legs and crippling himself for life. By the 11th century, the abbey con-tained the second-largest library in Europe before being dissolved by Henry VIII in 1539. Subsequently its walls were pockmarked with bullets from the English Civil War, during which it changed hands seven times. The graveyard contains the body of Athelstan (AD941), the first king of a united England.

OPEN   Daily 10am–4pm.

AMENITIES   £

⑭ LEARN ABOUT THE DEATH OF A HOT-AIR BALLOONING MP AT THE ATHELSTAN MUSEUM

Malmesbury, Wiltshire SN16 9BZ (📞 **01666 829258**, www.athelstanmuseum.org).

Find out about two flying town legends – the 10th-century monk Elmer, who leapt from the top of Malmesbury Abbey (see p. 117) believing his home-made wings would turn him into a bird, and avia-tor MP Walter Powell, who perished in a hot-air balloon over the channel while attempting to promote ballooning as a safe form of air travel. Exhibits include photos of Powell taking off in his balloon from Malmesbury in the 1880s plus a painting of Elmer's doomed flight. Other famous local men remembered here include the world's first political philosopher, Thomas Hobbes, author of the snappily titled *Behemoth: the History of the Causes of the Civil Wars of England and of the Counsels and Artifices by which they were carried on from the year 1640 to the year 1662*, and also artist Thomas Girtin. He was an

18th-century artist, contemporary and friend of JMW Turner, who magnanimously said of the man after he died of consumption, 'Had Tom Girtin lived, I should have starved'. There are lace-making demonstrations at the museum on Mondays.

OPEN   Daily 10:30am–4:30pm.

AMENITIES   ☕ 🛍 £

⑭ SEE WHERE MR DARCY MET ELIZABETH IN LACOCK VILLAGE

Lacock, Chippenham, Wiltshire SN15 2LG (✆ **01249 730459**, www.nationaltrust.org.uk/lacock).

You might not know its name but you'll doubtless recognise its high street because the village of Lacock has featured in more period dramas than any other in the country. With its lime-washed, half-timbered stone houses dating from the 13th century, most owned and carefully preserved by the National Trust, it is the perfect backdrop for all manner of movies and TV series including *Cranford, Pride and Prejudice, The Other Boleyn Girl, Randall and Hopkirk (Deceased), The Mayor of Casterbridge, Moll Flanders, Emma* and a sprinkling of Harry Potters. The favourite filming locations are on the high street, where overhead wires and satellite dishes are banned, the Red Lion pub, the façade of which represented the assembly rooms when Colin Firth's Darcy met Elizabeth in the 1995 *Pride and Prejudice* movie, and the medieval tithe barn on East Street. If you can dodge the film crews and bonnet-wearing actresses blushing behind their fans, there are some great tea shops to sniff out, while Lacock Abbey, home of William Henry Fox Talbot, who invented the photo negative in 1835, is also worth a visit (although there is an admission charge). The Fox Talbot Museum (again chargeable) is also dedicated to the village's most famous son. It was his descendents who donated the abbey and most of the houses in the village to the National Trust.

OPEN   All year round.

AMENITIES   🍴 🥤 🛍 £

What you Can Bring with You

There are a number of restrictions when visiting the Stonehenge site for the summer solstice. For instance, the amount of alcohol allowed onto the site is limited to four cans or one bottle of wine per person (although that doesn't stop crafty people leaving extras in their cars so they can go back and forwards). There's no glass allowed so decant your wine into plastic bottles. Rucksacks and, oddly, duvets are barred as they are apparently a tripping hazard.

⓯ CELEBRATE THE SUMMER SOLSTICE AT STONEHENGE

Two miles (3.2km) west of Amesbury, Salisbury, SP4 7DE (ⓒ **0870 333 1181**, www. english-heritage.org.uk).

More than 30,000 druids, pagans, New Age hippies, pensioners, loved-up couples, lonely singletons, nutters, weirdos, accountants – in fact just about anyone from every walk of life imaginable – descend every year on the country's most famous Neolithic monument to draw power and inspiration from the sunrise on summer solstice. Revellers begin to gather at the 5,000-year-old site, believed to be a place of sun worship, a healing sanctuary or a burial site, at around 7pm near to 21 June when the ropes around the stone circle are removed. Party-goers mill about all night drinking, banging drums, reciting poetry, chanting and even knitting, although also occasionally getting pulled off the stones by police. Everybody waits for the sunrise, normally expected at around 4:56am (although it's been obscured by cloud for the last five years) and the great cheer that greets it. There is a car park a short walk away across the hillside with room for 6,500 vehicles that fills up fast. A shuttle bus operates from Wiltshire train and bus stations ferrying crowds to the site until 1:15am. They restart at 5am to take people back again. There's further free but managed access to the site on the winter (December), spring (March) and autumn (September) solstices although the gatherings are smaller and entry to the stones is limited generally to around one hour before the expected sunrise.

Robin Hood Statue, Nottingham.

MIDLANDS

The top free things to do in the Midlands include visiting the three nuclear bombers at the Royal Air Force Museum in Shifnal, a trip to Bosworth battlefield, the site of the last conflict in the War of the Roses and the Coventry Transport Museum that's home to the land-speed world record breaking car, Thrust SSC. Elsewhere you can learn a new religion at the Jain Centre in Leicester, see the Major Oak in the Sherwood Forest Country Park near Nottingham – legend has it Robin Hood famously hid in and visited the eerie beauty of the plague village of Eyam. One of the world's greatest collections of Pre-Raphaelite paintings is housed at the Birmingham Museum and Art Gallery while in the village of Much Wenlock you can get an early taste for the 2012 London Olympics attending the village's Olympian Games, the forerunner and inspiration for the modern day Olympics. Other great museums include the shoe museum in Northampton and the Stoke-on-Trent Potteries Museum and Art Gallery with its diverting exhibition about the local wallabies that used to live in these parts. Outdoor highlights include pond-dipping for kids at the Marston Vale Millennium Country Park in Bedford and great walks at the Worcester Countryside Centre. Two famous pubs we suggest stopping for a pint in are Ye Olde Trip to Jerusalem in Nottingham that was once Richard II's local and The Old Bull pub in the village of Inkberrow, the setting for the Radio 4 series *The Archers*.

⑭ HAVE A PICNIC AMONG THE RUINS OF HOUGHTON HOUSE

Hazelwood Lane, Ampthill, Bedfordshire MK45 2EZ (© **0870 3331181**, www.english-heritage.org.uk/audio).

This stirring Gothic ruin of a house was where the Dowager Countess of Pembroke, Mary Herbert, died of smallpox in 1621; it was gutted in 1794 to furnish the nearby Swan Inn. It may have been the inspiration for the 'House Beautiful' in John Bunyan's 17th-century *Pilgrim's Progress* and was so finely designed many believe it to be the work of architect Inigo Jones. There is a free audio download for your MP3 player or iPod with information about the roofless house available at the web address above (you'll find it under East of England). Originally a hunting lodge, Houghton was extended in the 17th century when it became the main family home of the wealthy Bruce family. Have a wander around the ruins, then enjoy a picnic in the grounds and a game of hide-and-seek with your children.

OPEN   All year round.

AMENITIES   P

⑭ POND-DIP AT MARSTON VALE MILLENNIUM COUNTRY PARK

Marston Moretaine, Bedford MK43 0PR (© **01234 767037**, www.marstonvale.org).

Our daughter caught a newt pond-dipping (nets are supplied from the visitor centre for free) at this 250-hectare park and wetland reserve and tried to sneak it home. Based at a former brickworks and quarry, this man-made park is home to birds including bitterns, sparrow-hawks, yellow wagtails and kestrels. Observe the wildlife from specially constructed hides, enjoy the smells in the sensory garden and follow the five-mile (8km) cycle trail through the park, which also has woodland and wetland walks. The Visitor Centre offers interactive displays on the environment, and, rather strangely, a full-size Nissan Micra suspended from its ceiling. We are not sure exactly why but suspect it is something to do with the Marston Vale Trust's quest to lower carbon emissions.

OPEN   Summer 10am–6pm; winter 9am–5pm.

AMENITIES   ☕ 🏠 🅿

149 WATCH FAWLTY TOWERS AT QUAD

Market Place, Cathedral Quarter, Derby, DE1 3AS (✆ **01332 290 606**, www.derby quad.co.uk).

Watch free classic movies like *Brief Encounter* at this new, glass, cube-shaped building housing a cinema, gallery, café and workshop in an old quarter of Derby. Although it's primarily an arts cinema (tickets £6), more than 1,500 pieces of film have been digitalised from the archive of the British Film Institute and visitors can book a two-hour slot in one of the five two-seater booths at the QUAD's spin off, BFI Mediatheque. The films are shown on large computer screens and you can book ahead, although you have to join the British Film Institute first (this is also free). Sitcoms such as *Fawlty Towers* are also on offer, plus a host of documentaries and film footage dating back to the 1890s. There is also a gallery here featuring temporary exhibitions, including work by Turner-prize nominated artists Jane and Louise Wilson.

OPEN   Gallery Mon–Sat 11am–6pm, Sun 12pm–6pm; Mediatheque Mon–Sat 11am–8pm, Sun midday–8pm.

AMENITIES   ☕ 🍷 £

150 TIRE OF HEARING ABOUT MATTHEW MACFAYDEN AT CHATSWORTH HOUSE

Chatsworth, Bakewell, Derbyshire DE45 1PP (📞 **01246 565300**, www.chatsworth. org).

Owned by the Duke and Duchess of Devonshire for 450 years, Chatsworth House is instantly recognisable as the famous setting for many period movies including *Pride and Prejudice* starring Keira Knightley, and more importantly for my wife, Matthew Macfayden. While the formal gardens and the house have an admission charge, the 1,000-acre estate sits on the banks of the river Derwent in the Peak District National Park and is free to enter. Designed by Capability Brown in the 1760s and full of great walks, views, lakes and bridges, there are plenty of perfect picnic spots here; our favourite is in Stand Wood, which looms behind the main house and has views across the surrounding park and moorland.

| OPEN | All year round. |

| AMENITIES | ☕ 🛍 🐔 £ |

151 VISIT THE PLAGUE VILLAGE OF EYAM & SEE THE RILEY GRAVES

Eyam Museum, Hawkhill Road, Eyam, Derbyshire S32 5QP (📞 **01433 631371**, www. eyammuseum.demon.co.uk, www.eyamplaguevillage.co.uk).

The Derbyshire village of Eyam in the Peak District is the site of one of the most courageous and heart-breaking stories of the 17th century (see box, p. 127). The plague hit hard here and there are information boards throughout the village telling the story of its progress, indicating which houses were affected – the so-called Plague Cottages on Church Street have plaques outside them. In the churchyard on the same street you'll find the grave of Catherine Mompesson, the vicar's wife, while there is also a museum telling the story in more detail (£2 admission) with an appropriate rat-topped weather vane. The best way to appreciate this incredible story is by walking a mile or so from the village towards Grindleford up a lonely track marked by a blue sign pointing to the Riley Graves. Enclosed in a simple stone circle, the graves are of the husband and six children of Elizabeth Hancock, who buried them all within days of each other. Almost 350 years

Plague Story

When the plague arrived in Eyam in 1665, the people of the village voluntarily cut themselves off from the rest of the world in an unprecedented act of selfless bravery to prevent the infection spreading to neighbouring areas. It's believed the disease arrived at the village on second-hand clothes from London delivered to local tailor George Vickers. The cloth was damp and Vickers placed it in front of the fire to dry it, releasing the plague-bearing fleas. A few days later he and a cluster of people around his address were dead. It was William Mompesson, the local vicar, who advised villagers to quarantine themselves. From then until the disease passed 14 months later, church services were held outdoors at nearby Cucklett Delf and the villagers buried their own dead, surviving on food handouts from the Earl of Devonshire at nearby Chatsworth. If they wanted to buy goods, they left money in vinegar-soaked holes in a boundary stone in a field between Eyam and Stoney Middleton; to see it head up the Lydgate on your way out of the village. All in all the plague caused 260 deaths – three-quarters of the village's population.

later, a remembrance service is held every Plague Sunday (the last Sunday in August) at Cucklett Delf, Eyam.

OPEN   Museum Mar–Nov Tues–Sun 10am–4:30pm. Village open all year round.

AMENITIES

❻ WANDER ROUND THE BOSWORTH BATTLEFIELD HERITAGE CENTRE & COUNTRY PARK

Sutton Cheney, near Market Bosworth, Nuneaton, Leicestershire CV13 0AD (✆ **01455 290429**, www.bosworthbattlefield.com).

We enjoyed a contemplative afternoon mooching around the site of one of Britain's most famous battlefields imagining Richard III's men streaming down Ambien Hill to attack Henry VII's men. While there is a new exhibition centre (£6 to get in), where children can handle weapons and dress up in medieval armour, there is a free 1.2-mile

(2km) walk around the famous site where it is probable (but not certain) that the houses of Lancaster and York fought the final battle of the War of the Roses in 1485. There are flags denoting where King Richard's men gathered, and also marking the disputed positions of Henry Tudor and Sir William Stanley's assembled troops. The Battle of Bosworth Field, one of the most significant on English soil, resulted in Richard III's defeat, the end of the Plantagenet dynasty and the ascension of Henry Tudor to the throne. The battle was immortalised in Shakespeare's play, Richard III, when just prior to his defeat, unhorsed, betrayed and surrounded by his enemies, Richard famously shouts 'a horse, a horse, my kingdom for a horse'.

OPEN Country Park daily 8:30am–5:30pm (Oct–Mar 4:40pm).

AMENITIES ¶¶ ♦ £

⓱ LEARN A NEW RELIGION AT THE JAIN CENTRE

32 Oxford Street, Leicester LE1 5XU (✆ **0116 2541150**, www.jaincentre.com).

This temple was once a Methodist chapel and is now the only Jain house of worship in Europe. A series of elaborate carvings have been stuck rather incongruously onto the exterior and inside there are 44 elaborate hand-carved sandstone pillars decorating the prayer room, which weigh over 250 tons and took over 100,000 man-hours to complete. These, along with the dome and mirrored walls, achieve the impression, bearing in mind that the temple is just off the busy Leicester ring road, of suddenly feeling like you're in a peaceful forest clearing. This tranquillity even affected our children who amazingly hardly complained when asked to leave their crisps behind as food is not permitted upstairs in the temple. The relaxed attitude to children meant our one year old only very slightly put off the devotees in attendance by trying to pull down images of the 16th and 23rd tirthankaras. Dr Ramesh Mehta, who showed us around – ring ahead for a personal tour – took time out to teach us the main concepts of his religion: non-violence (both in word and deed), multiplicity of viewpoint and the careful limiting of your possessions. Buggy-pushers beware: there's no lift, and menstruating women are not allowed upstairs.

OPEN Mon–Fri 2–5pm.

AMENITIES   £

⓪ CHECK OUT THE WAISTCOAT OF THE ONE-TIME FATTEST MAN IN THE WORLD AT THE NEWARKE HOUSES MUSEUM

The Newarke, Leicester LE2 7BY (℃ **0116 2254980**, www.leicester.gov.uk).

Telling the story of Leicester through the ages, this museum is worth visiting if only to learn about the one-time fattest man in the world, Leicester's Daniel Lambert. At a hulking 52st 11lbs, Lambert, who died in 1891, was so famous in his day that he was introduced to King George III, and mentioned in the works of Dickens, Melville and Thackeray. Because of his prodigious size he became a symbol for the strength of the English during the Napoleonic Wars and was so large he'd float down the river Soar on his back with children hitching a ride on his stomach. At this museum you can see Lambert's waistcoat, stockings and a portrait of him by Ben Marshall, although be careful – our daughter ('Daddy, he ate too many sweets didn't he?') set off a sensitive alarm trying to get too close to Lambert's mementoes. There is

Does my Bum Look Big in These?

1. Shoes were traditionally hidden away from view in houses to protect their inhabitants from evil and misfortune.
2. The patron saint of shoemakers is Crispin.
3. The average increase in the protrusion of a woman's buttocks is 25 per cent when she wears high heels (Harper's Index).
4. Each foot has 125,000 sweat glands, which excrete half a pint of moisture a day.
5. Heels were invented in the Middle East to lift the foot away from burning sand.
6. In Hungary, the groom drinks a toast to his bride out of her wedding slipper.
7. The first lady's boot was designed for Queen Victoria in 1840.

also a toy gallery full of old-fashioned playthings including board games and hoops.

OPEN   Daily Mon–Sat 10am–5pm; Sun 11am–5pm.

AMENITIES

⑮ TREAT THE CHILDREN TO AN EXHIBITION ON THEIR FAVOURITE SUBSTANCE AT THE ABBEY PUMPING STATION

Corporation Road, Leicester LE4 5PX (℗ **0116 2995111**, www.leicester.gov.uk).

★ ♙ ☂

Leicester's Museum of Science and Technology is housed in a colourful brick pumping station and relates the story of the city's industrial heritage, but there is only really one main reason for visiting. Toddlers mired in lavatorial fascination (our daughter) can watch spellbound as human excrement progresses from a Leicester toilet via a see-through pipe as it heads on its journey to Wanlip sewage works. This is an absolute must for any self-respecting child under the age of six. It was at this station, used in the 19th century to pump Leicester sewage to a treatment works in Beaumont Leys, that our son was allowed to put his hand down a toilet for the first time without us telling him off. It is not only ideal for children, however. Also here is possibly the least likely museum exhibit in England: 'Stand or crouch – how posture assists bowel movement'. There are also four beam engines for steam buffs; these were originally used to pump the sewage and three have been carefully restored. Check the website for activity days, when the engines are displayed under steam.

OPEN   Daily Feb–Oct 11am–4:30pm.

AMENITIES   P

⑯ SEE A MEAT-MAKING DEMO AT YE OLDE PORK PIE SHOPPE

10 Nottingham Street, Melton Mowbray, Leicestershire LE13 1NW (℗ **01664 482068**, www.porkpie.co.uk).

At the oldest original pork pie manufacturer in the country, you can see demonstrations of pies being 'hand-raised', enjoy a free sample of the world's original fast food and start mentally adding extra letter 'e's to the end of words that don'te warrante iteeee. The pork pies of Melton Mowbray distinguish themselves by using cured pork and a secret recipe that produces pies consumed down the years by royalty and 'celebrities, although we cannot reveal their names, I'm afraid'. The 15-minute demonstrations include a history lesson about the invention of the pie, which was devised as a snack for huntsmen; the pastry was originally used as a means of protecting the meat from dirt and was discarded like packaging. The business has been producing pork pies since 1851, and owners Dickinson and Morris receive around 250,000 visitors a year.

OPEN   Mon–Sat Jan–Feb 8:30am–4pm; Mar–Dec 8:30am–5pm.

AMENITIES   £

⟨157⟩ VISIT THE COUNTRY'S PREMIER SHOE COLLECTION AT THE NORTHAMPTON MUSEUM & ART GALLERY

Guildhall Road, Northampton NN1 1DP (℡ **01604 838111**, www.northampton. gov.uk).

Northampton is the shoe capital of Britain. The town has been selling shoes as far back as 1266 when King John rode here to buy a pair of riding boots for 9d. Henry III bought shoes here. Tony Blair wore a lucky pair of Northampton-made shoes to every Prime Minister's Questions, and James Bond wore footwear from the town in *Casino Royale*. The town shod the entire British army, navy and air force during both world wars. The town's football team is even called the Cobblers and yet this museum of shoes is called the Northampton Museum and Art Gallery. Why? To start with, it has 12,000 shoes in the world-famous collection in the Life and Sole Gallery, telling the history of footwear going back 8,000 years to the world's first-ever shoe. There is a recreated shoe factory and a useful archive where, if you tap in your shoe size, you can discover how small or large your feet are compared to the rest of the world's population. The Followers of Fashion Gallery takes a look at shoe design down the ages, featuring the work of contemporary designers Manolo Blahnik and Christian Louboutin and a scary selection of fetish wear. The art gallery does have a large number of Italian paintings dating from the 15th to 18th centuries and there's also a gallery telling the story of the town since Neolithic times, but the humble shoe steals the show.

OPEN   Tues–Sat 10am–5pm; Sun 2pm–5pm.

AMENITIES

ⓝ LEARN ABOUT ROBIN HOOD AT THE GALLERIES OF JUSTICE

The Lace Market, Nottingham NG1 1HN (✆ **0115 9520555**, www.galleriesofjustice.org.uk).

Inside the cabinet of crime at Nottingham's old courthouse and jail you can view a camouflage jacket worn by one of the Great Train Robbers, torture implements and a set of gallows. Meanwhile, in a gallery named Robin Hood the Legendary Outlaw Returns, learn about the development of the city's famous myth and see pictures and artefacts from the various films made about the arrow-firing man in Lincoln-green. Dr Isaac Massey's Emporium of Curiosities is part of the HM Prison Service Collection, which is jauntily showed off to the accompaniment of circus music and includes weapons confiscated from prisoners and a hangman's box containing all the implements a travelling executioner needed to do his job. There are also tours of the former court and cells (adults £8.75).

OPEN   Daily 10:30am–5pm.

AMENITIES

ⓝ VISIT RICHARD I'S LOCAL, THE YE OLDE TRIP TO JERUSALEM

Brewhouse Yard, Nottingham NG1 6AD (✆ **0115 947 3171**, www.triptojerusalem.com).

This is believed to be the oldest pub in Britain, open since AD1189, and was where the Knights Templar in King Richard I's day met for a drink and overnight rest before embarking on the Crusades. It is even claimed that Richard himself downed a few pints here. More importantly for me, it is also where my wife accidentally sat on an antique chair said to make all women who sit on it pregnant ('I don't want any more children, thank you'). The pub is also famous for its caves, carved out of the soft sandstone rock beneath Nottingham Castle, against which the building rests. The ground-level caverns form the pub's rear drinking rooms and there's a network of caves underneath the floor. As well as the pregnancy chair, there is a *cursed galleon* in one of the bars – a small wooden model of a ship. It's claimed that all who have cleaned it have met a mysterious death. Landlords have refused to allow anyone to dust the ship over the years, allowing inches of thick grime to build up on it. It's now encased in glass to prevent large clumps of dust falling into unsuspecting drinkers' pints.

OPEN   Sun–Thurs 10am–11pm; Fri-Sat 10am–midnight.

AMENITIES   P

⓰ SEE THE FAMOUS ROBIN HOOD TREE AT SHERWOOD FOREST COUNTRY PARK

Edwinstowe, near Mansfield, Nottinghamshire NG21 9HN (ⓒ **01623 823202**, www. nottinghamshire.gov.uk).

The best thing to do here is take pictures of your family in some very silly felt-feathered green hats (available for £1 from the Visitor Centre) in front of the Major Oak, where Robin Hood supposedly hid to elude the evil Sheriff of Nottingham. Stand jauntily for the snaps and whack your raised knee with one flat hand for extra outlaw authenticity. The Major Oak is about a 20-minute walk from the Visitor Centre, and is disappointingly fenced off, with its important branches supported by scaffolding props. There is an exhibition about Robin Hood at the Visitor Centre, where we found out that he preyed primarily on travellers on the Great North Road (now the A1), was first mentioned in 1261 and, through a dangerously inaccurate interactive display, that it's safe to eat deadly nightshade while wandering around the 450-acre park. There are way-marked trails among the 900 aged oaks, sheep and cattle grazing and lots of bird and insect life to spot. Just don't eat the deadly nightshade.

OPEN   Daily May–Sept 10am–5pm; Oct–Apr 10am–4:30pm.

AMENITIES   ⑪ 🪑 P

⑯ SEE THE BABY GHOST AT RUFFORD COUNTRY PARK

Ollerton, Newark, Nottinghamshire NG22 9DF (✆ **01623 821310**, www. nottinghamshire.gov.uk/ruffordcp).

At this 150-acre park, home to the foreboding roofless 12th-century ruins of Rufford Abbey, apparently haunted by a black monk, a white lady and a baby who likes to 'snuggle up to female visitors', you can have fun hiding from your wife in the crypt while whimpering in an infantile yet increasingly aggressive voice: 'I want a cuddle. I *want* a cuddle'. In the grounds around the Cistercian abbey there are woodland walks, formal gardens full of herbs and flowers as well as 20 sculptures, including iron work by Roger Lee and the famous *Man & Ewe on Park Bench* by Sioban Coppinger. There's also a pretty lake and a children's play village.

OPEN   Daily 9am–5:30pm.

AMENITIES

⑯ HATCH A CONSPIRACY WHERE THE GUNPOWDER PLOT WAS CONCEIVED

St Andrew's Church, Main Street, Stoke Dry, Rutland LE15 9JG (✆ **01572 822717**).

★

'Remember, remember, the fifth of November, gunpowder, treason and plot'. Yes, of course you do. But did you know that the Gunpowder Plot to blow up Parliament in 1605 (and the origin of fireworks every 5th November) was apparently hatched in this tiny church because one of the plotters, Sir Everard Digby, lived in the village. The story goes the Gunpowder Plot was dreamt up in a room above the porch reached by a narrow staircase. The plan ended in failure; the traitors were rounded up and executed, with their leader Guy Fawkes burnt at the stake. The Norman church here was largely rebuilt during the 13th and 15th centuries and has an interesting 15th-century oak rood screen, and fascinating medieval wall paintings which show the martyrdom of St Edmund and the churchyard is a good spot for a picnic.

OPEN   All year round.

AMENITIES

⑯ MAKE DIVE-BOMBING STUKKA NOISES AT THE ROYAL AIR FORCE MUSEUM COSFORD

Shifnal, Shropshire, TF11 8UP (✆ **01902 376200**, www.rafmuseum.org.uk/cosford).

In the Cold War Exhibition at Cosford there are, among the 70 aircraft on display, three nuclear bombers that would have been used to retaliate against a Soviet strike on Britain. This thoughtful display about the war that never (thankfully) went hot features a Checkpoint Charlie area telling of life behind the Iron Curtain, tanks from the era and biographies of the key characters such as Reagan and Gorbachev, who were involved in the eventual thawing of relations between East and West. Elsewhere in the museum there's an interactive area where children can learn how to fly planes and a collection of missiles, including a Polaris. In the War Planes Hangar, there are the obligatory Spitfires and Messerschmitts from World War II, allowing you the opportunity to demonstrate your realistic dive-bombing Stukka noises.

| OPEN | Daily 10am–6pm.

| AMENITIES |

Gutted Plotter

Sir Everard Digby (1578–1606) was one of the plotters involved in the abortive 1605 Gunpowder plot to assassinate King James I of England and VI of Scotland along with members of the Parliament of England and he is also notorious for the manner of his death. Digby was hanged for 'only a very short time', and was certainly alive when he went to the quartering block to be disembowelled. Sir Francis Bacon told that when the executioner plucked out his heart and held it aloft exclaiming, as custom commanded 'Here is the heart of a traitor', Digby summoned up the superhuman strength to challenge, 'Thou liest'.

⑯ SEE THE LIKELY HOME OF ROBIN HOOD AT WHITTINGTON CASTLE

Castle Street, Whittington, Shropshire SY11 4DF (✆ **01691 662397**, www.whittington castle.co.uk).

Owned and run by the local community, Whittington Castle is touted as the former home of the 'real' Robin Hood. Fulk FitzWarin III, a man sounding so American it is virtually impossible not to picture him in slacks sat on a golf buggy on a Florida links, built the now-ruined castle in 1197, but was ousted from his baronial seat by King John and became an outlaw. FitzWarin, like the Robin Hood of legend, gathered a band of men about him who robbed from the rich to give to the poor. It was he, whose castle was eventually restored to him, who forced King John to sign the Magna Carta. Nowadays the castle, which has been derelict since 1760 and was acquired on lease by villagers in the 1980s, has lots of swans and ducks on the moat to feed bread crusts to, while the 12 acres of grounds contain interpretation boards telling you what the castle looked like in its glory days. Other myths and legends surrounding the partially restored Norman ruin concern Dick Whittington, the Lord Mayor of London, who some believe hailed from the village, and also the Holy Grail, which according to gossip (admittedly only in the tea shop) was supposedly once stored in the castle's private chapel.

OPEN Mar–Oct Wed–Sun 10am–4pm; Nov–Feb Fri–Sun 10am–4pm. Castle grounds open all year round.

AMENITIES

⓯ SAMPLE A ROMAN LITTLE CHEF AT LETOCETUM ROMAN BATHS & MUSEUM

Watling Street, Wall, near Lichfield, Staffordshire WS14 0AW (℅ **0121 625 6820**, www.english-heritage.org.uk).

This is the Roman equivalent of Newport Pagnell Service Station and Days Inn Milton Keynes Hotel – basically a staging post for soldiers to have a rest, a bath and a bite to eat on their way to Wales along Watling Street. Letocetum, quite literally in Latin meaning 'Little Chef' (ok – 'wooden area' really) is considered the finest excavated site of its kind in the country. The foundations are all that's left of the bath-house and Roman inn, although you can see some of the artefacts archaeologists have uncovered at the site including pottery, bronzes and weapon fragments in the free museum next door.

OPEN Daily Mar–Oct 10am–5pm; last weekend of each month all year 10am–5pm.

AMENITIES

⑯ LEARN ABOUT THE STAFFORDSHIRE WALLABIES AT THE POTTERIES MUSEUM & ART GALLERY

Bethesda Street, Cultural Quarter, Stoke-on-Trent, Staffordshire ST1 3DW (℃ **01782 232323**, www.stoke.gov.uk/museum).

♦♦ ↗

Known primarily for its nationally important 5,000-piece strong ceramics collection, this absorbing museum also has fine-art galleries and others on archaeology and natural history. Highlights of the exhibitions include the rare 17th-century Ozzie the Owl slipware pottery jug uncovered on TV's *Antiques Roadshow*, a stuffed Staffordshire wallaby (we are not making that up) and a full-size Battle of Britain Spitfire designed by Stoke's most famous son, Reginald Mitchell. Learn about the unlikely wild wallaby population of Staffordshire, which grew up after a number were released from a private zoo after World War II – they hopped about the area until the climate, a little different from Australia's, killed them all off in the 1980s. Our daughter's favourite exhibits were the 400 cream jugs made in the shape of cows arranged along one wall, and our son made plane noises for three days after coming face to face with the Spitfire. In addition, there are one-off events ranging from knitting workshops to meeting and collecting the autographs from Stoke City's new-season signings, plus children's trails and family activities during the school holidays.

OPEN Mon–Sat 10am–5pm; Sun 2pm–5pm.

AMENITIES ☕ 🎒 🅿

⑰ HEAR THE LAST POST AT THE NATIONAL MEMORIAL ARBORETUM

Croxall Road, Alrewas, Staffordshire DE13 7AR (℃ **01283 792333**, www.thenma.org.uk).

This national site of remembrance was established in 2001 over 150 acres of an old gravel works and contains more than 50,000 trees, including dawn redwoods and Douglas-firs, and more than 150 memorials to the 16,000 armed forces who have lost their lives serving their country since World War II. For me, the highlight was the Shot at Dawn Memorial to the 306 British and Commonwealth brothers executed for desertion or cowardice during World War I. Their treatment is marked by a 10-ft (3m) statue of a blindfolded solider tied to a stake; it was modelled on a 17-year-old private, Herbert Burden, who had lied about his age to join up. The Last Post is sounded daily at 11am, followed by the Reveille and a two-minute silence in the Millennium Chapel of Peace. The children got a kick out of the Polar Bear Memorial, a tribute to the 49th Infantry West Riding Division stationed in Iceland, which was used as a staging post to ferry American materials to the front during World War II.

OPEN   Daily 9am–5pm.

AMENITIES   ¶¶ 🛍 ⓥ £

⓱ VISIT THE HOME OF THE MODERN-DAY OLYMPICS AT MUCH WENLOCK

Much Wenlock, Shropshire (✆ **01952 727907**, www.wenlock-olympian-society. org.uk).

It's a little known fact that the revival of the multi-billion-pound modern Olympic Games, the biggest sporting event in the world, was inspired by the efforts of Dr William Penny Brookes (see box, p. 139) from this small Shropshire town. He organised his own Olympian Games here in 1850, 44 years before the revival of this Ancient Greek spectacle. The Olympian Games are now staged here every year on the second weekend in July at the Gaskell Recreation Ground. They are free to attend and guests in the past have included the Queen, triple-jump gold medallist Jonathan Edwards, and the former middle-distance runner, Tory politician Lord Sebastian Coe. The games include track and field events, a cricket match and golf tournament. They differ slightly from the 1850 version of the games in that the 'fun event', which used to include perhaps a wheelbarrow race, has been dropped. In accordance with the Ancient Greek ethos of improving mind and body, there is an artistic Olympian event in Much Wenlock on the second weekend of March, when medals are awarded for poetry, writing and singing. Pick up the free brochure on the Olympian Trail from the Guildhall and Wenlock Tourist Information Centre, complete with a map. The trail takes visitors on a 1.5-mile (2.4km) walk through the town, highlighting the important sites relating to Brookes and the Olympian Society, including the Much Wenlock Museum (free) where there are photos of Dr Brookes, the beautiful

16th-century Guildhall where he was a magistrate, his grave at Holy Trinity, his former home and the site of the Games itself.

OPEN   July (check times).

AMENITIES   P

⓳ CHECK OUT THE CUTLERY DINOSAUR AT THE MILLENNIUM GALLERY

90 Surrey Street, Sheffield, South Yorkshire S1 1DA (✆ **0114 2211900**, www.sheffield. gov.uk).

This site of 5,000 domestic greenhouses, Sheffield's answer to the Eden Project, contains more than 2,500 plants and is the largest temperate glass house built in Britain in the last 100 years. The Winter Garden is a restful city-centre hangout with miniature waterfalls and ponds as well as free classical music and jazz concerts, with Wednesday Live events taking place from June to September between 5pm–8pm. The gardens are connected to the excellent Millennium Gallery, where you'll find a vast collection of writing and paintings by Victorian art critic and painter John Ruskin, who was responsible for bringing JMW Turner to public attention. The highlight of the collection is, however, an enormous dinosaur made of knives and forks, paying homage to Sheffield's former incarnation as 'Steel City'. There's also an interactive area where children are encouraged through play to learn about the history of the cutlery (first there was the

Rekindling the Flame

Dr William Penny Brookes (1809–1895) was the scholar, physician, magistrate and all-round good egg who reintroduced the notion of the Olympics to England in 1859, the same decade that the Games were reintroduced in Athens. He founded the Wenlock Olympian Society, which held games annually, and later became President of the National Olympian Association, which led to the staging of the first Olympic Games, held in 1866 at the Crystal Palace in South London. Competitors included cricketer WG Grace, who came first in the hurdles, but the Games only attracted 250 entrants and about 10,000 spectators.

fork, then the knife and finally we cracked it with the spoon) that was so interwoven with the history of Sheffield as a major industrial city.

OPEN   Daily 8am–6pm.

AMENITIES   ☕ £

170 RIDE THE SINGING LIFT AT THE IKON GALLERY

1 Oozells Square, Brindleyplace, Birmingham, Warwickshire B1 2HS (℃ **0121 248 0708**, www.ikon-gallery.co.uk).

The highlight of this contemporary gallery, housed in a 19th-century school, is the singing lift in which our children rode up and down for almost half an hour listening to the harmony rising with each floor level. The lift was designed by Turner Prize-winning Martin Creed and is one of the few permanent pieces at the gallery, which stages new temporary exhibitions every seven or eight weeks. Highlights in the past have included anything from traditional painting to the woodland photography and angular sculptures of Italian artist Giuseppe Penone. There are children's workshops aimed at those aged five and over on the first Saturday of each month between 2pm–5pm, featuring arts and crafts relevant to the current exhibition.

OPEN   Tues–Sun 11am–6pm.

AMENITIES   ☕ 🛍 £

171 SEE THE PRE-RAPHAELITE ART COLLECTION AT BIRMINGHAM MUSEUM & ART GALLERY

Chamberlain Square, Birmingham, Warwickshire B3 3DH (℃ **0121 303 2834**, www.bmag.org.uk).

This Victorian purpose-built museum was founded in 1887 and has the best collection of Pre-Raphaelite works in the world (1,000 drawings and more than 100 finished paintings), featuring big names such as Dante Gabriel Rossetti, William Holman Hunt and locally born Edward Burne-Jones. In addition the museum is home to millions of other exhibits and is especially rich in glass and ceramics, amassed here in the 19th century from all over the world with the specific aim of inspiring local craftsmen to get back to their workshops with renewed creative vigour. There's a strong contemporary art collection and regular visiting exhibitions from the likes of Bridget Riley and photographer Stephen McCurry. There are hands-on children's galleries featuring a variety of talking bronze heads, including one of Albert Einstein who addresses, for reasons we could not decipher, a camel herder.

OPEN   Mon–Thurs, Sat 10am–5pm; Fri 10:30am–5pm; Sun 12:30pm–5pm.

AMENITIES

⑰ SEE CRAFT DEMOS AT THE MUSEUM OF THE JEWELLERY QUARTER

75–79 Vyse Street, Hockley, Birmingham, Warwickshire B18 6HA (✆ **0121 554 3598**, www.bmag.org.uk).

Recently topping St Mark's Cathedral in Venice and Notre Dame in Paris in a poll of Europe's top free attractions, this museum is based at the 19th-century Smith and Pepper jewellery factory. It is preserved so faithfully that the jar of Marmite left out to make the workers' sandwiches remains where it was on the day the doors were bolted shut in 1981. The museum recounts the story of 250 years of jewellery production in Birmingham, from its height in 1914 when 60,000 were employed, to the present day with just 6,000 in the trade. There are hourly guided tours (more frequent during busy periods), during which you'll check out the container of white potassium cyanide crystals dangerously close to the sugar in the tea-making area and see several pieces of machinery in operation, including polishing machines and drop stamps. The second floor 'Earth's Riches' gallery showcases jewellery made from natural materials such as whale teeth and coral. There are 10-minute demonstrations at the jeweller's bench and regular family events during school holidays. Check the website for details.

OPEN   Tues–Sat 10:30am–4pm.

AMENITIES

⑰ BREAK THE LAND-SPEED RECORD AT THE COVENTRY TRANSPORT MUSEUM

Millennium Place, Hales Street, Coventry, Warwickshire CV1 1JD (✆ **024 7623 4270**, www.transport-museum.com).

At one of the largest museums of its kind in Europe, there are many opportunities to get separated from your wife, enabling me to sneak back at least three times to the Spirit of Speed Gallery to have a go in the simulator for the Thrust SSC, the car in which Andy Green broke the land-speed record and the sound barrier in 1997. The museum honours the city of Coventry, where there were once more than 600 companies making motorcycles and cars. Its highlights include an Austin Metro once belonging to Lady Diana Spencer, the Humber staff car used by General Montgomery during World War II and a display about the Michael Caine movie *The Italian Job*, which was partly filmed (yes, I am really going to say this), and not a lot of people know this, near Coventry. Elsewhere there are demonstrations about bicycles in the Cyclopedia area, which involved a costumed member of staff perching our daughter precariously on top of a hay-fork tricycle from 1880. Children get to draw their own cars at a circular table with crayons and there's a small quirky display where you get to guess, from photos of the staff, which mode of transport they come to work by.

OPEN   Daily 10am–5pm.

AMENITIES

⑱ WEBB ELLIS RUGBY FOOTBALL MUSEUM

5–6 St Matthews Street, Rugby, Warwickshire CV21 3BY (✆ **01788 567777**, www.warwickshire.gov.uk).

Based in a small Victorian terrace where rugby balls have been produced for more than 160 years, this museum charts the progress of the game invented here by Rugby schoolboy, William Webb Ellis (see box, p. 143). Highlights include memorabilia from players, a signed ball by Martin Johnson, and the chance to meet John Batchelor, who is the world's oldest rugby-ball stitcher and has made test-match balls for over 60 years. See the materials used to make the famous oval balls, from pigs' bladders right up to the synthetic rubber used today and accidentally fling a spinning bag of sandwiches at your unsuspecting wife in the middle of the room. The Rugby Art Gallery and Museum (closed Mondays) next door is free and also worth a visit for its 20th-century art collection showcasing LS Lowry and Barbara Hepworth.

OPEN   Mon–Sat 9am–5pm.

AMENITIES

⑰ DISCOVER THE TRUTH ABOUT 17TH-CENTURY CONDOMS AT WALSALL LEATHER MUSEUM

Littleton Street West, Walsall, West Midlands WS2 8EQ (✆ **01922 721153**, www.walsall.gov.uk/leathermuseum).

At the country's home of leather (the town has three warrants to supply leather to the Royal family) you can learn about 17th-century leather condoms, how dog dirt was used in the tanning process and see the Walsall-made football used during the town's famous victory over Arsenal in the 1933 FA Cup. Telling the story of how Walsall became associated with the leather trade, the museum showcases goods made here down the years from 17th-century saddles to today's designer handbags. Tanning demonstrations and talks take place daily on an *ad hoc* basis and it's the same with the hand-stitching displays. If he's around, seek out 85-year-old Ron, who'll tell you how to seal animal skins for tanning

Rugger Rugger

William Webb Ellis (1806–1872) was born in Lancashire and attended Rugby public school, where he was credited with inventing the game of rugby in 1823 by catching a ball (allowed) and running with it, a practice hitherto outlawed in football. After leaving school, Webb Ellis got a scholarship to Brasenose College, Oxford before entering the Church and becoming chaplain of St George's, Albermarle Street, London. He never married and moved to the south of France for his health, where he died in 1872. His grave in 'le cimetière du vieux château' at Menton in the Alpes-Maritime was rediscovered in 1958 by Ross McWhirter of *The Guiness Book of Records* fame, and was renovated by the French rugby union.

and also about the leather condoms found during an archaeological dig of a nearby Civil War site.

OPEN   Apr–Oct Tues–Sat 10am–5pm; Nov–Mar Tues–Sat 10am–4pm.

AMENITIES   ☕ 🛍 🎪 ☀ £

⓲ LEARN ABOUT GLOVES AT THE WORCESTER COUNTRYSIDE CENTRE

Wildwood Drive, Worcester WR5 2LG (✆ **01905 766943**).

◑

A good place for a relatively untaxing ramble, this was where, on a 45-minute trail through an ancient oak copse in Nunnery Wood, we saw squirrels, various birds and a foxglove that our daughter couldn't grasp wasn't an actual glove. There are carved sculptures for children to stand on and slip off when their shoes get muddy, another trail through meadows, some biodiversity themed interactive displays at the Visitor Centre and a recently redeveloped play park next to a café serving organic produce.

OPEN   Countryside Centre 10am–5pm.

AMENITIES   ☕ P

⓱ DRINK IN THE ARCHER'S LOCAL, THE OLD BULL PUB

Village Green, Inkberrow, Worcester WR7 4DZ (✆ **01386 792428**).

While there is not much to see here, the village of Inkberrow is the famous setting for the unmissable (if you are my wife) radio series *The Archers*, all about everyday country folk who speak very loudly because of the tumultuous birdsong in the background, which has been running on Radio 4 since Roman times. To bolster the experience, time your arrival to coincide with the show playing on the radio. That way you can listen to it in the car feeling surreally like you might suddenly feature in the very episode you're listening to. More fun still is winding down the window and shouting established *Archer* catchphrases at the locals. After this we recommend you take a little pootle down to The Old Bull pub for an 'Archers special' – a bowl of home-made soup and a sliced white-bread sandwich. The black-and-white half-timbered Tudor pub has a signed picture of the cast on the wall and the actors regularly meet up there for reunions.

OPEN   Daily 11:30am–midnight.

AMENITIES **P**

Streetlife Museum of Transport, Hull.

NORTH-EAST

In the north-east and Yorkshire there's plenty to do for free. Highlights here include patting a pit pony at the National Coal Mining Museum in Wakefield, cycling the North York moors made famous by the Brontë sisters, as well as experiencing the Egyptian afterlife at the Great North Museum in Newcastle. You can ride a hansom carriage in Hull, learn about Catherine Cookson in South Shields, and sword-fight at the Royal Armouries Museum in Leeds. For train buffs there's the chance to ride a steam train at the Stephenson Railway Museum in North Shields, while in York you can see over 100 locos at the National Railway Museum. Other museum high spots include the famous stuffed lion at the Sunderland Museum and

Winter Gardens and slavery exhibitions at the Wilberforce House Museum in Hull. Durham Cathedral is one of the grandest in the world, while for art lovers there's the 1853 Gallery in Saltaire with its collection of Hockneys. Outdoors Bamburgh beach on the stunning Northumberland coastline is a jewel, while a bike ride through the Dalby forest makes for a wonderful day out.

⑱ SEE THE WORLD'S OLDEST LIFEBOAT AT THE RNLI ZETLAND MUSEUM

The Esplanade, Redcar, Cleveland TS10 3AH (℡ **01642 494311**, www.rnli.org.uk).

The oldest lifeboat in the world, *The Zetland*, is on display here. Built in 1802, the clinker-built rowing boat was based at Granville Terrace and is so old it was launched from a wooden carriage pulled by horses. The boat saved some 500 lives over 78 years of service and was crewed by volunteers, mainly Redcar fishermen, who were summoned to their stations by a boy beating a drum to the tune 'Come Along Brave Boys, Come Along'. Next to the lifeboat is a fragment of the rudder of the Irish brig, *Jane Erskine*, which washed up on the beach at Redcar in 1992, 142 years after the ship sank and her 52-strong crew were rescued by *The Zetland*. Downstairs in the museum is a display of photographs, models and other exhibits associated with the history of sea-rescue in the north of England, while upstairs you can see life-saving equipment past and present as well as a reconstruction of a fisherman's cottage.

OPEN   May–Oct Tues–Sun 12pm–4pm.

AMENITIES

⑲ VISIT DURHAM CATHEDRAL IN BILL BRYSON'S CAR

The College, Durham DH1 3EH (℡ **0191 386 4266**, www.durhamcathedral.co.uk).

According to travel writer and Anglophile Bill Bryson, Durham has the best cathedral on earth. In fact Bryson was so enamoured of this place when he visited that he offered to lend his car to anyone who wanted to see it. Founded in 1093, the cathedral is considered the finest example of Romanesque architecture in Europe and took a record 40 years to build. It has been eulogised by writers Nathaniel Hawthorne and Sir Walter Scott, who stopped short of offering his horse and cart for visits but did write a poem in its honour. The highlights of the cathedral, voted by Radio 4 listeners as the most popular building in Britain, include the tombs of St Cuthbert (behind the high altar) and the Venerable Bede (the Galilee Chapel) along with the huge sanctuary knocker on the north door, the rasping of which gave a medieval fugitive 37 days' grace inside with the monks before facing prosecution or voluntary banishment from the nearest port. To climb the tower (325 steps) with excellent city views costs £3 (children £1.50). Guided tours are £4 and to see the shrine of St Cuthbert (see box) is £2.50. Children's quiz available.

OPEN Daily 9:15am–5pm, Sun 9:15am–3pm.

AMENITIES ☕ 🏠 £

Cuddy & the Otters

St Cuthbert, known affectionately as Cuddy in the north-east, may have been Scottish and pitched up at Lindisfarne Priory in 651 after spells in monasteries at Melrose and Ripon. He was so devout that he converted many people to Christianity and so holy that legend dictates otters would dry his feet after he prayed in the North Sea. He ended his life as a hermit and died in 687 on Farne Island. Some 11 years after his death, Cuthbert's body was dug up to make his bones into reliquaries for veneration and his body was found still miraculously intact. A cult grew up around him and when Lindisfarne was abandoned to Viking raiders his body was moved from the priory. For 100 years or so it was ferried hither-and-thither around Northumberland before he eventually wound up in Durham Cathedral, which was founded in his honour.

⑱ SEE THE FAMOUS TRAIN FROM THE RAILWAY CHILDREN AT LOCOMOTION

Shildon, County Durham DL4 1PQ ((**01388 777999**, www.locomotion.uk.com).

Based at the station from which the first-ever steam-hauled passenger train departed, this huge warehouse of a museum houses more than

Still Railing

In 1829 the Liverpool and Manchester Railway, the world's first 'Inter-City' line, was under construction. As a way of encouraging passengers to take to the railways, a race was staged for pioneers to show off their steam trains. The Rainhill Trials proved a watershed moment for rail transport and were won by Stephenson's *Rocket* despite the fact that Timothy Hackworth's *Sans Pareil* was travelling faster than the *Rocket* when a vital cylinder broke on the engine. As this had been cast at Stephenson's factory, the incident fuelled controversy that Hackworth was nobbled.

50 large trains including every buff's favourite, the world's first tilting train, the APT-E. Among the top exhibits are the original *Sans Pareil* steam locomotive raced by Timmy Hackworth against George Stephenson's *Rocket* in the 1829 Rainhill Trials (see box). Other highlights include the saddle tank engine used for filming weepie classic *The Railway Children* as well as, slightly bizarrely, the first car to drive on a British motorway. A shuttle bus takes visitors to the warehouse from the car park. Before this you can walk round the former home of Timmy Hackworth, which is given over to family-friendly, fun interactive exhibits that informed our daughter that 19th-century railway-men liked to eat parakeets and also enabled my wife and I to complete a railway-man themed game modelled on Splat the Rat involving hammering in rivets.

OPEN   1 Apr–4 Oct Mon–Sun 10am–5pm; 5 Oct–31 Mar Mon–Sun 10am–4pm.

AMENITIES

⑱ LEARN HOW A MONKEY WAS HANGED AS A FRENCH SPY AT THE MUSEUM OF HARTLEPOOL

Jackson's Dock, Maritime Avenue, Hartlepool, County Durham TS24 0XZ (© **01429 860077**, www.hartlepoolmaritimeexperience.com).

This museum is based in the same complex as the Maritime Experience (adults £7.75) and recounts the history of the town from prehistory to present day. However, it should be visited solely to hear the legend of how a monkey washed ashore from a shipwreck was hanged during the 19th-century Napoleonic Wars for being a French spy. Townsfolk today, far from being ashamed of this disputed fact, rejoice in it. Hartlepool United football team even have H'angus the monkey as their mascot. The museum also has great facilities for children; dressing up, magnifying glasses to examine fossils and hidden treasure to discover in sandpits, as well as a real 5,000-year-old human skeleton and a fully restored paddle steamer, the *PSS Wingfield Castle*, to explore.

OPEN   Daily Mar–Oct 10am–5pm; Nov–Feb 10:30am–4pm.

AMENITIES

182 WALK THE WILLIAM WILBERFORCE TRAIL

Hull, East Yorkshire HU1 (Hull Development Education Centre *C* **01482 224019**, www.wilberforcetrail.co.uk).

★

A walking tour of Hull's old town, dedicated to the anti-slavery campaigner William Wilberforce, takes in Wilberforce House Museum (see p. 152) as well as his old grammar school (now the Hands-on History Museum) and a monument to the Victorian do-gooder. The trail takes walkers back to 1807, the year the transatlantic slave trade was abolished, to a time when Hull was heavily involved in the sugar and tobacco trade and tall ships used to sail up and down the rivers Hull and Humber. Download the tour and map from the above web address, which includes a brief description of several points of interest along the way, including the wall of

The Force is Strong in this One

Born in Hull, William Wilberforce (1759–1833) was a small, sickly, delicate child with poor eyesight who nevertheless grew up to be an MP, committed philanthropist and leading abolitionist. As a young man he was an inveterate gambler and socialite, who bribed his way into Parliament on the advice of his friend William Pitt (later to be Prime Minster), and was once described as the 'wittiest man in England'. Later in life he had an evangelical epiphany and changed his ways, becoming heavily involved with anti-slave-trade activists, leading the campaign for many years before the Slavery Abolition Act was finally signed in 1883, coming into force three days before Wilberforce died. He's buried in Westminster Abbey.

honour in Hull's Peace Garden to all those involved in the cause of human freedom and the Assembly Rooms of Trinity Square where William Wilberforce (see box, p. 151) used to hang about with his pals discussing issues of the day. It concludes at the 102-ft (31m) Wilberforce column, one of only six in Britain dedicated to non-military men.

OPEN   All year around.

AMENITIES   ☕ 🍴 🍸 🛍️

⒇ EXPERIENCE SLAVERY AT THE WILBERFORCE HOUSE MUSEUM

23–25 High Street, Hull, East Yorkshire HU1 1NQ (© **01482 613902**, www.hullcc.gov.uk).

Containing the Bible, letters and frockcoat of the town's famous anti-slavery campaigner William Wilberforce, this museum also tells the story of black emancipation and displays slave collars, whips and the famous model of a slave ship Wilberforce waved in Parliament to highlight the barbarity of the trade. Also at this 17th-century house are damning plantation records from the West Indies cataloguing the names and values of slaves as well as fashionable anti-slavery merchandise of the 19th century, such as ladies' brooches bearing the Josiah Wedgwood logo of a slave on bended knees and bearing the legend 'Am I not a man and a brother?'. The museum's new galleries look at contemporary aspects of West African culture, from music to crafts, as well as highlighting the present-day campaign against international slavery and people trafficking.

OPEN   Mon–Sat 10am–5pm; Sun 1:30pm–4:30pm.

AMENITIES   🛍️ £

⒈ RIDE A HANSOM CARRIAGE AT STREETLIFE

23–25 High Street, Hull, East Yorkshire HU1 1NQ (© **01482 616435**, www.hullcc.gov.uk).

Visitors experience the invigorating claustrophobia of a pitch-black night-time 18th-century carriage ride at this 1980s' built transport museum, pumped full of realistic horse smells (manure) and bygone sound affects (begging children). There are more than 10 carriages on display as well as bicycles ranging from Victorian boneshakers to the rebellious Harley-Davidson-inspired 1970s' Choppers I used to ride no-handed down hills in fingerless gloves thinking I was Marlon Brando from *On The Waterfront*. Displays include a 1940s' cobbled street with old shops you can go into, and an automobile collection going right back to a turn-of-the-century Daimler. During the three-minute simulated carriage ride, expect to be shaken about so vigorously that in the words of my wife, you will need to 'sit down for a moment'.

OPEN   Mon–Sat 10am–5pm; Sun 1:30pm–4:30pm.

AMENITIES

185 DODGE SCARY TRAIN BUFFS AT THE NATIONAL RAILWAY MUSEUM

Leeman Road, York, North Yorkshire YO26 4XJ (✆ **08448 153139**, www.nrm.org.uk).

Containing more than 100 locomotives, including the Flying Scotsman, the record-breaking Mallard and a replica of Stephenson's *Rocket*, this is the largest museum of its kind in the world and it's affiliated to Locomotion (see p. 149). Other highlights here include the futuristic Japanese bullet train and carriages from the Royal Train, with their rather dated upholstery and patterned tea services. You'll find kitchen carriages, open wagons, mineral wagons, cattle wagons, dining cars and private saloons, plus the steam engine *Agnoria* from Shutt End Colliery, and rather bizarrely, a lock of Robert Stephenson's hair. Film shows about the development of rail travel over the last 200 years are held in the Platform 4 theatre, but be wary of entering the Warehouse Room, where we got hopelessly lost amongst the aisles of railway memorabilia in the company of over-enthusiastic train buffs in brightly coloured pac-a-macs.

OPEN   Daily 10am–6pm.

AMENITIES

⑱ LEARN ABOUT THE CITY OF YORK DURING A WALKING TOUR

York, North Yorkshire YO1 (✆ **01904 640780**, www.visityork.org).

Take a two-hour guided walk to learn about the city's illustrious history, from Roman occupation through the Viking period right up to the canonisation in 1970 of butcher's wife St Margaret of Clitherow, who was crushed to death with rocks for harbouring a Jesuit priest. The one-mile (1.6km) stroll starts in Exhibition Square (leaving 10:15am daily, also 2:15pm Apr–Sept and additional tours at 6:45pm June, July and Aug) and ends in the cobbled Shambles, which is the city's narrowest street and has atmospheric hanging gables. There is a shrine here to St Margaret, who lived in the street, and whose arm is now a reliquary kept at the Bar Convent, just outside Micklegate Bar, the medieval west entrance to the city. The walks are organised by the Association of Voluntary Guides of the City of York and take in the medieval city walls, the exterior of the Minster, Holy Trinity Church, the Treasurer's House and Monk Bar (the north-east gate of the medieval walls), and include some historical snippets such as this one: Did you know two Roman emperors, Septimius Severus (AD211) and Constantius Chlorus (AD306), the father of the great Emperor Constantine, both died in York?

OPEN   All year round.

AMENITIES   ¶¶ ⅄ ▪

⑱ MOUNTAIN BIKE THROUGH THE DALBY FOREST

Low Dalby, near Thornton-le-Dale, North Yorkshire YO18 7LT (✆ **01751 460295**, www.forestry.gov.uk).

There are more than 30 miles (50km) of scenic trails running through North Yorkshire's Dalby Forest, which are graded according to their level of difficulty. The toughest red-graded routes include hazards such as jumps, steps, steep inclines, and teenage boys who'll throw their back wheels through puddles in front of your face to splash you with mud. (Thanks for that, boys.) There are blue trails for intermediates, while the green one we chose was a gentle two-and-a-half-mile (4km) family meander that started and ended at the Dalby courtyard.

The highlights included: getting off the bike to sit in an animal hide and look for squirrels, voles (even though we don't know what one looks like) and badgers (none seen), having a woodland picnic (ham sandwiches), as well as releasing my daughter from the bike seat at the end so that she'd finally stop saying, 'Dad, it's *tooooo* bumpy'.

OPEN Daily 7am–dusk.

AMENITIES ☕ 🚲 🛍 £

⑱ VISIT OUR FAVOURITE BEACH IN ENGLAND: BAMBURGH

Bamburgh, Northumberland NE69 7DF (Alnwick Tourist Information Centre ℂ **01665 511333**, www.northumberland-coast.co.uk).

★ ♀ ◐

This is probably the loveliest and most deserted beach in Britain, with three golden miles (5km) of sand that are set off perfectly by the dramatic backdrop of Norman Bamburgh Castle, from where Henry VI ruled England in the 15th century. The bracing North Sea winds keep most tourists away but are ideal for kite flying, while the dunes support rare flora and fauna and have been designated an SSI. We found the beach by accident – lost on the way to Lindisfarne – like huge ignoramuses we had never heard of it and felt like we'd discovered it ourselves. We've felt a loyalty to the beach and to the whole of the little-known yet wonderful Northumberland coastline ever since and never tire of boring people about it. To get to this un-signposted Blue Flag beach, drive down The Wyndings (signposted to the golf course) and park in the bays behind the dunes. From here, you can walk down towards the castle.

OPEN All year round.

AMENITIES 🅿

⑲ SKY-GAZE IN KIELDER WATER & FOREST PARK

Kielder, Northumberland NE48 1ER (ℂ **01434 220616**, www.visitkielder.com).

☺

Kielder Forest has walks and cycle tracks and all sorts of water sports as well as a scattering of art installations among the trees. 'Skyspace' is a flashy title for a small, round stone chamber containing a couple of seats below a hole in the roof, which allows you to look up and see a framed view of the sky. This particular creation is by James Turrell and is located on a rocky outcrop overlooking Kielder Water. In daylight hours when illuminated by natural light through the roof aperture, the chamber could well focus your attention onto quiet contemplation of the sky, but is less enticing if you have two children under five round your knees demanding that you leave immediately because 'I've seen the sky, Dad. Please can we play mini-golf now?'. At dusk and dawn, the lighting system in the chamber sparks up and visitors prepared to sedate their children with chocolate will see an extraordinary light show reflecting on the night sky through the three-metre-wide hole. To get to Skyspace, follow the C200 road past Kielder Water towards Kielder village; it is a one-mile (1.6km) walk up the forest road from the car park. If you want to drive right up to the artwork, you need keys to get through a forestry gate. These are apparently available from the Kielder Visitor Centre, the Anglers Arms in Kielder village, and from somewhere called the Calvert Trust, although they might as well have been lodged with a munchkin living in a tree hollow, for all the success we had finding them.

OPEN All year round.

AMENITIES £

⑲ EXPERIENCE THE EGYPTIAN AFTERLIFE AT THE GREAT NORTH MUSEUM

Barras Bridge, Newcastle-upon-Tyne, Tyne and Wear NE2 4PT (℃ **0191 222 6765**, www.twmuseums.org.uk).

Under one roof at this newly opened museum, you'll come face to face with a 60-ft (18m) T-Rex skeleton, journey through a snake-filled tunnel to the Egyptian afterlife and check out a 76-ft (23m) scaled replica of the entire length of Hadrian's Wall. An amalgam of the Hancock, Antiquities and Shefton museums plus the Hatton Gallery, other highlights include live pythons, lizards and leaf-cutting ants as well as two Egyptian mummies. The £26-million museum is split between the Hadrian's Wall area, where touch-screen computers tell the story of the famous Roman fortification, and the Living Planet

The Best Light-bulb Jokes

Q: How many thought police does it take to screw in a light bulb?

A: None … There never 'was' any light bulb, don't you remember?

Q: How many psychologists does it take to change a light bulb?

A: One, but the light bulb has to really want to change.

Q. How many existentialists does it take to screw in a light bulb?

A: Two: one to screw it in and one to observe how the light bulb itself symbolises a single incandescent beacon of subjective reality in a netherworld of absurdity reaching out toward a cosmos of nothingness.

Q: How many Polish ballet dancers does it take to screw in a light bulb?

A: None, they like Danzig in the dark.

area, where the live lizards and insects mingle somewhat oddly with a stuffed elephant and other dead creatures. There's also a palaeontology gallery housing the T-Rex model and upstairs a mocked-up Afterlife Tunnel, through which ancient Egyptians believed they passed on their way to either a cosy eternity or one associated with a pit of fire. Expect to see projected images of snakes at your feet and for your young son to run out shouting 'snakes in there!'. The planetarium has a £2.50 charge.

OPEN Mon–Sat 10am–5pm; Sun 2pm–5pm.

AMENITIES

⑲ CRACK LIGHT-BULB JOKES AT THE DISCOVERY MUSEUM

Blandford Square, Newcastle-upon-Tyne, NE1 4JA (✆ **0191 232 6789**, www.tw museums.org.uk).

This award-winning hands-on family museum is based at a former Victorian Co-op HQ and is home to the 19th-century *Turbinia*, once the fastest ship in the world. It's themed around science and the history of the north-east and holds regular exhibitions about the region's music scene, its experiences during the world wars and Newcastle's shipbuilding past, as well as lots of interactive button-pressing for children. Look out for science shows conducted by Professor Brainstorm, and check out the Play Tyne water play area. Other highlights at the museum include early examples of light bulbs, invented by Joseph Swan and inspiration for thousands of jokes (see box, p. 157), plus the regimental museum of the 15th/19th The King's Royal Hussars and The Northumberland Hussars, which displayed enough weaponry for our son's favourite sentence to go from 'Thomas is blue', to 'I going to shoot you dead' in the space of an afternoon.

OPEN   Mon–Sat 10am–5pm; Sun 2pm–5pm.

AMENITIES   ☕ 🛍 £

⑲ GET THE CHILDREN INVOLVED AT THE BALTIC CENTRE FOR CONTEMPORARY ART

Gateshead Quays, South Shore Road, Gateshead, Tyne and Wear NE8 3BA (© **0191 478 1810**, www.balticmill.com).

👫 ⛱

A huge art space housed in a 1950s' grain warehouse, BALTIC enjoys superb views over the river Tyne and attracts temporary exhibitions by top names such as Antony Gormley, Damien Hirst, Anish Kapoor, the skittish Sam Taylor-Wood and even Yoko Ono, plus retrospectives of the CoBrA group of artists and Patti Smith's photography. Based over six floors and covering 3,000 square metres, there's a small cinema here showing short arty pieces, and a learning zone (Sat–Sun 2pm–4pm) aimed at encouraging children aged up to 13 to explore some of the themes of current exhibitions through their own work and the help of resident artists. There are Toddler Tuesday sessions (£3 per child) between 10:45am–11:45am, where under twos are encouraged by in-house artists to explore their own creativity through the mediums of shape, colour and shouting 'I want the blue pen, that's mine'. There's a library and archive here but no permanent collections; the temporary exhibitions change three to four times a year.

OPEN   Wed–Mon 10am–6pm; Tues 10:30am–6pm.

AMENITIES   ☕ 🍴 🛍 £

❿ SEE THE ARTS & CRAFTS AT THE SHIPLEY ART GALLERY

Prince Consort Road, Gateshead, Tyne and Wear, NE8 4JB (✆ **0191 477 1495**, www. twmuseums.co.uk).

Showcasing the greatest collection of contemporary craftwork, Oriental ceramics, furniture and glassware outside London, the highlights here include the collections of Newcastle silver, Tyneside pottery and William Irving's 1903 *The Blaydon Races*. Housed in a Grade II-listed Edwardian building, the majority of the collection was donated to the city in 1909 by wealthy patron of the arts Joseph Shipley, while many of the ceramics came from the collection of Henry Rothschild. The museum has lots of interactive exhibits on which you can design your own living room on a computer screen using a horrible hotchpotch of period and modern furniture to create in my wife's Sarah Beeny-like words 'a shabby chic look that would appeal to young professionals'. There are also regular visiting exhibitions on anything from the Story of The Supremes to making a ball gown for your teddy bear.

OPEN   Mon–Sat 10am–5pm; Sun 2pm–5pm.

AMENITIES

❿ SEE THE STUFFED LION AT THE SUNDERLAND MUSEUM AND WINTER GARDENS

Burdon Road, Sunderland, Tyne and Wear SR1 1PP (✆ **0191 553 2323**, www.tw museums.org.uk).

Modelled on Crystal Palace and extended with lottery cash in 2001, this eclectic museum includes the first Nissan car off the line at the local Washington factory in 1986, with its licence plate JOB 1, and an exhibition on my wife's favourite cookware, Pyrex, which was first produced in the region. There are also more Lowry paintings than anywhere outside of Salford (see p. 176), while the museum's fabulous glass-domed winter gardens are home to 1,500 varieties of plant you can inspect from a treetop-level walkway. Our favourite exhibit was undoubtedly Wallace the Lion, once part of a touring Victorian menagerie, who was stuffed in 1875 a few years after mauling his trainer Martini Maccomo. Wallace is found in the Time Gallery and had his finest hour some 40 years after his death, when he was ridden around the streets of Sunderland by a woman representing Boadicea in a victory parade at the end of World War I. Other exhibits at this, the first municipally-funded museum outside London, include Sunderland Heroes – campaign medals and a small memorial to the 197 men of the 125th Anti-Tank Regiment who were killed or imprisoned at the fall of Singapore; some 1920s' divers' suits; and a half-ton slab of coal mined for the 1929 North-East Coast Exhibition which towers above a scale model of a pithead. There are hands-on activities for children.

OPEN   Mon–Sat 10am–5pm; Sun 2pm–5pm.

AMENITIES   ☕ 🛍 £

⑲ RIDE A STEAM ENGINE AT THE STEPHENSON RAILWAY MUSEUM

Middle Engine Lane, North Shields, Tyne and Wear NE29 8DX (✆ **0191 200 7146**, www.twmuseums.org.uk).

👫 ☂

Dedicated to local father-and-son railway pioneers George and Robert Stephenson, here you get to see one of the world's oldest steam locomotives, ride on a steam train for just £1 and, on event days, hear themed storytelling sessions in a luggage carriage. The steam train *Billy* was made by the Stephensons in 1826 and predates the *Rocket* by three years. The steam train rides start at Middle Engine Lane by the museum, shunt for 30 minutes up to Percy Main and then return. They're available between Easter and October. There are also Heritage Open Days in September where you can explore behind the scenes and see volunteers restoring old engines in the workshops at the back of the museum. Other events in peak times include Victorian theme days and teddy-bear picnics and lots of children's arts-and-crafts activities.

OPEN   Daily 11am–4pm in school holidays; Easter–end Oct Sat–Sun; Nov–Easter closed.

AMENITIES   🛍 🅿

⑲⑥ WALK AROUND THE RECONSTRUCTED ARBEIA ROMAN FORT AND MUSEUM

Baring Street, South Shields, Tyne and Wear NE33 2BB (✆ **0191 4544093**, www.twmuseums.org.uk).

Every December (check for times) there are free candlelit tours of the best-reconstructed Roman fort in Britain. The tours are designed to coincide with the Roman festival of Saturnalia and must be booked in advance. They take place in the lavishly reworked commanding officer's quarters, kitted out in the style of the second century BC. The five-acre site of the fort was developed to guard the entrance to the river Tyne and was built in AD 120; the name 'Arbeia' translates as 'fort of Arab troops' in recognition of the fact it was garrisoned by a squadron of Syrian and Iraqi boatmen from the river Tigress, who would have been naturalised into the Roman army. In all 400 men were probably stationed here at the height of the Roman occupation of Britain, guarding against invasive assaults by the Picts along the north-east coast. A small museum is attached to Arbeia and the main draws here are two monuments. One commemorates Regina, a British woman of the Catuvellauni tribe (from what is now Kent), who was first the slave, then the freedwoman and subsequently the wife of Barates, a Palmyrene merchant, who erected the gravestone after her death aged 30. The second commemorates Victor, another former slave, freed by Numerianus of the First Asturian Cavalry, who arranged his funeral when Victor died at the age of 20.

OPEN   Apr–Oct Mon–Sat 10am–5:30pm, Sun 1pm–5pm; Nov–Mar Mon–Sat 10am–3:30pm.

AMENITIES   🛍 🅿

⑲⑦ LEARN ABOUT CATHERINE COOKSON AT THE SOUTH SHIELDS MUSEUM & ART GALLERY

South Shields, Tyne and Wear NE33 2JA (✆ **0191 456 8740**, www.twmuseums.org.uk/southshields).

This museum celebrates the life of the city's most famous local writer, Catherine Cookson, who sold more than 123 million books in her lifetime and was for years the most widely read author in Britain. The museum has recreated her writing room, including her desk and dict-aphone. There are also clothes, awards she received and, touchingly, the decorations that adorned her wedding cake on the day she married Tom Cookson, who died heartbroken 17 days after his wife's death in 1996. As Cookson, whose romantic-history novels about worn-down characters from the north-east, lived for most of the 20th century, her experiences are also used as a backdrop to the story of South Shields. There is an old kitchen here, designed to look like the one in her childhood home, with a Cookson-esque voiceover, plus two further galleries, one containing an exhibition of fine art and another, Changing Faces, telling the story of South Shields from the Bronze Age to the start of the 20th century. This includes a display on the world's first-ever lifeboat, designed in South Shields in 1789 by William Wouldhave, and another on William Jobling, one of the last men in England to be gibbeted (hung at the gallows and then left to rot in an iron cage after execution) for murder in the 1830s.

OPEN   1 Apr–31 Oct Mon–Sat 10am–5:30pm, Sun 1pm–5pm; 1 Nov–31 Mar Mon–Sat 10am–5pm.

AMENITIES

⑲ SWORD FIGHT AT THE ROYAL ARMOURIES MUSEUM

Armouries Drive, Leeds, West Yorkshire LS10 1LT (℃ **0113 220 1999**, www.royal armouries.org).

You can try on medieval chain-mail or handle antique weapons and children can have a go at sword fighting with wooden weapons at the country's national collection of guns and armour. Housing more than 8,500 exhibits, this vast museum's highlights are spread over four floors and include the world's largest elephant armour, dating back to 1600, armour worn by Henry VIII at the Field of Cloth of Gold in 1520, and an 1848 Colt Dragoon revolver. The museum has five themes – War, Tournament, Self-Defence, Hunting and the Arms and Armour of the Orient – and uses film and role-playing actors to tell its stories. The handling of weapons occurs during peak times in the school holidays, when there are also arts and crafts activities for children. Chargeable extras include the crossbow range, jousting and Tudor horsemanship demonstrations as well as falconry events in the Tiltyard.

OPEN Daily 10am–5pm.

AMENITIES ☕ 🎁 ♿

⑲ PAT A PIT PONY AT THE NATIONAL COAL-MINING MUSEUM FOR ENGLAND

Caphouse Colliery, New Road, Overton, Wakefield, West Yorkshire WF4 4RH (✆ **01924 848806**, www.ncm.org.uk).

A visit to the once-defunct pit complex encompasses the colliery buildings, now an interactive science display, exhibitions of machinery and a peek at the pithead baths. Kick off with a guided tour 140 feet (43m) below ground in Hope Pit, led by an ex-miner. Visitors carry safety lamps and hard hats and descend in a pit cage, with the tour lasting about an hour and 20 minutes. Back up top your children get to meet a retired drift-mine pony named Robbie ('Can I have a drift-mine pony, Dad?') and a Shire horse called Colonel, who in days gone by was used to pull coal tubs. There are displays on how the mining industry has changed from Victorian times to the present day and interactive exhibitions about the lives of miners, a gallery focusing on 1842, the year when women and children were banned from going down mines, and a nature trail around the 17-acre site.

OPEN Daily 10am–5pm.

AMENITIES ☕ 🎁 ♿

⑳ CYCLE THE MOORS MADE FAMOUS BY THE BRONTËS

Penistone Hill, West of Haworth, West Yorkshire BD22 9RH (behind the Bradford City Council car park) (✆ **01274 432666**, http://recreation.yorkshirewater.com/?OBH=3743).

Pretend to be that black-eyed 'imp of Satan' Heathcliff, chasing after his beloved Cathy on the desolate moors, on a circular 13-and-a-half mile (22km) cycle route. The Haworth & Denholme Cycling Route offers spectacular views over the valleys and hills of West Yorkshire, taking in Thornton Moor and the Stubden and Leeshaw reservoirs, and skirting Haworth, where the Brontë family lived. There's a good map showing the various staging points along the way available from the website above; the path is a mixture of moorland and tarmac and some areas are remote, so go in pairs rather than cycling alone.

OPEN   All year round.

AMENITIES

FOLLOW MR SPOON AT THE NATIONAL MEDIA MUSEUM

Pictureville, Bradford, West Yorkshire BD1 1NQ (✆ **0870 7010200**, www.national mediamuseum.org.uk).

★ ➤ ☺

The TV Heaven Archive has over 900 children's TV programmes, encompassing the last 60 years of television broadcasting history. It was in a private booth here (ring ahead to book one) that my wife and I solved a long-running dispute about the neighbours of the Meekers in *Rentaghost*, which ran between 1976–1984. They were the Perkins family of course. After this we watched *Chorlton and the Wheelies* (ho, ho, ho), *Fenella the Kettle Witch*, which upset our son, and then we gorged ourselves on an episode of *Button Moon*. As well as childhood favourites there are sit-coms, soaps and hard-hitting documentaries in the archive, plus three IMAX cinemas (with admission fees, unfortunately) and excellent free displays relating the story of TV and photography.

OPEN   Tues–Sun 10am–6pm.

AMENITIES

YORKSHIRE SCULPTURE PARK

West Bretton, Wakefield, West Yorkshire WF4 4LG (✆ **01924 832631**, www.ysp. co.uk).

◐

Set in 500 acres, this open-air art gallery includes 60 outdoor pieces by Henry Moore (the hole guy), Elizabeth Frink, Antony Gormley, Barbara Hepworth, and our *Skyspace* friend James Turrell (see p. 155). When you have tired of seeing art outside, go inside and see some more. There are four galleries here in all featuring, when we visited, some work about 'the expectation of the three-dimensional form' by

Peter Randall-Page that we enjoyed but did not understand a word of. More accessible was the exhibition in the Longside Gallery by Peter Randall-Page, who was catapulted into the public consciousness in 2003 when he won the Turner Prize and accepted his award dressed as his transvestite alter-ego, Claire. Back outside in the park, struggling to make sense of all this creativity, there are mammals (Highland cows), amphibians (frogs) and birds (black ones), all of them three-dimensional, for your children to appreciate, while you speculate on what your own transgender alter-ego might dress like to receive an art prize.

OPEN   Daily grounds 10am–5pm, galleries 10am–4pm.

AMENITIES   ¶¶ ▯ £

⓼ SEE THE DAVID HOCKNEYS AT THE 1853 GALLERY

Salts Mill, Victoria Road, Shipley, Saltaire, West Yorkshire (✆ **01274 531163**, www.saltsmill.org.uk).

Salts Mill, once the largest industrial edifice in the world, was built by Victorian philanthropist Titus Salt between 1851–1876 at the same time as he constructed Saltaire as a refuge for his workers from the 'satanic mills' of Victorian Bradford. Today the mill is a part of a UNESCO World Heritage Site and contains several art galleries, including the world's largest single collection of David Hockneys. Among the 300-plus works here by the artist, who was brought up locally before he headed for sunnier climes in California, there's everything from his early drawings right up to more recent watercolours. Elsewhere in the massive building there are opera sets on display and a wonderful bookshop above the galleries, where there are lots of tables for children to sit and read at. This has become something of a meeting point for local mums and toddlers because of the child-friendly café and the series of high-end boutiques selling everything from jewellery to Hockney prints.

OPEN   Mon–Fri 10am–5.30pm; Sat–Sun 10am–6pm.

The Lowry Centre, Salford.

NORTH-WEST

For free in this region you can do anything from entering the World Gurning Championships in Egremont, Cumbria to visiting the classic railway station at Carnforth where the black and white weepy *Brief Encounter* was set. Other highlights include lifting a mini at the MOSI in Manchester, witnessing the Blackpool illuminations and popping into an ancient temperance bar. There are bike trails in the Grizedale Forest, Lowry paintings to see in Salford, the Roman walls of Chester to walk around, as well as Anthony Gormley's *Another Place* art installation on Sefton beach, a perfect spot to eat a picnic.

⁂ WALK AROUND CHESTER CITY WALLS

Chester Tourist Information, Northgate Street, Chester CH1 2H5 (✆ **01244 351609**, www.chestertourist.com).

Walk round the most complete city walls in Britain, and if you're in a bad mood, murder a Welshman with a bow and arrow while you're at it (see box below). The best way to approach the one-hour, two-mile (3.2km) walk is from the famous Eastgate Clock on Eastgate Street. Head north towards King Charles Tower and the Shropshire Grand Union Canal. The walk is mostly flat and the wall, part Roman, part Saxon and part Victorian, ranges from a few feet high up to 15 feet (4.5m) in places. Highlights on the hike include the ruins of the old Norman castle, the Roman amphitheatre (leave the walls at Newgate Arch for a better look) and the steps in front of the watchtower by the river Dee; according to legend if you can ascend these steps in one go without drawing breath, you can make a wish that will come true. There are information boards along the route or splash out 99p on *Walkabout*, a book highlighting points of interest along the way and available from the tourist office. There are ramped sections for buggies and wheelchairs but not all the wall can be walked. If you're really keen, and we mean really keen, there are free Blue Badge walks of the walls on Christmas Day. They leave at 10:30am from the tourist information centre above.

OPEN   All year round.

AMENITIES

Killer Wales

An archaic bylaw of Chester states that any Welshman loitering within the city walls after sunset may be killed by decapitation or shot with a longbow. The law was originally imposed by King Henry V following the Welsh Revolt from 1400–1415. This order was never repealed and still officially stands on the statute to this day, although it probably no longer provides much protection against prosecution for murder, so best not to be too blatant about it.

⁂ CONTORT YOUR FACE IN THE WORLD GURNING CHAMPIONSHIPS

Egremont Crab Fair and Sports, Market Hall, Egremont, Cumbria CA22 2DF (✆ **01946 821220** (after 6pm), www.egremontcrabfair.org.uk).

The antithesis of Miss World, the aim here is to contort your face inside a horse collar into something so grotesque you draw groans of disgust from the 1,200-strong crowd that gathers to watch this event. This is a fun event, usually won by the rubber-faced Tommy Mallinson – nine times so far – and it's entertaining to turn up and say to everyone you meet, 'Wow, you should enter. Oh sorry – that's your normal face, isn't it?'. The panel of judges awards points for the *transformation* of the face rather than its resting repulsiveness, so anyone has a chance of winning. The gurning draws competitors from all over the world and is the culmination of an ancient three-day fair first held in 1267, which also features horse and pony leaping, ferret

Gurning

To 'gurn' means to 'snarl like a dog, look savage, or distort the countenance'. Down through the centuries the Cumbria gurning competition has had various titles. In 1852 it was the '**Grin for Tobacco**', while by 1884 it had become '**Grinning for 'bacca**'. In the 20th century it morphed into '**Gurning Through a Braffin**' (horse collar) and is now known simply as the **World Gurning Competition**. Gurning may have originated from the mockery of the village idiot – the townsfolk would throw a horse's collar over him and make him pull funny faces in exchange for ale.

shows, horn blowing contests, dog classes and music in the streets. All this festivity takes place in September around Harvest Festival.

OPEN   Check dates on website.

ⓩ WITNESS THE WORLD WORMING CHAMPIONSHIPS

Willaston Primary School, Willaston, near Crewe, Cheshire (ℂ **01270 663 957**, www.wormcharming.com).

☻

This is one of those events that can only happen in Britain, and must be seen to be believed. On the last Saturday in June, around 300 likeminded people gather in a field and use an assortment of techniques (trumpets, tuning forks and bouncing space hoppers are just a few) to try and charm as many worms as possible from the earth within half an hour. The record was set in 2009 when 567 wrigglers were lured

The Worm Turns

In recent breakthrough research, an American neuroscientist called Professor Kenneth Catania, who specialises in sonic phenomena, discovered that the vibrations created by the most successful worm-charmers replicated those produced naturally by moles. Moles are every worm's nemesis, with the shovel-footed creatures able to eat their weight in worms every day. As worms are afraid of moles, the theory goes, they spring to the top of the soil to escape whenever they feel a mole's vibrations.

to the surface of a three-metre-square area by a garden fork repeatedly inserted 15cm into the turf and 'twanged'. This smashed the long-standing record of 511 worms set in the inaugural championship in 1980 by one Mr Shufflebottom. The rules of the competition are administered by (this is true) the International Federation for Charming Worms and Allied Pastimes, and forbid any digging or the use of water, although music is permitted and the squeamish can nominate a second to handle the worms. Charmed worms are humanely released after the birds have gone to roost in the evening, and the winner is presented with a coveted trophy in the shape of a 'golden rampant worm'. There is also a trophy awarded to whoever catches the heaviest worm, the record standing at 6.6g since 1987. The event was originally designed as a fundraiser for the local primary school and now attracts large crowds of worm-fanciers. It costs £1 to see the spectacle and £3 to enter.

OPEN   Check dates on website.

AMENITIES

⑳ LEARN ABOUT SHIPBUILDING IN THE NORTH-WEST AT THE DOCK MUSEUM

North Road, Barrow-in-Furness, Cumbria LA14 2PW (☎ **01229 876400**, www.dockmuseum.org.uk).

Based over a graving dock (where barnacles are traditionally burned off ships' hulls), the Dock Museum charts the history of shipbuilding and iron- and steel-working in Barrow. You'll find out about some of the famous ships that set sail from here, including the world's first pre-dreadnought battleship, the *HMS Mikasa*, the *HMS Invincible* and also the *SS Oriana*, launched in 1957 and at that time the largest cruise ship built in England. There are photos, films and boards out-lining the history of Barrow's spectacular growth from a small fishing village before the Industrial Revolution into the base of the country's largest steelworks and in the 1960s, the country's nuclear-powered submarine production as well. There are also interactive family-friendly displays and temporary exhibitions.

OPEN   Nov–Easter Wed–Fri 10:30am–4pm; Sat–Sun 11am–4:30pm.

AMENITIES   ☕ 🎒 🅿

⑳⑧ BIKE AROUND GRIZEDALE FOREST PARK & VISITOR CENTRE

Grizedale, Hawkshead, Cumbria LA22 0QJ (✆ **01229 860010**, www.forestry.gov/grizedaleforestpark).

On a nine-and-a-half mile (15km) ramble through this oak and coni-fer woodland you'll see dozens of outdoor sculptures of snails, sheep, foxes and owls, plus a giant woodsman with an axe, witness views on a clear day to Morecambe Bay and Coniston Fells, and if you're lucky you might see red and roe deer, buzzards and maybe even an elusive red squirrel. Covering 12,000 acres, the forest has a host of cycle routes and walks ranging from the red-graded nine-mile (15km) North Face mountain-bike course, right down to the untaxing buggy-friendly one-mile (1.6km) long trail we chose that saw us take in around 15 art works. If you want to see more art, including Andy Goldsworthy's famous wriggling *Stone Wall* weaving between the trees, try the *Star Trek*-sounding Silurian Way.

OPEN   Visitor Centre daily summer 10am–5pm; winter 10am–4pm. Forest daily dawn to dusk.

AMENITIES   ☕ 🚲 🎒 £

HAVE A BRIEF ENCOUNTER AT CARNFORTH STATION

Warton Road, Carnforth, Lancashire LA5 9TR (📞 **01524 735165**, www.carnforth station.co.uk).

★ 😃

Me (being Trevor Howard playing decent family man, Dr Alec Harvey): 'I love you. I love your wide eyes, the way you smile, your shyness, and the way you laugh at my jokes.'

My wife (being Celia Johnson playing awfully nice housewife Laura Jesson): 'Please don't.'

Me: 'I love you. I love you. You love me too. It's no use pretending it hasn't happened because it has.'

My wife: (checks her mobile after a text bleeps through) 'Sorry, that was Bev about the babysitting.'

Me: 'We've been here an hour drinking a cup of tea talking rubbish and the woman behind the counter is staring at us.'

My wife: 'Ok, let's go.'

Act out the famous scene from *Brief Encounter* for yourselves at the very Victorian Refreshment Room where Laura and Alec first meet in the 1945 classic. The clock on the station platform where Alex removes the dust from Laura's eye is also still there, while a free Visitor Centre (open Tues–Sun 10am–4pm) retells the movie's story.

OPEN   Visitor Centre daily 10am–4pm (not Mondays Oct–Easter). Refreshment Room daily 9am–4pm (but not Mondays Easter-Sept).

AMENITIES

⑳ ATTEND THE WORLD BLACK PUDDING THROWING CHAMPIONSHIPS

Royal Oak, Bridge Street, Ramsbottom, Lancashire BL0 9AD (📞 **01706 822786**, www. worldblackpuddingthrowing.googlepages.com/).

This bizarre culinary take on the 15th-century War of the Roses involves hurling Lancashire black puddings at stacks of Yorkshire puddings piled up on a 20-ft (6m) podium. It is enacted annually at the Royal Oak pub, with competitors coming from as far afield as Hong Kong, Africa and Sweden to take part. Entrants with names like Rollercoaster Rudge are required to lob (under arm) three 6-oz puddings swaddled in lady's tights (what else?) at their targets, each throw accompanied by loud cheers and whoops. The winner (last year five Yorkshire puddings were dislodged) receives a medal and trophy that is kept at the pub. The contest, nicknamed 'Pudstock' as it also features local bands in the evening, takes place in September and dates back to the 1850s and the revival of that old Lancashire–Yorkshire rivalry.

OPEN   Sun–Thurs midday–midnight; Fri–Sat midday–1am. (No date yet for this year's chuck.)

㉑ ENJOY A CORDIAL AT FITZPATRICK'S TEMPERANCE BAR

Bank Street, Rawtenstall, Rossendale, Lancashire BB4 6QS (✆ **01706 231836**, www. mrfitzpatricks.com).

It looks like a pub and it sounds like a pub, but is in fact the oldest original temperance bar in Britain. When Fitzpatrick's opened in 1890, temperance bars were ten a penny. There was no alcohol tax – every hour was happy hour. Alcoholism was rife and so in 1832 Preston cheese-maker Joseph Livesey took matters into his own hands and the Temperance Movement was born. Initially avoiding spirits was enough for membership, but after a while 'taking the pledge' broadened to mean no alcohol whatsoever. In fact, the word 'teetotal' is said to come from these times, when one member with a stammer said that nothing was acceptable except 'tee-tee-total abstinence'. Temperance bars grew to become the focal point of many communities, locals gathering for a quick cordial as Band of Hope children sang uplifting songs. At this time the Fitzpatrick family, renowned herbalists, ran a chain of temperance bars throughout Lancashire. Now under new ownership, visitors to the old-fashioned wooden temperance bar can enjoy award-winning homemade cordials like sarsaparilla (an age-old cure for syphilis that apparently tastes a bit like root beer), blood tonic and dandelion and burdock. The shelves in the bar are full of jars bearing strange-sounding ingredients like comfrey and borage, and for the less adventurous there are traditional sweets such as Uncle Joe's Mint Balls.

OPEN   Mon–Wed 9:30am–4:30pm; Thurs–Sat 9am–5pm.

AMENITIES   🄿

⓬ SEE MARADONA'S SHIRT AT THE NATIONAL FOOTBALL MUSEUM

Sir Tom Finney Way, Preston, Lancashire PR1 6PA (✆ **01772 908 442**, www.national footballmuseum.com).

Based at Preston North End's ground (the oldest surviving football league ground in the world), in this museum of two halves you get to see the ball from the first World Cup Final in 1930, the shirt Maradona wore when he scored his infamous 'hand of God' goal against England and Bobby Moore's shirt from his legendary game against Pele's Brazil in the 1970 World Cup finals, all on the ground floor. On the hands-on first floor Gary Lineker invites visitors to become panellists on a special edition of Match of the Day, which gets played back on screen, you can see the oldest FA Cup trophy and explore the Hall of Fame, where greats from the game are honoured, with new players inducted each year. Other highlights at the museum include the Shrewsbury Coracle, a tiny boat used by Shrewsbury Town football club during home games, to retrieve the ball when it went over the stand and into a local river, and the neck-brace Bert Trautman (see box, p. 175) wore in the 1956 Cup Final.

OPEN   Tues–Sat 10am–5pm; Sun 11am–5pm.

AMENITIES   ☕ 🔒 👟 🅿

⓭ BE ELECTRIFIED BY THE BLACKPOOL ILLUMINATIONS

Promenade, Blackpool, Lancashire FY1 (✆ **01253 478222**, www.visitblackpool.com).

Dubbed the greatest free show on earth, the Blackpool Illuminations see six miles (10 km) of the town's seafront lit up with more than one million bulbs. Staged every year since 1879 – when the lights were known as 'artificial sunshine' – the Big Switch-On ceremony attracts tens of thousands of visitors, including my wife when she lived in nearby Widnes as a child. The spectacle runs for 66 nights from 3 September to 7 November from Starr Gate at the South Promenade to Bispham to the north and is probably best seen close to the Blackpool Tower. Recent celebs switching on the lights have included Alan Carr and Kate Thornton, followed by a concert featuring Madness, Tony

Christie and *The X Factor* creation JLS as well as Paloma Faith, who sang her single, *Stone Cold Sober,* somewhat ironically in the binge-drinking capital of Britain. Concerts are staged each year in a make-shift arena in the car park behind Bonney Street Market and attract around 20,000 music fans on a first-come, first-served basis.

OPEN Winter nights.

AMENITIES

❹ CHECK OUT THE URBIS MUSEUM

Cathedral Gardens, Manchester M4 3BG
(✆ **0161 605 8200**, www.urbis.org.uk).

This bright chunk of sleek glass in Manchester city centre is given over to the concept of modern city living, and exhibitions in the past have included those on Manchester's Hacienda (at the height of the rave scene, the most famous nightclub in the world), city ghosts, hip-hop and, when we visited, one on guerrilla gardening (see box, p. 176) that included a *Gardeners' Question Time* shed where my wife asked for advice on 'when to plant my lupins'. Opened in 2002 and designed by Ian Simpson to resemble New York's Flatiron Building, the Urbis runs a variety

A German Pain in the Neck

Bernhard Carl 'Bert' Trautmann OBE (born 22 October 1923) is the only former Luftwaffe paratrooper to have played in topflight English football. After three years fighting the Eastern Front, and with an Iron Cross to his name, he was one of only 90 men in his 1,000-strong regiment to survive World War II. He settled in Lancashire following his release from a prisoner-of-war camp and his signing as a goalkeeper for Manchester City in 1949 sparked a 20,000-strong demonstration, although by the end of the season and after a string of fine performances Trautmann had been well and truly accepted. Named Footballer of the Year in 1956, Trautmann entered folklore with his display in that year's FA Cup Final. With 17 minutes remaining Trautmann suffered a serious injury after diving at the feet of Birmingham City's Peter Murphy. Despite this he continued playing, making crucial saves to preserve his team's three–one lead. His neck was noticeably crooked as he collected his winner's medal; three days later an X-ray revealed it to be broken. How did the Germans lose the war?

Flower Power

Guerrilla gardening is a political form of direct action practised by environmentalists that had its origins in New York in the 1970s. The concept relates to land rights. Activists take over ('squat') an abandoned piece of land, usually at night, to grow crops or flowers on it. Guerrilla gardeners believe in redefining ownership to reclaim land from perceived neglect or misuse. A famous example of guerrilla gardening took place in May 1996 when 500 activists occupied 13 acres of derelict land belonging to Guinness & Co on the banks of the river Thames in Wandsworth, South London. A community grew up on the site called 'Pure Genius' (named after the Guinness advertising slogan) and survived there for five and a half months before they were pushed out overnight by the police.

of guided walking city tours costing £3 on subjects ranging from musical Manchester to the city's medieval past.

OPEN   Daily 10am–6pm.

AMENITIES   ☕ 🍴 🛍 🅿

⑮ SEE STICK FIGURES AT THE LOWRY

The Lowry, Pier 8, Salford Quays, Manchester M50 3AZ (✆ **0870 787 5780**, www.thelowry.com).

Set in a magnificent waterside location at the heart of redeveloped Salford Quays, this award-winning stainless-steel blue, purple and orange building opened in 2000 and was designed by Michael Wilford. It holds the largest public collection of LS Lowry's work in the world. The 350 pictures and drawings of smoking factory stacks, portraits and less well-known seascapes are sampled in changing exhibitions, often in tandem with the work of visiting artists. There's a film about Lowry, a family corner with drawing materials and children's books as well as a hide-and-seek trail available from the information desk. Three theatres stage anything from dance and drama through to comedy with ticket prices starting at around £5 a head, while the wonderful café is the place for some quiet reflection on Lowry's work.

OPEN   Sun–Fri 11am–5pm; Sat 10am–5pm.

AMENITIES   ☕ 🍴 £

㉖ LEARN ABOUT ANIMALS IN WAR-TIME AT THE IMPERIAL WAR MUSEUM NORTH

Salford Quays, Trafford Wharf Road, Trafford Park, Manchester M17 1TZ (℃ **0161 836 4000**, www.north.iwm.org.uk).

👫 🏖

In an award-winning building designed by Daniel Libeskind to represent a globe shattered by conflict, you can see the field gun that fired the first British shells in World War I, the compass that helped Oliver Philpot to escape from the infamous Stalag Luft III (see box, p. 178) during World War II and a searchlight that once sat on a watchtower guarding the Berlin Wall. The museum's highlight, however, is its 'total immersion theatre' in the main gallery, where the lights are dimmed every hour for 20 minutes and film and sound are projected into the museum around three themes: Children at War, Weapons of War and War at Home, each outlining the human cost of conflict in various ways. The museum charts these themes from 1914 to the present and there are handling sessions twice a day (12:30pm and 3:30pm) when museum guides open display cabinets and explain selected exhibits such as gas masks to children at Time Stack stations. Family sessions on Sundays feature regular talks on war themes that children can relate to, including Animals at War focusing on the Dickin Medal, the George Cross equivalent issued to brave animals in war-time. For 95p scale the air shard, a 180-ft (55m) high funnel open to the elements at the top, with a viewing platform 95 feet (29m) up that gives great views over Salford Quays and the Manchester Ship Canal.

OPEN   Daily Mar–Oct 10am–6pm; Nov–Feb 10am–5pm.

AMENITIES   ☕ 🛍 ♿

㉗ SEE OLD-FASHIONED UNDIES AT MANCHESTER ART GALLERY

Mosley Street, Manchester M2 3JL (℃ **0161 235 8888**, www.manchestergalleries.org).

👫 🏖

Home to a well-regarded collection of Pre-Raphaelite paintings and more contemporary works by Lucien Freud and David Hockney, it was at the costume gallery we saw our favourite exhibit – a pair of close-fitting M&S purple-patterned underpants from the 1970s. Yes, Dante Gabriel Rossetti's *The Bower Meadow* (1850) is full of poetic melancholy and, of course, we admired Ford Maddox Brown's work inspired by the writings of Thomas Carlyle, but they stood no chance against a pair of psychedelic knickers. There is also a decorative-arts gallery here featuring textiles, dolls' houses and glass. Temporary exhibitions are regularly staged and have included works by Da Vinci and Holman Hunt. Free activity backpacks are available for family groups with children aged between seven and 12, and there is an interactive gallery with dressing up and dancing. For younger children there are special bags available, containing a story to read, a blanket to sit on and games to play.

OPEN   Tues–Sun 10am–5pm.

AMENITIES

⑳ LIFT A MINI AT THE MUSEUM OF SCIENCE & INDUSTRY

Liverpool Road, Castlefield, Manchester M3 4FP (✆ **0161 8322244**, www.mosi. org.uk).

Here you get the chance to lift a Mini with your little finger, walk through a Victorian sewer and compare your Palm Pilot to the world's first enormous computer, nicknamed 'The Baby'. Other high spots include listening to a talk by Manchester scientist John

---

The Great Escape

Of the 70 people who escaped during World War II from Stalag Luft III in East Germany, only three made it to safety. Oliver Philpot was a World War II Beaufort RAF pilot shot down over the North Sea and was one of the three who managed to escape. In scenes used for the movie *The Great Escape*, this is how it happened: a hollow vaulting horse was used as a cover to dig a tunnel. The tunnel (starting about 90 feet (27m) from the wire) was excavated with bowls and, apart from the first few yards, had no shoring. Philpot and two others dug for 114 days while the other officers vaulted the horse, until the finished tunnel stretched for about 100 yards (90m) beyond the boundary. The breakout was on 29 October 1943. A week later, disguised as a Norwegian margarine salesman, Philpot and his trusty compass (on display at Manchester's Imperial War Museum) reached a ship to neutral Sweden via the Danzig train. All three men then made home runs from Sweden.

Dalton, who discovered atomic theory, and trying on goggles in the child-centric Experiment Gallery that fool your eyes into seeing everything back to front. Based at the old Liverpool Road Station, the museum tells the story of the area's contribution to science and industry and houses full-size locomotives and replica tri-planes. There's also a good café with a menu serving children's portions.

OPEN   Daily 10am–5pm.

AMENITIES   ☕ 🛍 ♿

㉑⑨ LEARN ABOUT THE WOMEN'S MOVEMENT AT THE PANKHURST CENTRE

60–62 Nelson Street, Chorlton on Medlock, Manchester M13 9WP (📞 **0161 274 4979**).

At the Georgian home of former suffragette Emmeline Pankhurst (1858–1928), you can see her piano, some gender-stereotypical embroidery I got in trouble with my wife for scoffing at, and the typewriter she wrote her autobiography on. There's also a film about the Women's Movement that my wife watched with clenched fists (she was feminist of the year in her halls of residence at Leicester University), and the recreated parlour where the campaign for women's suffrage was orchestrated. There's a library for research into feminism as well as a drop-in facility every Thursday between 11am–2pm for any woman (no transgenders allowed), with a home-cooked lunch (£2 suggested donation).

OPEN   Mon–Thurs 10am–4pm.

AMENITIES   ♿

㉒⓪ SEE TITANIC MEMORABILIA AT THE MERSEYSIDE MARITIME MUSEUM

Albert Dock, Liverpool, Merseyside L3 4AQ (📞 **0151 478 4499**, www.liverpool museums.org.uk).

👫 ☂

We could easily have spent a whole week at this museum, which charts the many ways the port of Liverpool has influenced both the city and the wider world. The basement Seized Gallery focuses on the role of the city's revenue and customs officers by displaying some of their stranger discoveries, while the Emigration Gallery tells the story of the nine million people who left Liverpool between 1830 and 1930 for a better life in the 'new worlds' of Australia and America. The Liverpool World Gateway Gallery focuses on the ships and companies that used the port over the last 200 years, highlighting the tragic tales of the *Titanic*, the *Express of Ireland* and the *Lusitania*; all three ships sank between 1912 and 1915, marking the end of Liverpool's Edwardian heyday. On show is a life jacket worn by a survivor of the *Titanic* as well as the builder's 20-ft (6m) model of the ship. My favourite section was the Battle of the Atlantic Gallery, telling the story of Liverpool's role in World War II. The city provided the entry point for 4.7 million troops and saw the construction of over 100 warships, including HMS *Ark Royal*. The 68 bombing raids over Liverpool killed 4,000 people, bearing testament to her importance as the UK's main war-time port.

OPEN   Daily 10am–5pm.

AMENITIES   ☕ 🍴 🛍 ⋀ £

㉑ SEE TRIBAL MASKS IN THE INTERNATIONAL SLAVERY MUSEUM

Albert Dock, Liverpool, Merseyside L3 4AQ (© **0151 478 4499**, www.liverpool museums.org.uk).

👫 🏖

Based on the third floor of the Maritime Museum, this fab little exhibition charts the story of Liverpool's role in the slave trade, which saw Africans shipped via Liverpool to America to work on the plantations. The first gallery concentrates on life in West Africa before the arrival of the slave traders, with examples of art and tribal masks on display, and the second gallery is on the enslavement itself – the dangerous voyages that saw many slaves dead on arrival – although more interesting is the Legends of Slavery section, discussing the black civil rights movement in America, the progress towards equality and racial stereotyping. You can see a Ku Klux Klan robe from Orange County, New York, a tube of 'Darkie' toothpaste and postcards depicting the piccaninny stereotype of the little black child. The museum culminates with the Achievers' Gallery, featuring successful people of African descent like Kelly Holmes and Muhammad Ali.

OPEN   Daily 10am–5pm.

AMENITIES

㉒ DISCOVER THE AVERAGE WEIGHT OF FLIES YOU'LL SWALLOW IN A LIFETIME AT THE WORLD MUSEUM

William Brown Street, Liverpool, Merseyside L3 8EN ((℃) **0151 478 4393**, www.liverpool museums.org.uk).

Here you get to watch leaf-cutter ants in action, visit a 62-seat planetarium, dress up like an Eskimo and handle 5,000-year-old fossils. Vague but grandiose, the museum's title put us off initially (how can you have a museum about the entire world?), but after a day here we realised there is no other way to describe such a vast museum; there are over 1.2 million zoological specimens alone, ranging over such diverse subjects as natural history, space and how the average human accidentally swallows half a kilo of insects in their lifetime. The museum is a fantastic place to take children, with hands-on activities everywhere, including a six-and-a-half feet (2m) long animatronics fly as well as Molly the Friendly Blue Whale story-telling sessions in the Treasure House Theatre. Arrive early to get a seat in the planetarium, showing films on the solar system, the infinity of space and children's shows.

OPEN   Daily 10am–5pm.

AMENITIES

㉓ CHECK OUT HOCKNEY'S 'BOTTOM' PICTURE AT THE WALKER GALLERY

William Brown Street, Liverpool, Merseyside L3 8EL ((℃) **0151 478 4199**, www.liverpool museums.org.uk).

Notable pieces at this gallery encompass works from the 13th century to the present day and include masterpieces by Rubens, Rembrandt and Turner. There is also sculpture and a craft-and-design gallery featuring everything from glassware to enamel trinkets, while in the Big Art for Little Artists area on the ground floor of this beautiful Neo-Classical building there's dressing up and games for children. However, our favourite moment was our daughter's biting analysis of David Hockney's cheeky naked portrait *Peter Getting Out of Nick's Pool*; 'Dad, I can see his bum'.

OPEN Daily 10am–5pm.

AMENITIES ☕ 🛍 £

❷❷❹ TAKE SOME TIME OUT AT SUDLEY HOUSE

Mossley Hill Road, Liverpool, Merseyside L18 8BX (**℃ 0151 7243245**, www.liverpool
museums.org.uk).

Sudley House offers the only art collection of a Victorian merchant (in this case sugar merchant George Holt) still in its original setting and features two childhood rooms – including a huge dolls' house our daughter asked to 'borrow for a while'. There are Pre-Raphaelite pictures including work by Edward Burne-Jones on the walls, plus several Turners, a Gainsborough and a Reynolds, as well as videos to watch about various Holt family members, while the Costume Room displays a selection of over 700 outfits dating from the 1880s to the 1920s. The house – a quiet place to take time out – was donated to the city of Liverpool in 1883. There are some relaxing grounds to flop down upon outside.

OPEN Daily 10am–5pm.

AMENITIES ☕ ✿ 🅿

❷❷❺ SEE THE DROWNING STATUES AT ANTONY GORMLEY'S ANOTHER PLACE

Crosby Beach, Sefton, Liverpool, Merseyside L23 6SX (**℃ 0845 1400845**, www.
sefton.gov.uk).

Antony 'Angel of the North' Gormley's 100 cast-iron art figures stretch over half a mile (1km) out to sea at Crosby Beach in Sefton, making an arresting spectacle that we would have picnicked in front of if it hadn't been so freezing when we visited. Made from casts of the artist's own body, the figures are either slowly revealed or gradually submerged by the sea as the tide ebbs and flows. Stretching along almost two miles (3km) of beach, the installations were due to be removed in 2006 but won planning permission to stay and are now a permanent fixture, much to the annoyance of local water-sports enthusiasts (sinking hazard) and prudes (they have small simplified penises). The figures stare out at the horizon and are apparently a 'poetic response to the individual and universal sentiments associated with emigration – sadness at leaving, but the hope of a new future in another place'.

OPEN   All year round (but don't come at high tide).

AMENITIES   **P**

⓰ FEED NUTS TO DISCERNING MAMMALS AT FORMBY POINT RED SQUIRREL RESERVE

Victoria Road, Freshfields, Formby, Liverpool, Merseyside L37 1LJ (© **01704 878591**, www.nationaltrust.org.uk).

◔

Along a peaceful stretch of sandy coast, you have the outside chance of spotting an endangered red squirrel in one of only three refuge sites for the creature in the country. This National Trust area, perfect for a picnic or a wander through the pinewoods, is home to around (at last count) 1,000 of the remaining 160,000 red squirrels left in the country. Needless to say when we visited we didn't spot a single one. Told they were so tame they'd take peanuts from our hands, we came equipped with a family bag of nuts and didn't get so much as a nibble. We were led to believe this was because of a devastating recent pox outbreak that had reduced their numbers, although we met a

Telltale Squirrel Signs

❶ Chewed pine cones.

❷ Scratches on tree bark.

❸ A strange 'chuk-chuk' noise.

The Soap Star

1 William Hesketh Lever is credited in marketing circles for the famous quotation: 'Half my advertising money is wasted. The problem is that I don't know which half!'

2 He got up at 5am to exercise and take a cold shower then worked every day until 5:30pm, resting for a 15-minute lunch-break. He built a glass canopy supported by stilts on the roof of his house, with only minimal protection from the weather, and slept there every night.

3 In 1930 Unilever was created by the merger of Dutch margarine company Margarine Unie with Lever Brothers. Nowadays, the Anglo-Dutch giant is one of the world's biggest manufacturers of household goods, including ice-cream, spreads, frozen foods, tea, mayonnaise, soap, soap powder and detergents.

4 The inhabitants of Lever's hometown Bolton were not forgotten – the town was provided with its own country park, which Lever stocked with zebras, flamingoes and even a lion, so that its citizens might have 'free and uninterrupted enjoyment'.

couple from Oldham in the car park who bragged about the success they'd had with a different variety of nuts. Red squirrels evidently know their nuts. Audio guides are available from the entrance kiosk (£2).

OPEN   Daily dusk–dawn.

AMENITIES

227 WALK AROUND THE LADY LEVER ART GALLERY

Port Sunlight Village, Wirral, Merseyside CH62 5EQ (© **0151 478 4136**, www.liverpool museums.org.uk).

Named after his wife, this museum houses the private collection of the former 1st Lord Leverhulme, William Hesketh Lever, who started collecting art in the 19th century, which he used to brand and advertise his Port Sunlight soap. Soap had been traditionally cut from large blocks and sold, so Lever was the first industrialist to have the idea of packaging it. He then decided to choose artwork to help sell his soap, so he bought paintings featuring pretty women and used them to adorn the packaging and added advertising slogans such as 'As good as new', or 'Whiter than white'. Sometimes he'd blot out objects in paintings and replace them with pictures of soap bars. Lever came accidentally to love art and by the end of his life he was a discerning collector. His company went from strength to strength, employing 85,000 people worldwide at one time, but he never forgot his roots. He was a grocer's son and ex-Liberal MP for the Wirral when he decided to build a village for his employees at Port Sunlight. The Lady Lever Gallery houses some 20,000 works by, among others, Waterhouse, Stubbs, Turner and Reynolds, lots of Chinese decorative arts and porcelain by Wedgwood. Lectures are based around the featured painting of the month and there are children's quizzes, but there are also almost too many tapestries, items of furniture and ceramics here that it took a while to unglaze our vapid eyes.

OPEN   Mon–Sat 10am–5pm; Sun midday–5pm.

AMENITIES

Wales Millenium Centre and Pierhead Building, Cardiff Bay.

WALES

Some of the great free highlights in Wales include descending 300 feet into a former coal mine in Torfaen, visiting the famous Merthyr Mawr sand dunes where *Lawrence of Arabia* was filmed, and a Dr Who tour of Cardiff. Elsewhere you can see a lock of Nelson's hair in the Nelson Museum and Local History Centre in Monmouth, hear a choir service at St David's Cathedral and shout "behind you" at the Llandudno Punch and Judy show. The town with the longest name in the world – Llanfairpwllgwyngyllgogerychwyrndrobwllllantysiliogogogoch – is here as is the Baked Bean Museum of Excellence in Port Talbot. If that doesn't hit the right note you can climb Mount Snowdon, see paintings by Rolf Harris's grandfather in Merthyr Tydfil, or visit Britain's most complete Roman amphitheatre in Newport. Other activities to enjoy include learning circus tricks at Cardiff's Millennium Centre, and if you don't mind getting your hands, and the rest of your body, dirty there's the World Bog-Snorkelling Championships in Powys to enter. For the really hardy the Boxing Day Swim in Tenby is worth a day out and for wildlife enthusiasts there are the rare butterflies and cashmere goats of The Great Orme Country Park. And that's not to mention the magnificent beaches including the fabulous Rhossili Bay in the Gower peninsula.

㉘ VISIT THE TOWN WITH THE LONGEST NAME IN THE WORLD

Station Site, Holyhead Road, Llanfairpwllgwyngyllgogerychwyrndrobwllllantysiliogogogoch, Anglesey LL61 5UJ (☏ **01248 713177**).

You cannot come to the north-west of Wales and miss the opportunity of queuing behind a coach party of pensioners from Bolton to have your picture taken in front of the longest place name in the world – Llanfairpwllgwyngyllgogerychwyrndrobwllllantysiliogogogoch. The 51-letter place name, best snapped on the Holyhead-bound platform of the station or above the doors of the nearby Edinburgh Woollen Mill,

> **Pronunciation Tip**
>
> The 'll' in Welsh is a voiceless lateral fricative, or to you and me a sound that does not occur in English and is sometimes approximated as 'thl' as in 'athlete'.

was contrived by a local tailor in the 1860s as a publicity stunt to give the town the longest-named railway station in the world. The tongue twister means 'The church of St Mary in the hollow of white hazel trees near the rapid whirlpool by St Tysilio's of the red cave'. You can get your passport stamped in the gift shop, which is also home to the Tourist Information Centre if you haven't had enough of the joke yet. To get to Anglesey, take either the A5 across the Menai Bridge, built by Thomas Telford in 1826, or Robert Stephenson's Britannia Bridge, continuing the A55 from Chester.

OPEN   All year round.

AMENITIES

❷❷❾ SEE PUFFINS AT ELLIN'S TOWER
RSPB SEABIRD CENTRE

Plas Nico, South Stack, Holyhead, Anglesey LL65 1YH (℃ **01407 764973**, www.rspb.
org.uk/southstack).

Watch one of only 200 pairs of choughs in Britain through a live cam-
era in a spectacularly beautiful setting 300 feet (90m) above the Irish
Sea. In a castellated former folly, once part of Liberal MP William
Stanley's estate and now owned
by the RSPB, the cameras are
also trained on colonies of puf-
fins, razorbills and guillemots.
The plate-glass platform on the
first floor of Ellin's Tower (named
after Stanley's wife) has views to
South Stack lighthouse and on a
clear day across 60 miles
(100km) to Ireland. The Visitor
Centre on this 600-acre reserve
has displays about local wildlife
and members of staff are on-hand
to help locate birds on its cameras and telescopes. The best time to
come is from late-April to mid-July, when there are 4,000 seabirds
nesting in the cliffs.

> **Useful Welsh Phrases**
>
> 'Brensiach y bratia, mae hi'n
> bwrw glaw eto!': Oh bloody hell,
> it's raining again.
>
> 'Ti wedi bwyta darn olaf o pizza
> fi, mae rhaid i ti farw': You have
> eaten my last piece of pizza, you
> must die.

OPEN   Ellin's Tower daily Easter–mid-Sept 10am–5pm. Reserve all year round.

AMENITIES   ☕ 🍴 🅿

❷❸⓿ TRY YOUR HAND AT SPINNING AT
THE NATIONAL WOOL MUSEUM

Dre-fach-Felindre, near Newcastle Emlyn, Llandysul, Carmarthenshire SA44 5UP
(℃ **01559 370929**, www.museumwales.ac.uk).

Nicknamed (unkindly or respectfully, we are not sure) the 'Hudders-
field of Wales', the picturesque village of Dre-fach Felindre in the
rolling green Teifi Valley was once the centre of a thriving woollen
industry. The museum based at this former mill tells the story of wool
production from fleece to fabric, in what was historically the most

important industry in Wales. Shirts and shawls, blankets and bedcovers, woollen stockings and socks were all made here and sold throughout the world. You can see historic machinery including looms and something called an Open Width Scourer and Filtration Trough, which we had fun mentioning on postcards home. There is a raised walkway for viewing the textiles in production and some unusual 19th-century knitted socks, while families can have fun following a specially designed trail called 'A Woolly Tale', trying their hands at carding, spinning and sewing along the way.

OPEN   Daily Apr–Sept 10am–5pm; Oct–Mar Tues–Sat 10am–5pm.

AMENITIES

㉛ CURSE THE MR BLOBBY SEESAW AT THE GREAT ORME COUNTRY PARK

Great Orme, near Llandudno, Conwy LL30 5XS (☎ **01492 874151**, www.conwy.gov. uk/greatorme).

Our children are aged just five and two, although that still seemed very little excuse for their flagrantly heathen-like attitude to the natural wonders of the Great Orme. Designated an SSI, the Great Orme is named after the Norse word for 'worm' and is a limestone outcrop 679 feet (200m) above the pretty seaside town of Llandudno. Two miles (3.2km) long and a mile (1.6km) wide, the Orme is a walker's paradise, home to rare wildflowers, birds, curly-horned cashmere goats and a butterfly (the silver studded blue) that exists nowhere else in the world. Yet despite this and the Visitor Centre (open Easter to October), where you can learn about the area's unique geology, all our children wanted to do was go on the Mr Blobby seesaw (30p) in the Summit Complex arcade. If you don't want to walk to the summit of the Orme, a tramway runs up to the top, costing £5.50 for adults and £3.70 for children. Carriages on the only cable-hauled road tramway in the world leave every 20 minutes and save a lot of leg work clambering up the hill. Halfway up the Orme near the second tramway station there is a 2,000-year-old copper mine (☎ **01492 870447**, www.greatormemines.info, £6 for adults), which has an excellent second-hand bookshop next to its ticket booth. We spent an hour

Look Behind You

1. The Punch and Judy show features a hunchbacked Punch, with a hooked nose, the cruel and boastful husband of his nagging wife, Judy. The show can trace its roots back to 16th-century Italian *Commedia dell'arte*.

2. Punch speaks in a distinctive squawking voice produced by a contrivance known as a 'swazzle', which the professor holds in his mouth, transmitting his gleeful cackle 'That's the way to do it'.

3. The term 'pleased as Punch' is derived from Punch's gleeful self-satisfaction.

4. A Punch and Judy puppeteer has been known as a professor since Victorian times.

browsing in here to keep out of the incredibly strong winds, and were lucky enough to hear the nerdiest man in Wales say to his two embarrassed teenaged sons, 'A 2,000 year old Iron-Age mine, a tea shop AND a second-hand bookshop. We've lucked out, boys.'

OPEN   All year round.

AMENITIES

⓬ WATCH THE PUNCH & JUDY SHOW ON LLANDUDNO PIER

Promenade, Llandudno, Conwy LL30 2LP (☎ **01492 879523**, www.llandudno-tourism.co.uk).

That's the way to do it. This puppet theatre has been run by the Codman family since 1860. It was started by the late 'Professor' Richard Codman, a former bare-fisted fighter, who performed for Queen Victoria and Queen Mary among others. The theatre is now run by his great granddaughter Jackie Millband-Codman, her husband Morris and their son Jason. The puppets used are the 19th-century originals carved from local driftwood. Always attracting large crowds, these true professionals put on their shows through wind and rain. We should know. We watched a performance through a horrendous storm last summer, which our children, who are accustomed to the monotonous whimsy of TV programmes *In the Night Garden* and *Waybuloo*, couldn't believe they were allowed to watch. As our daughter remarked for days afterwards, 'Punch was so naughty, Dad'.

OPEN   Easter–Sept shows at midday, 2pm and 4pm.

AMENITIES

㉝ SEE THE BEST-PRESERVED AMPHITHEATRE IN BRITAIN AT THE NATIONAL ROMAN LEGION MUSEUM

High Street, Caerleon, Newport, Gwent NP18 1AE (✆ **01633 423 134**, www.museum wales.ac.uk).

★ ♁

Based at the site of one of only three permanent Roman fortresses in Britain, this far-flung former outpost of the Empire has the most complete amphitheatre in Britain and the only remains of a legionary barracks in Europe. In AD75 the Romans built a fortress at Caerleon that stood guard over the region for more than 200 years. Today at the remains there's a Roman garden to wander around, where we discovered something shocking about the leek – it's actually not native to Wales. At weekends and during school holidays or if you come after 3pm on a weekday (although check ahead) children can try on replica armour in the barrack room and experience life as a Roman soldier. This museum also preserves and displays an internationally regarded collection of more than half-a-million objects (ceramics, jewellery, weaponry) from the fortress and its environs; the highlight here is the oldest example of writing in Wales – a query written on a wooden tablet by a legionnaire concerning his pay.

OPEN   Mon–Sat 10am–5pm; Sun 2pm–5pm.

AMENITIES

❷❸❹ FIGHT OVER SELWYN GRIFFITHS AT THE NATIONAL SLATE MUSEUM

Llanberis, Gwynedd LL55 4TY (📞 **01286 870 630**, www.museumwales.ac.uk).

With tools lying around and workshop sound effects, this museum is based at the former slate quarry of Dinorwig and tells the story of the once-great Welsh industry. The whole complex is frozen in time at the ending of the last shift in 1969. Our son loved the loco shed containing a steam train, while our daughter got to design a slate table mat (£1) in the activity room before promptly shattering it on the cobblestones outside. The highlights of a visit are the regular slate-splitting demonstrations, where you watch a genial former quarryman (winks, banter, lilting voice) break down a block of stone into slices of slate so fine you could almost roll them up like ham. There are films about the quarry's past and its controversial closure, plus a chance to snoop around former quarrymen's basic houses, although if you're unlucky your children might unaccountably begin fighting over who is going to be Selwyn Griffiths, a quarryman we saw in a photograph. ('No, Charlie, you're the brother Glyn Griffiths. I'm Selwyn because I'm the biggest.') There's also a waterwheel to watch whirling around and a great family-friendly café with pens and drawing books for children serving excellent millionaire shortbread.

OPEN   Daily Easter–Oct 10am–5pm; Nov–Easter Sun–Fri 10am–4pm.

AMENITIES

❷❸❺ SEE THE ARTWORK OF ROLF HARRIS'S GRANDFATHER AT CYFARTHFA CASTLE MUSEUM & ART GALLERY

Brecon Road, Merthyr Tydfil CF47 8RE (📞 **01685 723 112**, www.merthyr.gov.uk).

The world's first steam locomotive to pull a load, the 1804 *Penydarren*, is on display at one of the stateliest buildings of industrial South Wales; a castle complete with turrets and towers commissioned in 1824 by super-rich ironmaster William Crawshay. The rooms are

Strewth!

1. In 1992 Rolf Harris beat Lucien Freud, Damien Hirst and David Hockney to be named the world's most famous artist.

2. Harris's pop hits have included *Tie Me Kangaroo Down Sport*, *Sun Arise*, *Two Little Boys* and more recently *Stairway to Heaven*, which reached number 7 in the UK charts.

3. In 2005 Rolf painted Elizabeth II's portrait, in a calm pose with a 'nice friendly smile', emulating his great-grandfather who painted the Queen's grandfather George V inspecting troops.

4. Harris has played the didgeridoo on two albums by English pop singer Kate Bush, 1982's *The Dreaming* and 2005's *Aerial*.

5. In his appearance on the BBC's *Desert Island Discs*, Harris chose eight of his own records to take to his desert island.

stuffed with decorative arts but the highlights of the displays focus on Merthyr Tydfil's claims to fame. The first Labour MP, Keir Hardie, came from the town and the socialist red flag was first raised here following a workers' riot in 1831. Much later, and less successfully, the Sinclair C5 was made in Merthyr. There are paintings by Rolf Harris's Welsh-born grandfather George Frederick Harris (see box above), a local photographer and artist prior to his emigration to Australia, and Welsh landscape painter, Penry Williams. There are interactive displays throughout the museum, colouring-in sheets for children and hands-on family exhibits. The castle is set in 160 acres with wonderful sweeping lawns and a play area, where your children can happily swing and run around.

OPEN   Daily 1 Apr–30 Sept 10am–5pm; 1 Oct–31 Mar Tues–Fri 10am–4pm, Sat–Sun 12pm–4pm.

SEE A LOCK OF NELSON'S HAIR AT THE NELSON MUSEUM & LOCAL HISTORY CENTRE

Priory Street, Monmouth NP25 3XA (© **01600 710630**).

★ ♿

Although Admiral Horatio Nelson had little to do with Monmouth, or even Wales, in his lifetime and is buried in St Paul's Cathedral in London, Monmouth in Wales is home to one of the largest collection of Nelson memorabilia in the world. Among the exhibits found here is his naval sword from the Battle of Trafalgar (1805) as well as the two swords of the surrendering Spanish and French admirals. The museum has a ring fashioned out of hair believed to be from Nelson's head, letters and a glass eye that was proven to be a fake – contrary to received wisdom he never lost an eye or even wore an eye patch – he actually had a detached retina and wore a green flap on the front of his hat to shield his eyes from the glare of the sun off the sea. The collection, which also includes exhibits relating to Nelson's sole visit to Monmouth with the Hamiltons in 1802, was amassed by local peer Lady Llangattock, the mother of Charles Rolls (of Rolls-Royce fame), whose own boy's life story is also told here. Children can dress up in Edwardian sailor outfits and make a bi-cornered Nelson hat.

OPEN Mar–Oct Mon–Sat 11am–1pm, 2pm–5pm, Sun 2pm–5pm; Nov–Feb, 11am–1pm, 2pm–4pm, Sun 2pm–4pm.

AMENITIES

CATCH A CHOIR SERVICE AT ST DAVID'S CATHEDRAL

The Close, St David's, Pembrokeshire SA62 6RH (© **01437 720204**, www.stdavids cathedral.org.uk).

★

St David's is Britain's smallest city, thanks to its 12th-century cathedral built on the site of a sixth-century monastery. In medieval times this was a major place of pilgrimage, with two visits here considered the equivalent of a trip to Rome, although now it's the choir that puts the cathedral on the map. The main choir (there are four), first founded in 1132 and uniquely featuring female voices, has toured Europe many times and has album sales totalling more than one million in

America. Sung Evensong services are held from Tuesday to Friday at 6pm, or on Sunday at 11:15am and 6pm. Free tours of the cathedral itself (there is a suggested donation of £4) take place on Mondays at 11:30am and Fridays at 2:30pm.

OPEN Cathedral all the time, choir during services.

AMENITIES

② CHASE RABBITS AT BARAFUNDLE BAY

Stackpole, Pembrokeshire SA71 5LS (✆ **01646 661359**, www.nationaltrust.org.uk).

Barafundle was once voted the best place in Britain for a picnic, and is considered one of the world's Top 10 beaches. The breathtaking sandy sweep is reached via a cliff walk from the tiny harbour at Stackpole Quay, followed by a 15-minute walk to the beach past some stunning views of the Pembrokeshire coastline (there are about 40 steps). The final approach is through a storybook-style forest so dark and dense it reminded our children of Hansel and Gretel and my daughter wanted to drop Dolly Mixtures to find her way back to the car. On the beach the sand shines gold, there are caves to explore at low tide and distant views of Caldey Island and Exmoor to admire, so our daughter spent the whole day chasing rabbits in vain through the grassy dunes like Wile E. Coyote. The beach is amazingly tranquil and sheltered, and chances are you'll be alone there, probably due to the long walk from Stackpole Quay, which becomes its drawback when you have to carry Wile E. Coyote to the car.

OPEN All year round.

AMENITIES

② HOLD THE TURKEY AND GO FOR A BOXING DAY SWIM

Tenby, Pembrokeshire SA70 (Tenby Tourist Information Centre ✆ **01834 842402**, www.tenbyboxingdayswim.co.uk).

We all know Boxing Day morning is for scoffing mince pies and watching *Herbie Goes Bananas* in front of a roaring fire. Except, that is, for three years ago when we were staying in the Brecon Beacons over Christmas, when my pregnant wife, insane from her obsessive ginger intake, decided we should drive two hours to Tenby and take part in the Boxing Day swim in the freezing waters of Carmarthen Bay. The upshot, after a small protest from me, was our daughter in tears because 'the water's so cold it's hurting me', while my wife decided swimming in freezing water wasn't good for the baby, so yes, I had to go in. My daughter and I were given a free cup of hot soup and a medal to commemorate our achievements after our brief waist-high paddle. Considered one of the festival highlights of the Welsh calendar, the event draws crowds of thousands to Tenby's North Beach to enjoy the *schadenfreude* of observing 600 swimmers in fancy dress squealing with cold as they wade into the brine. The event is organised by the Tenby Sea Swimming Association and kicks off at 11am, raising around £20,000 a year for charity. There are prizes for the best costumes, and it is free to swim although many bathers are sponsored.

OPEN   Check website for details.

AMENITIES   £

ⓦ MARVEL AT THE WORLD BOG-SNORKELLING CHAMPIONSHIPS

Llanwrtyd Wells, Powys LD6 (Llanwrtyd Wells Tourist Information Centre ✆ **01591 610 666**, www.green-events.co.uk).

😮

Every August the smallest town in Britain plays host to the World Bog-Snorkelling Championships, which see more than 150 people don flippers and a diver's mask to swim two 55-metre lengths of a muddy trench. We attended the event last year at the Waen Rhydd Peat Bog with our children who couldn't believe what they saw – actual adults 'jumping in puddles of mud, Dad. Look!' An added complication to the rules is that the 200 entrants are not allowed to swim any recognisable stroke, meaning that they often look like they are drowning, although they can wear a wetsuit. Competitors, often in fancy dress, pay £15 to take part in the event, although watching, as hundreds do, is free. The record for the fastest swim stands at under 1 minute 35 seconds and there are also prizes for the best costume. The event takes place at the end of August.

OPEN   Check website for details.

AMENITIES

㉑ JUDGE THE PAINTINGS AT THE MUSEUM OF MODERN ART

Y Tabernacl, Heol Penrallt, Machynlleth, Powys SY20 8AJ (© **01654 703355**, www. momawales.org.uk).

Based alongside a performing arts centre in a converted chapel, MOMA has four light-filled galleries and an excellent reputation for promoting contemporary artists. The museum displays works by Welsh landscapists Kyffin Williams and Dai Llewellyn Hall, artist and author Iwan Bala and more established work by Augustus John and Wyndham Lewis as well as pencil drawings of the poet Dylan Thomas (see p. 204) by Mervyn Levy. There are frequent new exhibitions and in July visitors (even our children had a go) can vote on around 200 entrants to the annual Tabernacle Art Competition, which sees participants from all over the world competing for prize money of £1,200. You can enter the competition yourself for £6.

OPEN   Mon–Sat 10am–4pm.

AMENITIES

㉒ SEE THE IMPRESSIONISTS AT THE NATIONAL MUSEUM CARDIFF

Cathays Park, Cardiff, South Glamorgan CF10 3NP (© **029 2039 7951**, www. museumwales.ac.uk).

As well as admiring masterpieces from the likes of Monet, Manet and Van Gogh in one of the most impressive Impressionist collections in Europe, visitors can see a reconstruction of how South Wales looked 200 million years ago in the Evolution of Wales Gallery. The museum also tells the story of Wales' national archaeology and geology and is home to some large, moving model dinosaurs. The Glanely Discovery

Gallery is useful for a peaceful closer look at some of the museum's 7.5 million exhibits, featuring anything from Bronze-Age goldwork to ancient shells and includes the opportunity to touch and study fossils and bones.

OPEN   Tues–Sun 10am–5pm.

AMENITIES   ☕ 🍴 🛍 £

㉔ DO THE DR WHO TOUR OF CARDIFF

The Red Dragon Centre, Hemingway Road, Cardiff, South Glamorgan CF10 4JY (☎ **02920 256261**, www.thereddragoncentre.co.uk).

😮

Ok sci-fi nerds – this one is for you. Pick up a free copy of a map of the city detailing key locations used during the filming of the revived *Doctor Who* series. These include Tredegar House from the second episode of the second series, *The Girl in the Fireplace*, as well as Dyffryn Gardens, used to represent 18th-century France in episode four of the same series as well as more than a dozen other sites. Cardiff has other associations with *Doctor Who*. Terry Nation (see box below),

Exterminate, Exterminate

Terry Nation initially worked in comedy, finding a way into the industry in 1955 after Spike Milligan bought a sketch he had written. Nation worked on hundreds of radio scripts for British comedians, including Terry Scott, Eric Sykes, Harry Worth and Frankie Howerd. His big break came in 1962 when he was commissioned to write for Tony Hancock, although he was later fired. Jobless and with a young family to support, Nation took up the offer of writing the second *Doctor Who* series, which introduced the Daleks to the world. Soon they became the show's most popular monsters and were responsible for the BBC's first merchandising boom. As well as contributing episodes of *The Persuaders* and *The Saint*, Nation also wrote *Survivors*, a merry tale of the few remaining humans on Earth, and *Blake's 7*, the sci-fi romp about political prisoners on the run in a stolen alien space ship and wearing some awful pastel-coloured uniforms.

the creator of the Daleks, was born here and his inspiration for the stair-shy masters of the universe is said to have come from observing the flashing red lights on a TV mast. For more information on film locations in Cardiff, visit bbc.co.uk/wales/southeast/sites/doctorwho/. For those really dedicated *Doctor Who* nuts, there is a related exhibition at the Red Dragon Centre (£6 adults, £4.50 children), which also features *Torchwood*.

OPEN   Daily 10am–6:30pm.

AMENITIES   ☕ 🍴 ♿

244 JOIN IN THE FUN AT THE CARDIFF BIG WEEKEND

Cardiff Civic Centre, Cardiff, South Glamorgan CF10 3ND (✆ **029 2087 2087**, www.cardiff-festival.com).

★

The UK's biggest annual free outdoor music festival attracts around 6,000 music fans, who roll up to hear acts that have included the Stereophonics, Aswad, the Lightning Seeds and the Zutons. Taking place over three days in late July or early August, the event also features the world's largest travelling funfair and spectacular firework displays at the end of each day's entertainment. The Big Weekend has been running since 1995 and traditionally kicks off at 5pm on a Friday. You cannot bring in alcohol but there are plenty of bars inside the venue.

OPEN   Check website for dates.

AMENITIES   ☕ 🍴 🛍 ♿

245 LEARN CIRCUS TRICKS AT THE WALES MILLENNIUM CENTRE

Bute Place, Cardiff, South Glamorgan CF10 5AL (✆ **02920 636400**, www.wmc.org.uk).

Most lunchtimes and evenings there are free demonstrations at Cardiff's smart new civic showcase, ranging from learning to perform Japanese circus tricks (no lion-taming to our son's disappointment) through to Afro-Caribbean storytelling and close harmony choirs. Other events at the Glanfa Stage in the centre foyer could be jazz, classical-music recitals or even brass brands, poetry readings and performances from the

Welsh National Opera. The shows start at 1pm and 6pm. They last between 45 minutes to an hour and there is no need to book ahead. Meanwhile, there are occasional free music concerts outside in the sunken Roald Dahl Plas, including – we are not making this up – rappers performing at an event asking children to 'stay safe on Welsh railways this summer'.

OPEN   Daily.

AMENITIES   ☕ 🍴 🍸 £

㉔ PRETEND TO BE LAWRENCE OF ARABIA AT MERTHYR MAWR SAND DUNES

Merthyr Mawr Road, Merthyr Mawr, near Bridgend, Mid Glamorgan CF3 0LT (✆ **0845 1306229**, www.ccw.gov.uk).

Parts of David Lean's classic movie *Lawrence of Arabia* were filmed at these sand dunes, once the largest in Europe. The system still boasts the second-highest dune in Europe, known locally as the 'Big Dipper'. Olympic hero Steve Ovett used to run up and down the dune as part of his training for the 1,500m and the Welsh rugby team still use it today. I raced up it with my children and afterwards my knees were so stiff I couldn't squat for a week. The huge network of dunes is situated about one mile (1.6km) outside the pretty village of Merthyr Mawr and roll for miles towards Ogmore and Porthcawl on the south coast. The dunes are popular with children who like to roll down the slopes, local wildlife enthusiasts and people who like to pretend they are TE Lawrence in the desert and wear baby muslins around their heads. A footpath from the dunes leads to Merthyr Mawr and on to Ogmore and its ruined castle (entry free), reached via a series of stones across the river Ogmore. Against the eastern edge of the dunes are the moody, ivy-strangled ruins of Candleston Castle; this is actually a fortified 14th-century manor house and is all that survives of the village of Treganlaw ('the town of a hundred hands'), which was lost to the smothering sands. Said to be haunted, the castle and surrounding area have a dark, eerie and melancholic atmosphere.

OPEN   All year round.

AMENITIES   £

❷❹❼ DON'T MENTION THE WORD VILLAGE AT ST FAGANS: NATIONAL HISTORY MUSEUM

St Fagans, Cardiff, South Glamorgan CF5 6XB (℗ **029 2057 3500**, www.museum wales.ac.uk).

We spent a day at this 100-acre open-air museum, wandering in and out of Welsh buildings from varying centuries. Sites include 2,000-year-old Iron-Age roundhouses, a row of ironworkers' houses from Rhyd-y-Car built in 1805, and St Teilo's Church, which was shipped to the museum stone by stone. Elsewhere in the park there's a cock-fighting pit, a farm with animals our children enjoyed petting, and a Land Train that costs 50p a ride. There are also demonstrations from a blacksmith and a weaver (both on their lunch breaks when we visited) as well as a chance to learn something about the Iron Age village:

Me: 'How many people lived in these houses?'

Member of staff: 'We have no way of knowing.'

Me: 'Ok. How long would these houses have survived?'

Member of staff: 'We have no way of knowing.'

Me: 'Did they have animals in here too?'

Member of staff: 'Again, we have no way of knowing.'

One word of warning: do not refer to the clump of shops and houses round the blacksmith's forgery as a village, because 'it is not a village. It is an assortment of houses from different eras of Welsh history arranged accidentally into the exact design of a village'. We can only assume this vehemence is because staff here know so little that when they do know something, they get very insistent about it.

OPEN Daily 10am–5pm.

AMENITIES ☕ 🏮 🪑 £

❷❹❽ CLIMB SNOWDON

Llanberis, Snowdonia LL55 4TY (Snowdonia National Park ℗ **01766 770274**; Betws-y-Coed Tourist Information Centre ℗ **01690 710426**, www.eryri-npa.co.uk).

My great-great-grandfather George Yeld, was renowned in Victorian Europe as the foremost authority on scaling the Alps. He wrote many books on the subject, some still in circulation among serious climbers. Unfortunately I am a complete coward who feels the air begin to thin

Snowdon or Snowdon't?

1. In Welsh, Snowdon is known as Yr Wyddfa, which fittingly means 'tomb'.

2. Before the Snowdon Mountain Railway opened in 1896, ponies used to cart tourists to the summit.

3. The summit can reach temperatures of 30°C (86°F) in high summer, and plummets to -20°C (-4°F) in the winter. Add to this wind speeds of up to 150 mph and it can feel more like -50°C (-58°F) degrees up there.

changing the hall light bulb when standing on the third rung of a step-ladder. However, in our quest to make this book well rounded, we decided to scale Mount Snowdon (3,560 feet/1085m). We took the easiest route – the Llanberis Path – known also as the Tourist Route. However, it is also the longest trail (five miles/8km) and our climb, which normally takes six hours, actually took us eight after I hurt my ankle and we realised we'd left our sandwiches in the car. We were advised not to take our children and my wife now thinks this advice should extend to husbands in trainers. It began to rain at the peak of Moel Cynghorion and without good walking boots I was soon slipping back half a tread for every forward step. On the plus side, highlights include the huge rock of Maen Du'r Arddu and craggy, desolate Clog-wyn Du'r Arddu, a welcome cup of tea at the 1,700-feet (520m) high Halfway House, and the amazing views of Anglesey and the Irish Sea beyond. Alternatively you can cheat and ride the Snowdon Mountain Railway to the summit and back. Adult return fares are £16.

249 GET MISTAKEN FOR A HOBO AT THE NATIONAL WATERFRONT MUSEUM

Oystermouth Road, Maritime Quarter, Swansea SA1 3RD (℡ **01792 638950**, www.museumwales.ac.uk).

This new £35-million museum is in a Grade-II listed warehouse and tells the story of industry and innovation in Wales over the last 300

years. It was here that I was mistaken for a hobo near Vincenzo Rac-cuglia's *Cardboard World* installation in the foyer of the museum. I was squatting by the exhibit (our children were hiding inside) when an old lady approached and gave 50p from her purse. The museum has a host of interactive gizmos, the best of which is in the History of Welsh Industry section on the first floor. Using the latest sensory technology, learn about freemasonry and trade unionism by activating a screen using only hand gestures. Meanwhile the Achievers Gallery features famous Welsh pioneers such as former prime minister David Lloyd George and rugby international Gareth Edwards. The Transport, Materials and Networks Gallery focuses on Welsh inventions that have changed the world and includes a pre-1914 amateur airplane hanging from the ceiling in recognition of Tenby man Bill Frost, who apparently carried out the first powered flight in 1894, nine years before the Wright Brothers took off at Kitty Hawk.

OPEN Daily 10am–5pm.

AMENITIES

㉚ DO NOT GO GENTLY INTO THE DYLAN THOMAS CENTRE

Somerset Place, Swansea SA1 1RR (℗ **01792 463980**, www.dylanthomas.com).

Based at the city's former guildhall, this museum tells the story of Wales' best-loved literary figure so well and infectiously it is almost impossible not to be moved by the great man and his verse. The museum's highlights include a chance to hear Dylan Thomas himself, the second-most quoted writer in English, reading some of his work, a rendition of his most famous work, *Under Milk Wood* set to a lewd cartoon, and the Man and Myth display illuminating amusing snippets about his life and loves (see box, p. 205). More popular since the recent film about his life, *The Edge of Love*, starring Keira Knightley and Sienna Miller, the museum has memorabilia such as an old drinks bill of Thomas's as well as a timeline of his debauched life. There's also a room full of memorabilia highlighting the influence Thomas has had on other writers and figures as diverse as Bob Dylan (who changed his name in honour of the poet), John Lennon, former US

Rage, Rage, Rage

1 Dylan Thomas exhibited an artwork entitled *Boiled String* at the 1936 Surrealist Exhibition in London. It was some string in a teacup.

2 Thomas was a bohemian drunkard who would happily drink 18 single whiskies a night and then take amphetamines.

3 He was the first poet to sign recordings of his work and was a celebrity in Britain and America.

4 His themes were life, death, sex, love, childhood and himself; his best-known line is 'do not go gentle into that good night, … rage, rage against the dying of the light,' written, some say, about his dying father.

5 Thomas was very dependent on his women. His wife, Caitlin, for example, used to chop the top off his egg every morning as his mother had done before her.

6 He kept a photo of himself winning a race aged 12 all his life as evidence of his own physical strength. He had it with him when he died in 1953.

president Jimmy Carter and the creators of *Coronation Street* (which takes its name from the location in *Under Milk Wood*).

OPEN   Daily 10am–4:30pm.

AMENITIES

251 HAVE THE ORANGE CARPET LAID OUT FOR YOU AT THE BAKED BEAN MUSEUM OF EXCELLENCE

6 Flint House, Moorland Road, Sandfields Estate, Port Talbot, Swansea SA12 6JX (℗ **01639 680896** or **078038 72428**, www.bakedbeanmuseumofexcellence.org.uk).

To visit the world's only baked-bean museum, make a private appointment with Captain Beanie, formerly Barry Kirk. He changed his name by – wait for it – bean-poll. Voted by the discerning Mayfair Eccentric Club of Great Britain the 2009 Eccentric of the Year, Captain Beanie has set up the museum in the living room of his flat. It is registered with the Association of Independent Museums and contains around 250 examples of different baked-bean tins ('not just Heinz'), baked-bean posters and other bean-related memorabilia. The real draw here isn't the exhibits but the bald-headed Captain Beanie himself, dressed in a bright orange superhero cape and with a matching orange face. He has failed to get through nine auditions of *Big Brother* and became obsessed with baked beans after bathing in a tub full of them for a charity event in 1986. If you do call in, be sure to ask about the time he spent in the Department of Naturalisation when he visited New York shortly after September 11, dressed as Captain Beanie and with a picture of his orange-faced alter-ego as his passport photo.

OPEN   By arrangement.

A-BEAN-ITIES   Beans on toast

㉒ WALK TO WORM'S HEAD AT RHOSSILI BAY

Rhossili, Gower, Swansea SA3 1TR (✆ **01792 390707**, www.nationaltrust.org.uk).

Rhossili Bay is a majestic, sandy, three-mile (5km) sweep of beach backed by the downs, where the rolling waves are popular with surfers and families who've remembered to bring jumpers. The Hatch family spent a freezing morning here in T-shirts building sandcastles at an incredible speed to try and keep warm. Set on the Gower Peninsula, this beach was the first place in Britain to be designated an Area of Outstanding Natural Beauty and is often over-run by paragliders launching from the hills above. At low tide you can see the skeletal wreck of the cargo ship *Helvetia*, grounded here in the 19th century. There are great views of Worm's Head and a wonderful (and even windier) walk out to the promontory, which is only accessible at low tide. This walk in turn gives stunning views back over the arc of Rhossili beach and the precipitous drops into the sea below. There is a tiny coastguard hut part-way along the headland; you are welcome to pop in for a chat and warm-up in front of their fire. Back in the little white-washed village of Rhossili, there is a National Trust Visitors' Centre plus a few art galleries and craft shops.

OPEN   All year round.

AMENITIES

❷❺❸ GO DOWN A REAL MINE AT THE BIG PIT NATIONAL COAL MUSEUM

Blaenavon, Torfaen NP4 9XP (📞 **01495 790311**, www.museumwales.ac.uk).

👫 🌂 ☺

On a tour down the 300-ft (90m) deep mine at this former pit, dug in the 1800s, we were asked to turn off our helmet lights, and when it was so dark we couldn't see our hands in front of our faces, we were told by our chirpy ex-miner guide: 'That's what it was like when the candles blew out, although that wasn't the real problem. The real problem was the rats.' The abandoned coal mine at Blaenavon is now a UNESCO World Heritage Site and the tour underground lasts about 50 minutes, although with the stooping, the depressing talk of the working conditions (women and children under 11 worked here before the law was changed in 1842) and your wife panicking about rats it can seem considerably longer. It gets cold underground and very wet, with more than a million gallons of water passing through the shafts each day, so take sensible footwear and a jumper. Children under five are discouraged from the tour and no-one under one metre (39 inches) in height is allowed. After you've been hoisted back to the surface in the pit cage, taken off your hard hat and self-rescuer *and* checked your shoes for rat droppings, you get to walk into the side of a hill to see some of the heavier-duty cutting tools and a film high-lighting changing conditions underground. At the Pithead Baths there are exhibitions focusing on the 1984–85 miners' strike and the impact it had on mining communities.

OPEN Feb–Nov 9:30am–5pm (last tour 3:30pm); Dec–Jan 9:30am–4:30pm (call about tours).

AMENITIES 🍵 🛍 🅿

❷❺❹ HEAR A WELSH MALE VOICE CHOIR

Hafod Welfare Colliery Club, Queen's Street, Rhos, Wrexham (📞 **01978 845219**, www.rmvc.co.uk).

★

Twice a week more than 60 men aged from 17 to 79 from the small village of Rhos give up two hours of their time to rehearse for this famously proud Welsh male voice choir; Aled Jones once sang here as a young soprano. It's one of the most stirring sounds you'll hear; the valleys ring out from this room to the chorus of Welsh classics like *Take Me Away* and *Gwahoddiad* (Invitation) as well as operatic tunes and light arrangements such as *Unchained Melody*. The choir, frequently voted BBC Choir of the Year, were part of promotional material for the 1999 Rugby World Cup, regularly featured on Classic FM, and have been performing since 1891. There are two rehearsals a week that the public can attend, one at the above address on Monday nights from 7:15pm, and the second on Thursday at the same time just 20 yards away at the former Miners' Institute on Broad Street. If you like what you hear, the choir sing at an annual concert at William Aston Hall of Glyndwr University in Wrexham, normally in June, which has an admission fee. Their 'Best-Of' CDs are also available from the web address above.

OPEN   Check website for details.

AMENITIES

The Hermitage at Inver Dunkeld by the River Braan, Perthshire.

SCOTLAND

S cotland's reputation for meanness is undermined by its host of free activities which include the huge Museum of Transport in Glasgow, the wonderfully eclectic Kelvingrove Art Gallery and Museum and the People's Palace and Winter Gardens, where you can have a go at learning Glaswegian. That's not to mention the acclaimed Burrell Collection of art works and the Scotland Street School Museum that feature Victorian classroom re-enactions. In Edinburgh you'll find the famous, cloned Dolly the Sheep at the National Museum of Scotland, as well as the Museum of Childhood, while the Witchery by the Castle restaurant is a great place to celebrity-spot outside. Off the beaten track there's the creepy Munlochy Clootie Well, a magical spring said to cure all ills and dolphin-spotting at Chanonry Point. There's the World Stone-Skimming Championships to enter on Easdale Island and the amazing whispering walls of the Hamilton mausoleum to take in. If you have more energy you can climb Ben Nevis, or walk in the footsteps of Wordsworth on the Hermitage Trail. You can even sunbathe on the warmest Scottish beach at Nairn and if all else fails there's the chance of seeking enlightenment at the Kagyu Samye Ling Monastery and Tibetan Centre.

₂₅₅ CATCH ROYALTY DISEMBARKING FROM A TRAIN AT THE OLD ROYAL STATION

Station Square, Ballater, Aberdeenshire AB35 5RB ((℮ **01339 755306**, www.visit scotland.com).

OK, this isn't free, but trust us it is worth the £2 admission charge because at this old railway station you get to wear a realistic Queen Victoria mask and stroke a model of her pet collie, Sharp. This is where the Royal Family used to disembark from the 15-carriage, 600-feet (180m) long Royal Train on their way to their summer retreat at Balmoral Castle. The main draw is the replica of the carriage Queen Victoria travelled in; it's decorated as it was in her day while the station platform has been decorated with waxworks of Victoria and her daughter Louise alighting from the Royal Saloon. After disembarkation the Queen was greeted on the platform by a Guard of Honour from the Black Watch as well as thousands of well-wishers in Station Square before being escorted by a cavalcade from the Royal Scottish Greys along the beacon-lit Deeside road to Balmoral, with every church bell for miles

By Royal Appointment

If you're still bedazzled by the glamour of blue blood, try out some of the businesses sporting 'By Royal Appointment' and enormous royal crests above their doorways in Balleter. It was a great comfort making our lunch from a sandwich loaf manufactured by Royal-Approved Ballater bakers. You can also have a Royal Appointed windscreen washer replaced at the Ballater Garage and read *Closer* magazine by Royal Appointment from the local paper shop.

around ringing. The tradition of using the Royal Train for the annual pilgrimage to Balmoral began to wane with George VI, who preferred driving; it was killed off altogether by the Beeching cuts when many rail lines closed in the 1960s. The museum didn't over-excite our daughter,

> **Trainspotting**
>
> During World War II the Royal Train was repainted the same colours as ordinary trains so that it was not an obvious target for enemy bombers.

even when we explained that queens are the mothers of princesses (her favourite human form), although I was quietly pleased with a pair of gold-handled scissors encased in glass.

OPEN Daily July–7 Sept 9am–6pm; 8 Sept–June 10am–5pm.

AMENITIES 🛍 🅿

❷⁵⁶ HEAR ALARMING THINGS ABOUT SOLAR-FLARE CYCLES AT TOMNAVERIE STONE CIRCLE

Four miles (6.5km) north-west of Aboyne, off the B9094 Aboyne to Tarland Road, Aberdeenshire AB34 4YR.

This ancient stone circle, around 4,500 years old and about 30 feet (10m) in diameter, was over-run with Gothic teenagers when we visited. We were alarmed to hear them persistently mention something called 'the 11-year solar-flare cycle'. Up a relatively steep path from the car park below and set in some bleakish moorland, the circle's altar stone might have been used to sacrifice animals (or possibly humans), although nowadays if you brave the wind and the Goths (we also heard one say 'neuro-resonant field systems') you're treated to great views over Tarland to Lochnagar 20 miles (32km) away. As there is nobody around to tell you off, our daughter had fun climbing over the stones and playing hide-and-seek before we sacrificed her to a fertility god for refusing to return to the car.

OPEN All year round.

AMENITIES 🅿

㉗ SHOUT 'TOSSER' AT THE WORLD STONE-SKIMMING CHAMPIONSHIPS

Easdale Island, by Oban, Argyllshire PA34 4TB (Oban Visitor Information Centre ℂ **01631 563 122**, www.stoneskimming.com).

There are a handful of male activities that impress women. Descending a ladder with the baby you've rescued from a burning building is one of those. However, there are several male activities that we men know boost our appeal but which women pretend they don't care for, like the ability to barbecue ribs and watch Man Utd simultaneously on a portable TV. Or stone-skimming. Why do we do it? We do it because it's a power show to say 'Look at me – I can protect you in that cave – see how far my stone skimmed'. Nowadays living in a democracy with a welfare state, women are still secretly impressed. And nowhere can they be more impressed than on Easdale Island, where the annual World Stone-Skimming Championships are staged in a disused quarry. Stone-throwers get three skims, the stone must bounce at least three times and the winner is the person who skims the furthest. The competition began in 1997 and starts at midday on the last Sunday in September, with a pre-skim shindig on the Saturday night at Easdale Island Community Hall. You pay to enter (fees are between £1 and £4) but the competition is free to watch. There are around 200 entrants and more than 1,000 spectators so arrive early for the best views. The island is reached via a five-minute passenger ferry journey from Ellenabeich on the adjacent Isle of Seil, attached to the mainland by the Clachan Bridge. Call the ferry by pressing the buttons in the ferry shed on the pier at Ellenabeich. Return tickets are £1.60 for adults and 80p for children.

> ### Easdale
>
> Easdale is one of the most tranquil places in Scotland. It is the smallest inhabited island in the Inner Hebrides and has no cars, roads or street lamps. The wheelbarrow is the official means of transport, with individually identified examples lying on the grass by the slipway for the small ferry, awaiting their owners' return, or parked up outside cottages.

OPEN   See website for details.

⑳ AMAZE YOUR FAMILY AT THE ELECTRIC BRAE

On the A719 between Dunure and Croy Bay, Ayrshire KA19 8JR.

The Electric Brae is a phenomenon that fascinated American GIs stationed at Prestwick Airport during World War II as much it did General Eisenhower when he visited prior to D-Day. Park your car anywhere along the quarter-mile stretch of road from the bend overlooking Croy railway viaduct to Craigencroy Glen in the east. Switch off the engine and release the handbrake. Following this, step out of the car. Line your family up along the road and request they stare at the car. They will see the car appear to slowly roll *up* the hill. The optical illusion was totally lost on our children, who don't understand gravity, but is created by the lie of the surrounding land. The term 'Electric Brae' dates from a time when the phenomenon was incorrectly thought to be caused by electric or magnetic attraction. The spot is marked by a stone cairn inscribed with an explanation that you may or may not understand.

OPEN   All year round.

⑳ SEE JUSTICE BEING DONE IN SIR WALTER SCOTT'S COURTROOM

Market Place, Selkirk, Borders TD7 4PR (✆ **01750 20761**).

Playing homage to two famous sons of the Borders, this museum is set in the sheriff's court where novelist Sir Walter Scott dispensed justice as a magistrate. The exhibits tell his story and also that of comically inept local explorer Mungo Park (see box, p. 216). The courtroom remains as it appeared in Scott's time and even has a model of the great man presiding over a sentencing. In the display cases you'll find a lock of Scott's hair, his pistol, cloak and plaid brooch. Representing Mungo Park you'll find his red coat, walking stick and letters sent home from Africa.

OPEN   Mar–Sept Mon–Fri 10am–4pm, Sat 10am–2pm; May–Aug also Sun 10am–2pm.

AMENITIES

Mungo Jungo

Scottish explorer Mungo Park was born in Selkirk in 1771 and made two disastrous expeditions to Africa – although he did manage to find the source of the river Niger, despite being kidnapped for four months by a Moorish chief in 1796. He managed to escape, buck-naked apart from his pocket watch and hat, and in July of the same year reached the long-sought-after river at Segou in Mali. During his second expedition to Africa in 1805, Park took 36 bodyguards to prevent a repetition of his disastrous first trip but most of them died of fever and dysentery on the trek. Determined to navigate the Niger to the coast, in 1806 Park wrote in his final letter to the British Colonial Office 'set sail for the east with the fixed resolution to discover the termination of the Niger or perish in the attempt', which is exactly what he did when his party was set upon by hostile natives. He drowned in the Niger trying to escape.

㉖⓪ PAY HOMAGE TO THE HAGGIS POET AT BURNS HOUSE

Burns Street, Dumfries DG1 2PS (ℂ **01387 255297**, www.dumgal.gov.uk/museums).

This is the house where Robbie Burns died on 21 July 1796 aged 37. He lived with his long-suffering wife, Jean Armour, and the house contains the usual assortment of memorabilia – manuscripts, letters, his nutmeg grater and an old walking stick. In the larger bedroom one of the windows bears his signature scratched on the glass with a diamond ring. In the summer there are accompanied visits to the hideously ugly Burns Mausoleum, which looks like a fancy portaloo, at St Michael's Church. It's over the dual carriageway and opposite the statue of Jean Armour at the back of the creepy Gothic graveyard. Maps are available outlining where you can find the gravestones of the 45-odd Burns contemporaries buried here, including Jesse Lewers, who nursed him at the end of his life. Children are given activity packs with word-search puzzles and colouring-in books.

OPEN   Apr–Sept Mon–Sat 10am–5pm, Sun 2pm–5pm; Oct–Mar Tues–Sat 10am–1pm, 2pm–5pm.

AMENITIES   🛍 ♿

㉖ APOLOGISE FOR YOUR WIFE'S EFFRONTERY AT THE ROBERT BURNS CENTRE

Mill Road, Dumfries DG2 7BE (*℗* **01387 264808**, www.dumgal.gov.uk/museums).

☂

The Burns Centre is across the beautiful 15th-century Devorgilla Bridge over the river Nith from the poet's house. It's based at an old watermill and tells the unlikely story of Burns' rise from man of the soil to national icon, explaining it through the vernacular of the Scots in the 17th century as well as the country's rich history of music, verse and dance his poetry fed into. The fact that Robert Burns died young and had affairs gave him, of course, an added glamour, or as my wife (not a fan) put it: 'He'd be in *Closer* magazine today getting snapped outside the Met Bar with some girl-band slapper falling off his arm'. For children there are jigsaws of Burns's face to complete, as well as colouring-in sheets on the back of copies of Burns's most famous work.

OPEN   Apr–Sept Mon–Sat 10am–5pm, Sun 2pm–5pm; Oct–Mar Tues–Sat 10am–1pm, 2pm–5pm.

AMENITIES   ☕ 🛍 ♿

㉖ SEEK ENLIGHTENMENT AT THE KAGYU SAMYE LING MONASTERY & TIBETAN CENTRE

Eskdalemuir, Dumfries and Galloway DG13 0QL (*℗* **01387 373232**, www.samyeling.org).

☺

Wander around the peace garden at the West's first Tibetan Buddhist monastery, founded in 1967. Relax in the Tibetan tearoom, take in the temple with its golden roof and the beautiful Green Tara Statue representing fearlessness, before finally leaving after apologising in the Prayer Wheel House for the behaviour of your children who were shushed for disturbing students training their minds to live as a bodhisattva. There are daily tours (11am–3pm) of the Tibetan temple and grounds, requiring a minimum of 10 people, with meditation instruction. The charge for adults is £6 (children £3).

OPEN   Daily 6am–8pm.

AMENITIES

❷❻❸ SEE DOLLY THE SHEEP AT THE NATIONAL MUSEUM OF SCOTLAND

Chambers Street, Edinburgh EH1 JF (© **0131 2257534**, www.nms.ac.uk).

Designed by Benson and Forsyth and nominated for the 1999 Stirling Prize, much to Prince Charles's disapproval, the National Museum of Scotland houses some of the nation's most treasured possessions. Exhibits include Dolly the cloned (and now stuffed) sheep, Queen Mary's clarsach (harp) and also the spooky coffins from Arthur's Seat that my wife won't let me talk about after dark because they scare her. For those of you who have a higher terror threshold, the coffins were discovered in various stages of decomposition in 1837 on the volcanic slopes of Arthur's Seat and were made famous in one of Ian-Rankin's Rebus novels. They contained mysterious wooden figures thought to represent the victims of infamous serial killers (see box, p. 219) William Burke (1792–1829) and William Hare (1804–1829). On a less ghoulish note, a variety of themed guided tours of the museum, on anything from Scottish gold, weaponry through to bagpipes and the Romans run most days, while younger visitors can design a robot or test drive a Formula One car in the Discovery Zone. Outside, we suggest a restorative

A Dog's Life

The most frequently photographed statue in Edinburgh is not of a king, or even a writer – but of a small Skye terrier. Greyfriars Bobby's statue sits by the gates of Greyfriars Kirk reminding visitors of this famously loyal dog, who wouldn't leave the graveside of his owner, policeman John Gray, after he was buried in 1858. Bobby died 14 years of grave-watching later and his story went on to become a fairly morbid Disney film.

Body-snatchers

As medical science flourished in the early 19th century, demand rose sharply for cadaver available for the teaching of anatomy in British medical schools, including the University of Edinburgh. At this time the only legal supply of cadavers came from the bodies of executed criminals, the number of which fell due to a sharp drop in the execution rate brought about by penal reforms, so only about two or three corpses per year were *legally* available for a large number of students. This situation naturally attracted criminal elements. The first body sold by Burke and Hare to Dr Robert Knox, an anatomy lecturer at the Edinburgh Medical College, had died of natural causes and earned them £7/10. Thereafter Burke and Hare resorted to murder, massing 16 victims between 1827 and 1828, whose bodies were sold for dissection for up to £10 a time. When the crimes were eventually discovered Hare was offered immunity from prosecution in return for his testimony against Burke, who was sentenced to death and publicly dissected at the Edinburgh Medical School following his hanging. Dr Knox was never prosecuted. The Anatomy Act of 1832 changed all this, allowing bodies to be left to science or donated by relatives, effectively ending the reign of the body-snatchers.

stop at the sentimental statue to Scotland's favourite four-legged friend, Greyfriars Bobby (see p. 218).

OPEN   Daily 10am–5pm.

AMENITIES

❷❻❹ SEE THE REAL JEKYLL & HYDE AT BRODIE'S TAVERN

435 Lawnmarket, Edinburgh EH1 2AT (✆ **0131 225 6531**).

This old pub stands on the corner of Lawnmarket and the Royal Mile and is named after its most infamous local William Brodie, who was by day a respectable town councillor and Deacon of the Cabinetmakers' Guild and by night thief and gambler. He was the inspiration behind Robert Louis Stevenson's *Dr Jekyll and Mr Hyde* and made wax key impressions (check out the pub sign outside) while working in the homes of the wealthy and then returned at night to burgle them. When he was caught in 1788 he was sentenced to hang, ironically, on gallows he'd designed and built himself. A model of the fickle scoundrel in 18th-century garb, dressed half respectably and half disreputably, stands on the stairs up to the restaurant from the bar.

OPEN   Sun–Thurs 10am–midnight; Fri–Sat 10am–1am.

AMENITIES   £

ⓔ CELEB-SPOT AT THE WITCHERY BY THE CASTLE

352 Castlehill, Royal Mile, Edinburgh EH1 2NF (✆ **0131 225 5613**, www.thewitchery. com).

Who stays here? This famous eatery and hotel is based in a 16th-century merchant's house close to the gates of Edinburgh Castle and has been patronised by figures as diverse as Sir Andrew Lloyd-Webber, Joanna Lumley, Steve Coogan, Matt Groening, Michael Douglas and *X Factor* queen Dannii Minogue. It takes its name from the spot outside where witches were burnt until the 18th century; inside, the atmosphere is theatrically Gothic and entirely candle-lit, with Hogwarts-style oak panelling, tapestries and antiques.

Top tip: Don't take your children. At this über-cool hangout there'll be no sympathetic smiles if your toddler flips a soufflé to the floor in front of Jeremy Paxman.

OPEN   Mon–Sun midday–4pm and 5.30pm–11.30pm.

ⓕ SEE WHERE DICKENS'S SCROOGE WAS INSPIRED AT CANONGATE KIRK

153 Canongate, Edinburgh EH8 8BR (✆ **0131 556 3515**, www.canongatekirk.com).

The official kirk of Holyroodhouse Palace, this 17th-century church is used by the Royal Family when they are in residence at Hollyroodhouse Palace. It's also where Charles Dickens took his inspiration for the novel, *A Christmas Carol* (see box, p. 221). The church has a unique Dutch-style end gable and is also linked to Robert Burns as two of his most profound influences lie buried within the kirkyard: to the west, Robert Fergusson, an earlier poet whose gravestone Burns himself supplied; and to the east, Agnes Maclehose, known to Burns as 'Clarinda', whose correspondence inspired one of his most enduring love poems, *Ae fond kiss, And Then We Sever*. Other luminaries buried here include economist Adam 'Wealth of Nations' Smith.

OPEN   Dependent on services.

❷❻❼ GET NOSTALGIC FOR MOJOS AT THE MUSEUM OF CHILDHOOD

42 High Street, Royal Mile, Edinburgh EH1 1TG (✆ **0131 529 4142**, www.edinburgh. gov.uk).

This museum, the first of its kind in the world, was ironically set up by notorious child-hater Patrick Murray, who once proposed a memorial window to baby-slaughtering 'Good King Herod'. The museum charts changes in child-rearing since Victorian times, including a fascinating display on how naughty children used to be dosed with Epsom salts. Keep a look out for the creepy collection of waxen dolls with black glass eyes and real human hair on the second floor. The ones that gave my wife the nightmares were dolls 4, 8 (withered arm) and 12. This nostalgic, quietly

Bah Humbug

Thanks to Charles Dickens the name of Ebenezer Scrooge has come to represent avarice and meanness, but the character Scrooge was actually based on could not have been more different. *A Christmas Carol* came about after Charles Dickens gave a talk in Edinburgh in 1841 and afterwards came across a headstone in the Canongate Kirk graveyard that he misread because of failing light and his mild dyslexia. The headstone was for Ebenezer Lennox Scroggie, born in Kirkcaldy, Fife, a generous, rambunctious, slightly licentious man who threw wild parties and had once shocked the General Assembly of the Church of Scotland by 'goosing' the Countess of Mansfield. The headstone reads: 'Ebenezer Lennox Scroggie – meal man', in reference to his trade as a corn merchant, although Dickens mistook this for 'mean man'. He was intrigued by the description and two years later *A Christmas Carol* was published. Scroggie's final resting place was lost to redevelopment in 1932 and Ebenezer is no longer popular as a name.

Cuddly Toy Story

Former US President Teddy Roosevelt made teddy bears famous. It was his refusal to shoot a bear cub presented to him on a Mississippi hunting trip that kick-started the craze. The story of his reluctance to fire on the creature made it into the papers in 1902 and the incident was then immortalised in cartoons by Clifford K Berryman in *The Washington Post*, giving far-sighted New York shopkeepers Morris and Rose Michtom a brainwave. They made a replica of the bear and displayed it in their shop, naming it Teddy after the president. It was such a success with customers that they changed their shop's name to Teddy and eventually formed the Ideal Toy and Novelty Company. Teddy Roosevelt would have been surprised by his anti-hunt credentials as on an African safari in 1909 he and his companions killed or trapped 11,397 animals, including elephants, hippos and six rare white rhinos.

sweet collection is a must-see for 30-somethings like us not quite over the absence of Mojo sweets in their lives, even including the collection of Victorian board games, which showcases the very literal-sounding 'Virtue Rewarded, Vice Punished?'. There are steps for children to see high exhibits and activities range from teddy bear colouring-in while our son loved the potted history of *Thomas the Tank Engine*, although there was a huge tantrum when Toby could not be located.

OPEN   Mon–Sat 10am–5pm; Sun midday–5pm.

AMENITIES   🛍 £

❷⁶⁸ PLAN A ROBBERY AT THE HBOS MUSEUM ON THE MOUND

The Mound, Edinburgh EH1 1YZ (✆ **0131 243 5464**, www.museumonthemound. com).

At this altar to cash, based at the HQ of the Halifax Bank of Scotland, you'll find Scotland's oldest bank note, the world's first mechanical calculator and, more importantly, a display showing what a million pounds looks like in crisp new Scottish £20 notes (all unfortunately stamped cancelled). After 20 minutes spent imagining how you'd remove this stamp and steal the cash before fleeing to Mexico, you can locate your children sitting on the 1806 nightwatchman's chair. The tale of John Currie, who had his ear nailed to Tron Kirk on the Royal Mile after forging 20 shillings notes, will right your moral compass before you leave.

OPEN   Tues–Fri 10am–5pm; Sat–Sun 1pm–5pm.

AMENITIES

㉖⁹ OVERHEAR LAWYERS DISCUSSING MURDER CASES AT PARLIAMENT HOUSE

Parliament Square, Edinburgh EH1 1RQ (© **0131 225 2595**, www.scotcourts.gov.uk).

☂

Parliament House, the seat of Scottish government until the 1707 Act of Union with England, now accommodates Scotland's Criminal Court of Appeal and the Court of Session; this is the place to overhear lawyers communicating with defendants. Accessed via a metal detector in the lobby, the main attraction is the magnificent hammerbeam-roofed Parliament Hall and the Henry Raeburn portraits, although more interesting for us was watching the multiple tandems of lawyers pacing up and down the long room with clients in tow like swimmers doing lengths at a local leisure-centre pool. They're discussing cases and keep on the move for added privacy, although you can hear passing snippets if you sit on the benches at the sides of the hall. I was convinced I heard the word 'poison' and 'you killed her' but my wife claimed I'd been watching too much Taggart and the words were 'person' and 'your kilt, sir'.

OPEN   Mon–Fri 10am–5pm.

AMENITIES

㉗⁰ HAVE AN OPINION ON THE CONTROVERSIAL SCOTTISH PARLIAMENT BUILDING

Scottish Parliament, Horse Wynd, Edinburgh EH99 1SP (© **0131 348 5000**, www.scottish.parliament.uk).

The Scottish Parliament building won the Stirling Prize in 2005 – although its expense (£450 million) upset many. Designed by Catalan architect Enric Miralles, it is made entirely from almost all of Scotland's finest raw materials (except for shortbread). The design was based on Miralles using his well-honed architectural skills and years of training on spatial perception to drop a leafy twig onto a white piece of paper and make the building look like that. Guided tours are free, last one hour and are on the non-business days – Monday, Friday and Saturday. Arrive 20 minutes early and book ahead. Alternatively you can just wander about inside, where you could be forgiven for thinking you are in the local shopping centre, except in the futuristic garden lobby with its fabulous sky-lights. If your children aren't that interested in the difference between reserved and devolved powers, there's a free 10-place crèche for children aged six weeks to five years old (maximum stay four hours) operating between 8am–6pm (*✆* **0131 348 6192**).

OPEN   When Parliament is sitting.

AMENITIES

㉘ STROLL AROUND THE ROYAL BOTANIC GARDEN EDINBURGH

20a Inverleith Row, Edinburgh EH3 5LR (*✆* **0131 552 7171**, www.rbge.org.uk).

Founded in 1670 by Dr Robert Sibbald and Dr Andrew Balfour as a small area to grow medicinal plants, this 70-acre landscaped site was a popular hangout for Sir Conan Doyle, author of the Sherlock Homes stories, and nowadays is a favourite of the current Poet Laureate Caroline Duffy. Highlights include the 70-ft (21m) palm house, where an audio-guided biodiversity tour (50p) leads visitors through time from primitive ferns that pre-date the dinosaurs right up to complex flowering plants like the orchid. There's a memorial garden to the Queen Mother, which houses a grotto celebrating her life that my Royal-obsessed wife admired for a full 30 minutes, and a Rock Garden with more than 4,000 alpine trees. The recently opened £15-million Visitor Centre has interactive displays about global warming and other green issues, a wildlife viewing station with remote cameras to watch the birdlife in the gardens and a Real Life Science Studio, where visiting botanists and gardeners give regular talks on subjects as diverse as fungi to making children's toys out of witch hazel. There are nine Victorian glasshouses of rare plants that cost £5 to visit.

OPEN   Summer 10am–7pm; winter 10am–4pm. The Visitor Centre opens slightly earlier than this for breakfast.

AMENITIES   ☕ 🍴 📷 🅿

272 SEE DAMIEN HIRST'S PICKLED SHEEP AT THE SCOTTISH NATIONAL GALLERY OF MODERN ART

75 Belford Road, Edinburgh EH4 3DR (✆ **0131 624 6200**, www.nationalgalleries. org).

The highlights at this gallery, one of the most important modern-art galleries in Britain, are Damien Hirst's pickled sheep plus work by Tracey Emin, Andy Warhol, Henri Matisse, and David Hockney. The Scottish Colourists are very well represented with paintings by Fergus-son and Peploe. The gallery is home to around 5,000 works from 1900 to the present day, spread over 22 rooms and is based in a gorgeous Neo-Classical school dating from 1830. The building is fronted by impressive sculptures from Barbara Hepworth, Henry Moore and a landscaped ziggurat by Charles Jencks. You can drive to the gallery from the centre of Edinburgh although it's accessed best via an idyllic one-mile (1.6km) walk along the banks of the heron-rich Water of Leith from Stockbridge, just north of the New Town.

OPEN   Daily 10am–5pm.

AMENITIES   ☕ 📷 🅿

273 GET SURREAL AT THE DEAN GALLERY

73 Belford Road, Edinburgh EH4 3DS (✆ **0131 6246200**, www.nationalgalleries.org).

Sister to the Scottish National Gallery of Modern Art (see above), here you'll find a world-class collection of Surrealist art by greats such as Magritte, Picasso, Dalí and Max Ernst (not Bygraves as my wife referred to him in the café). Originally an orphanage designed in 1830 by Thomas Hamilton, the gallery now showcases the recreated studio of sculptor Eduardo Paolozzi; it contains his chair, bed, work and some of the children's toys and robots he gained inspiration from. Because Paolozzi liked to listen to BBC Radio 3 as he sculpted, the radio in his studio is tuned permanently to this station. Backing up the

The War Poets

Siegfried Sassoon and Wilfred Owen returned to active service in France following their stay at Edinburgh's Craiglockhart Psychiatric Hospital, and Owen was killed in 1918. Sassoon, despite his views on war, was promoted to lieutenant and then to acting captain, but relinquished his commission on health grounds in 1919. After the war, he became an acclaimed novelist and was instrumental in bringing Owen's work to the attention of a wider audience. His love life, however, was turbulent. Before marrying Hester Gatty and fathering a child by her, he sought emotional fulfilment from a succession of love affairs with men, including the actor Ivor Novello, the German aristocrat Prince Phillipp of Hesse and effete aristocrat the Honorable Stephen Tennant. Sassoon and Owen are both among the 16 Great War poets commemorated on a slate stone in Westminster Abbey's Poets' Corner.

permanent collection of paintings are temporary exhibits that change every three months.

OPEN   Daily 10am–5pm.

AMENITIES

② SEE THE WAR POETS' COLLECTION

Craiglockhart Library, Edinburgh Napier University, Edinburgh EH14 1DJ (✆ **0131 4554273**, www.napier.ac.uk/warpoets).

Craiglockhart, just south of Edinburgh city centre and famously the meeting place and source of inspiration of war poets Siegfried Sassoon and Wilfred Owen (see box above), was a military psychiatric hospital for the treatment of shell-shocked officers during World War I. Under the enlightened administration of doctors Arthur Brock and William Rivers, the patients could engage in therapy sessions where they talked about their experiences and were kept busy rather than undergoing the brain-fizzing electric-shock treatment still popular elsewhere. Brock persuaded Owen to edit the in-hospital magazine

Hydra and Sassoon to contribute his poems. The library is now home to the War Poets' Collection, full of letters, first editions and other solemn memorabilia associated with these famous names.

OPEN   Term time Mon–Thurs 8:45am–9pm, Fri 8:45am–8pm, Sat–Sun 10am–4pm; outside term time Mon–Thurs 8:45am–8pm, Fri 8:45am–5pm, Sat–Sun 10am–4pm.

AMENITIES

⓶⓻⓹ CHECK OUT THE POLICE-CONED DUKE AT THE GALLERY OF MODERN ART (GOMA)

Royal Exchange Square, Glasgow G1 3AH (📞 **0141 287 3050**, www.glasgow museums.com).

GOMA is based at a Neo-Classical 18th-century mansion and repre-sents the best of Glasgow's contemporary art as well as symbolising the city's flippant attitude to authority (see box below). Highlights include works by Fiona Tan, Richard Hamilton and George Roger as well as Scottish artist Ken Currie. There are free, drop-in children's art classes between 10am–1pm in the studio on the top floor, where activities for 3–10 year olds range from mobile-making to sculpting. The gallery houses a Learning Library in the basement, where there's children's storytelling on Friday afternoons at 2pm.

OPEN   Mon–Wed 10am–5pm; Thurs 10am–8pm; Sat 10am–5pm; Fri, Sun 11am–5pm.

AMENITIES

⓶⓻⓺ HAVE A PICNIC IN HISTORIC COMPANY ON GLASGOW GREEN

Greendyke Street, Glasgow G1 5DD (📞 **0141 287 5064**, www.glasgow. gov.uk).

Park rangers give free guided tours of the city's famous green, where James Watt is reputed to

---

Read About Glasgow for Free

All Glasgow museums run by Visit Glasgow have free leaflets downloadable from www. glasgowmuseums.com. These include the Kelvingrove, Gallery of Modern Art, the Museum of Transport, the People's Palace, the St Mungo Museum of Reli-gious Life and Art, Provand's Lordship, Fossil Grove Museum and the Burrell Collection in Pol-lock Country Park.

have thought up his steam engine brainwave, from the steps of the People's Palace (see below) at 2:30pm every Saturday and Sunday. They tell how Bonnie Prince Charlie reviewed his troops here before the defeat at Culloden in 1745, and how both Rangers and Celtic football teams have roots in this city space. Set amongst some unprepossessing housing estates, Glasgow Green is the oldest in Europe and was gifted to the people of the city by Royal Charter in the 14th century. Over the years, public executions, great Victorian temperance rallies and Chartist protests have all been staged here. The statue of Victorian temperance campaigner Sir William Collins is ironically now a popular late-night rendezvous for local winos. The ranger tours last 1 hour 15 minutes and include a walk along the banks of the river Clyde behind the Winter Gardens (see below) where, while our children fed geese the cheese from their lunch sandwiches, my wife and I contemplated the fates of the 71 people executed on Glasgow Green between 1814 and 1865; the most notorious of these was Dr Pritchard, who murdered his wife and mother-in-law and whose hanging drew crowds of 100,000.

> ### Wellington Meets His Waterloo
>
> The equestrian statue of the Duke of Wellington outside Glasgow's Gallery of Modern Art has a traffic cone more or less permanently on its head. For years the authorities removed the cones, only for them to be replaced (often the following night) by agile rebels climbing the 18-ft (5.5m) statue. Nowadays the cone is often simply left there.

OPEN   All year round.

AMENITIES

❷❼❼ LEARN GLASWEGIAN AT THE PEOPLE'S PALACE & WINTER GARDENS

Glasgow Green, Glasgow G40 1AT (❢ **0141 276 0789**, www.glasgowmuseums.co.uk).

Fronted by the Doulton Fountain, which is the largest terracotta fountain in the world and possibly the largest terracotta anything – the People's Palace is a quirky place to learn some undemanding social history, including Rab C Nesbitt's Glaswegian take on 'Stop complaining, you've got yourself upset now'. ('Quit whingein ye've got yersl in a righ fankle.') There are interactive exhibits about living in the city during the world wars, the old steamy public washhouses, and another entitled 'the bevy and crime'. Elsewhere discover how a family lived in a typical one-room tenement home of the 1930s and take a look at the banana boots Glasgow-born Billy Connolly wore on stage in the 1970s. The top floor of the palace houses the Glasgow History Mural by artist Ken Currie, commemorating the massacre of the Calton Weavers in 1787, an event that marked the birth of trade unionism. Inside the beautiful adjoining Winter Gardens, chirping birds fly among the tropical plants in the elegant Victorian glasshouse.

OPEN   Mon–Thurs, Sat 10am–5pm; Fri, Sun 11am–5pm.

AMENITIES   ☕ 🍴 🅿

㉗ COMPARE YOUR HEIGHT TO A GIRAFFE'S LEG AT THE KELVINGROVE ART GALLERY & MUSEUM

Argyle Street, Glasgow G3 8AG (✆ **0141 276 9599**, www.glasgowmusuems.com).

This museum, arguably the most popular tourist attraction in Scotland, has more than 8,000 objects on display including masterpieces by Dalí, Van Gogh, Monet, Rembrandt and Picasso. Located in picturesque Kelvin Park, the lower halls exhibit European Armour, Natural History, Prehistoric Animals and Egyptian Relics, while it has a fabulous 'Mini Museum' on the ground floor especially for children under five. Here youngsters can try on animal masks, compare their height against a giraffe's leg and see how many children weigh as much as a baby elephant. In discovery centres they can handle bird wings and draw their favourite animals (rabbits), while across the main hall they get to learn about

More Glaswegian Lessons

'Geiswanoyerfagsahvranoot' – could I have a cigarette, I seem to have run out.

'Whitasmasher' – that lady over there is quite attractive to me.

'Nae-borra' – That's quite all right.

'Stoatin aff the grun' – It's raining persistently.

colours and how artists such as Lowry and Constable used them. Organ music (recitals at 1pm daily and 3pm on Sundays) wafting through the beautifully restored Victorian halls lends a calming atmosphere crucial to your sanity when there are hundreds of school children roaming between displays smacking each other with their lunchboxes. There are free guided tours and the park itself, containing a statue of Lord Kelvin (see box, p. 231), is a great place for a picnic and a wander.

OPEN   Mon–Thurs, Sat 10am–5pm; Fri, Sun 11am–5pm.

AMENITIES   ☕ 🎒 🅿

㉒⑨ SEE EDIE MCCREDIE'S WHEELS FROM BALAMORY AT THE MUSEUM OF TRANSPORT

Kelvin Hall, 1 Bunhouse Road, Glasgow G3 8DP (✆ **0141 287 2720**, www.glasgow museums.com).

Telling the story of Scottish transport by land and sea through the ages you can see a display of Scottish-built cars, including every granny's favourite, the Hillman Imp, a recreated 1930s' cobbled street and an old-fashioned underground station. The Clyde Room tells the story of river transport with 300 ship models but our children's favourite activity was ducking under the guard ropes to clamber inside a 1931 vintage Rolls-Royce Phantom Landaulette. Elsewhere there's Edie McCredie's yellow bus from CBeebies favourite *Balamory* and the chance to send a postcard home from the oldest letterbox in the country.

OPEN   Mon–Thurs, Sat 10am–5pm; Fri, Sun 11am–5pm.

AMENITIES   ☕ 🎒 £

㉒⑧⓪ LEARN HOW MARY SHELLEY DREAMT UP FRANKENSTEIN'S MONSTER AT THE NECROPOLIS

50 Cathedral Square, Glasgow G4 0UZ (✆ **0141 552 3145**, www.glasgownecropolis.org).

Modelled on Père Lachaise Cemetery in Paris, there is a monument at the Necropolis to Scottish protestant reformer and firebrand preacher John Knox. Erected in 1825, it denotes the status of cemetery resident (the closer the grave to Knox, the richer the office holder in life). Ranger tours go from the entrance gates (check times ✆ **0141 287 5064**) and cover the problem of grave-robbing prior to the 1832 Act allowing people to donate bodies to medical science (see p. 219). You'll also hear how Mary Shelley of Frankenstein fame came up with her monster after a talk at Glasgow University on galvanism (shocking a corpse to produce physical movement) by Dr Jefferson, and an even stranger tale about Sir Arthur Conan Doyle helping a man called Oscar Slater, who is buried here, clear his name following a wrongful conviction for murder.

OPEN   7am until dusk.

AMENITIES

Fridge Magnate

Famous Scots physicist William Thompson was made 1st Baron Kelvin (after the river that flowed past his home) for inventing the absolute scale of temperature measurement that bears his name. An eccentric, Lord Kelvin asked his second wife to marry him by ship signal and lived in the first house in Britain lit by electricity. He redesigned the interior of the *Great Eastern*, Brunel's ocean-going paddle steamer, and had the world's first fridges, kelvinators, named after him. He also made several daft pronouncements, claiming aeroplanes would never work and that 'radio has no future'.

⟨281⟩ CAUSE AN UNSEEMLY SCENE AT THE ST MUNGO MUSEUM OF RELIGIOUS LIFE AND ART

2 Castle Street, Glasgow G4 0RH (✆ **0141 276 1625**, www.glasgowmuseums.com).

Looking for all the world like a medieval Highland castle, this museum was actually built in 1993. Heroically setting out to explore the importance of religion across the world and thus promote respect between people of different faiths and those with none, St Mungo's contains sculptures of gods, pictures and displays of religious practices such as the Mexican Day of the Dead (believe it or not, it involves eggy bread). Take the lift to the first floor for the view of the Necropolis (see p. 230), and head to the top floor, where there's a hands-on area for children, where our daughter, when it was time to leave, flung herself to the ground and went rigid with anger so we couldn't lift her. Luckily, there is a Zen Garden by the side of the museum, where the perfect proportions and views of Glasgow Cathedral calmed her tantrum and our shattered nerves.

OPEN   Mon–Thurs, Sat 10am–5pm; Fri, Sun 11am–5pm.

AMENITIES   ☕ 🛍 £

㉘ ARGUE ABOUT THAT ALMOND SLICE IN PROVAND'S LORDSHIP

3 Castle Street, Glasgow G4 0RB (*℗* **0141 552 8819**, www.glasgowmuseums.com).

🌂

Opposite St Mungo's and sounding more like an exclusive brand of shortbread, this is the name of the oldest surviving house in Glasgow. The baronial stone house was erected in the 14th century as part of St Nicholas's Hospital and is named after its former resident, the Lord of the Prebend of Barlanark, later corrupted to Lord of the Provand. The house was the home of the city's 18th-century hangman but it fell into disrepair until a partial restoration in 1903. Since then it has been used, variously, as a sweet shop, a drinks factory and a junk shop before becoming a museum in 1983. Inside, a series of echoing, wood panelled rooms are scantily furnished in 14th-century period style, with a frightening wax model of the Lord of the Provand perched on a throne in his chamber.

OPEN   Mon–Thurs, Sat 10am–5pm; Fri, Sun 11am–5pm.

AMENITIES   ✸ £

㉙ ENJOY THE BANTER AT BARRAS MARKET

Gallowgate, Glasgow G4 0TT (*℗* **0141 552 4601**, www.glasgow-barrowland.com).

A mix of covered and open stalls selling everything from antique furniture to computer games, Barras Market (see box, p. 233) has a reputation for selling counterfeit videos, CDs and DVDs before anywhere else in Europe, although crackdowns in recent years have made them scarcer. We bought a copy of the third season of *The Wire* for a tenner and up to episode eight and the showdown between Avon and Stringer Bell, the DVD has (fingers crossed) not skipped once. Cheaper, of course, and much more fun than the swanky shops of

Buchanan Street, the market is a great place to hear a little bit of Glasgow patter (see box, p. 229) as you try and knock down the price. A word of warning – if you're going to haggle, do it with a smile on your face. My wife tried to barter down a trader selling perfumed soap and was told to, 'walk on, lady', by a burly man in a sheepskin coat with two teeth missing.

OPEN Sat–Sun 10am–5pm.

AMENITIES

⓶⓼⓸ BEHAVE LIKE A DUNCE AT SCOTLAND STREET SCHOOL MUSEUM

225 Scotland Street, Glasgow G5 8QB (✆ **0141 2870500**, www.glasgowmuseums. com).

★ ♁ ⚐

The museum is appropriately housed in a former school designed by Charles Rennie Mackintosh between 1903–1906. Here you can write with a quill and wear a dunce's hat as you learn the story of Scottish education from Victorian times to the present day. In what proved a harrowing visit, I was shouted at in front of more than a dozen schoolchildren by a role-playing cane-wielding teacher for mis-spelling the word 'yacht'. Elsewhere in the museum children get to dress as bygone pupils in an old-style classroom, and there are drawing stations where I spent several minutes doodling soothingly irregular circles on a piece of A4 paper. Other highlights include listening to former pupils' recorded recollections of their schooldays and climbing

The History of Barras Market

The market was started by Maggie Russell, the daughter of an Ayrshire policeman, who discovered she had a head for business aged 12 when she looked after a fruit barrow on a street in Parkhead. She saved up enough money to open a fruit shop in the East End of Glasgow and after meeting her husband James McIver, they set up shop renting out horses and carts. They acquired ground in Moncur Street and rented out static barrows to traders on Saturday mornings – so the Barras Market was born in the early 20th century.

red-faced into your car to leave as your wife continues to shake her head about your spelling.

OPEN   Mon–Thurs, Sat 10am–5pm; Fri, Sun 11am–5pm.

AMENITIES   ☕ 🛍 🏪 P

㉘ BASK IN NATURE AT THE FOSSIL GROVE MUSEUM

Victoria Park, Glasgow G14 1BN (📞 **0141 950 1448**, www.glasgowmuseums.com).

In this, the city's prettiest park, you can view the remains of an ancient 350-million-year-old petrified forest. Discovered when this former quarry was being landscaped into a park, the metre-high fossilised tree stumps are preserved in the position they originally grew and are accessed via a viewing balcony. Elsewhere in the 50-acre park, created to mark Queen Victoria's golden jubilee in 1886, there are bowling greens, a boating lake and some formal-type gardens, through which your wife can glide, sniffing the flowers and exclaiming, 'Can you smell that? Isn't it beautiful? That's the spring.' There are also free-access tennis courts and a play area.

OPEN   Daily Easter–Sept 10am–3:30pm.

AMENITIES   P

㉙ VIEW THE BURRELL COLLECTION PRETENDING YOU HAD NOTHING TO DO WITH THE SMELL IN THE DÉGAS ROOM

Pollok Country Park, 2060 Pollokshaws Road, Glasgow G43 1AT (📞 **0141 287 2550**, www.glasgowmusuems.com).

This fabulous gallery was founded on the gift to the city of Sir William Burrell's (see box, p. 235) collection of 9,000 works of art and contains medieval art, tapestries, stained glass, English oak furniture, tapestries, works by Dégas, Cézanne, Epstein and Rodin and even an entire room transported from Burrell's home in the Borders. The L-shaped, light-filled and glass-fronted building housing the gallery in Pollok Park was designed by Barry Gasson and is very family friendly.

There's a quiz and treasure hunt for children, family backpacks and staff are scrupulously friendly with not an eye batted when our daughter had a little accident in the Dégas Room. There are also free guided tours and the park itself is a great place for a picnic.

OPEN   Mon–Thurs, Sat 10am–5pm; Fri, Sun 11am–5pm.

AMENITIES   🍵 🎒 🎧 💷

⑳ CLIMB TO THE TOP OF BEN NEVIS

Glen Nevis Visitor Centre, Glen Nevis, Fort William, Inverness-shire PH33 6ST (✆ **01397 705922**, www.bennevisweather.co.uk).

The Hatch family tried to reach the 4,409-ft (1344m) peak of Britain's highest mountain two years ago, although our push for the summit had to be abandoned due to a fatal underestimation of the mountain as evidenced in our inappropriate provisions – shorts, T-shirts and a bag of pick-n-mix. The most travelled route up the mountain is from the Visitor Centre in Glen Nevis. Cross the river and follow the well-trodden path up the south side of Ben Nevis. The climb can take around six hours for experienced Munro baggers but five hours up and three down is more realistic. The mountain is always a challenge, with gullies laden with snow even in the summer, so take a map (available from the Glen Nevis Visitor Centre), navigation equipment, proper climbing boots and better sustenance than strawberry-flavoured bon-bons. Good pieces of well-honed climbing advice from my great-great-grandfather (see p. 202):

Housing the Burrell Collection

Shipping magnate and philanthropist Sir William Burrell donated his vast collection of antiquities to the city of Glasgow in 1944 on condition that the art work was exhibited in a rural setting. Consequently nothing very much happened with the collection for 40 years until Glasgow City Council was gifted Pollok House and its 360-acre estate by the Maxwell MacDonald family in 1967. An architectural competition was held and winner Barry Gasson was commissioned a custom-build museum. The Burrell Collection finally opened here in 1983.

(1) On a mountain it is better to have and not need than to need and not have and (2) Don't look down.

If you make it up, the rooftop of Ben Nevis offers fabulous views on rare clear days to Perthshire and even the isles of Skye and Mull. There's a reliable daily weather forecast available.

OPEN　Glen Nevis Visitor Centre: daily Apr–June 9am–5pm; Jul–Sept 8:30am–5:30pm; Oct–Mar 9am–3pm.

AMENITIES　🛍 🅿

288 SUNBATHE ON SCOTLAND'S RIVIERA

Nairn, Inverness-shire IV12 (Nairn Tourist Information ℰ **01667 453476**, www.visit nairn.com).

At this award-winning beach, tucked behind sand dunes and the village cricket ground, and with views across the Moray Firth, from the shoreline you can regularly see one of the two resident schools of dolphins in Britain. With the longest sunshine hours in Scotland and low rainfall, the beach at Nairn, described as the 'Brighton of Scotland', has been popular with holidaymakers since Victorian times. Facilities for families include an outdoor children's pool and a playpark alongside the Links Tearoom, although we had the most fun playing hide-and-seek in the dunes before our daughter fell off some driftwood, got sand in her eyes and cried. She was eventually carried to the car under my arm like a plank of driftwood.

OPEN　All year round.

AMENITIES　☕ 🛍 🅿

289 LIVE WITH BENEDICTINE MONKS AT PLUSCARDEN ABBEY

Elgin, Morayshire IV30 8UA (www.pluscardenabbey.org).

☺

If you feel you have a genuine calling to serve the Lord or if you just fancy getting away from it all for a while and rather like Gregorian chanting, you can apply to the warden at Pluscarden for a place on retreat. Due to limited free spaces available – 12 guest rooms for

To Train to Be a Monk Here You Must:

1. be male.

2. be Roman Catholic.

3. have received the Sacrament of Confirmation.

4. be free from all binding obligations of family.

5. probably be having some kind of life crisis.

6. have lived a good, moral, Catholic life for a number of years.

7. have shown that you are capable of earning your own living.

8. normally be between 20 and 35 years of age.

women in the St Scolastica's annexe and 14 for men in a new wing – it's advisable to stress the strength of your faith when writing rather than your need to escape your wife's incessant discussion of *The X Factor*. Guests at the 13th-century abbey share lunch and supper with the monks in the refectory. In order to participate fully in the monastic life, you are expected to attend services and vigils (the first is at 4:45am), do your share of routine chores and maintain the silence code, so no loud mobile calls home about it being 'wickedly peaceful here'.

OPEN   Daily 4:30am–8pm.

AMENITIES   Lots of peace and quiet

290 SEE INTO AN OSPREY NEST AT THE DAVID MARSHALL LODGE VISITOR CENTRE

Queen Elizabeth Forest Park, Duke's Pass on the A821, Aberfoyle, Perthshire FK8 3SX (✆ **01877 382258**, www.forestry.gov.uk).

Part commercial forest, part ancient woodland, this 50,000 acre area was designated a park in 1953 to mark the coronation of Queen Elizabeth II. Treats along the scenic Loch Achray Trail include views of the summit of Ben Venue, the chance to see falcons soaring overhead and a glimpse of a red squirrel from a forest hide. Before you set off on this four-mile (6.5km) way-marked yomp through the Achray Forest, check out the osprey's nest near Lake Mentieth, visible through remote cameras at the Visitor Centre. The best time to see the chicks is July and August. Other wildlife on the walk includes buzzards, a red kite, eagles and a family who chucked their sandwich wrappers into the bushes after their picnic. There is a short 10-minute walk to a waterfall for those feeling less energetic, and for even lazier people who want to explore the Achray Forest by car, there's the Three Lochs Forest Drive. Open from April through to September, this follows seven-and-a-half miles (12km) of winding forest track and is accessed from the main road a mile or so north of the lodge.

 OPEN   Daily Feb–May 10am–5pm; June–Aug 10am–6pm; Sept–Oct 10am–5pm, Nov–Dec 10am–4pm.

 AMENITIES   ☕ 🛍 £

㉛ STROLL IN THE FOOTSTEPS OF WORDSWORTH AT HERMITAGE WALK

One mile (1.6km) north of Dunkeld off the A9, Perthshire PH8.

As parents to a toddler and a shilly-shallying five year old, we loved our gentle stroll along the rhododendron-clad banks of the river Braan to an idyllic waterfall that's overlooked by Britain's tallest tree – a magnificent 60-ft (18m) Douglas-fir. Once part of the Scottish Grand Tour, this three-quarter mile (1.2km) walk has been enjoyed by nature lovers (Wordsworth wandered lonely as a cloud here) for more than 200 years and what's more it's ideal for buggy-pushers apart from the tree roots before the stone-arched bridge. The focal point of the walk is the Black Linn Falls next to Ossian's Hall, a Victorian folly with a concealed door and an echoey chamber for our daughter to shout nonsense inside. Look at the woodland pool across the bridge, which, bathed in white petals when we visited, looked so like the Elysian backdrop of a Roman epic that we half-expected to encounter Narcissus falling in love with his reflection. Britain's tallest tree (now under dispute – there's a rival near Inverness) is unmarked to stop trophy hunters hacking chunks off, so you'll have to guess which giant it is. A little further along the banks of the Braan is Ossian's Cave, basically a roof over some large rocks that looks like the makeshift home of a hermit, giving the walk its name.

OPEN   All year round.

AMENITIES   P

292 THE FORTINGALL YEW TREE

Churchyard, Fortingall, Perthshire PH15 2NQ (www.forestry.gov.uk).

The yew tree of legend, traditionally a revered Christian symbol, is found in the churchyard of Fortinghall's village kirk. According to local mythology, Pontius Pilate was the son of a local Scottish woman fathered by a Roman ambassador and apparently played under this tree as a child before rising to become Prefect of Judea (AD26) and authorising the crucifixion of Jesus Christ. Impossible to age accurately because its trunk has hollowed with age – and actually not that impressive to look at – Fortingall's yew is protected by a fence and is estimated to be anything up to 9,000 years old. The journey to see the tree is worth the effort as it's possibly the earth's oldest living organism. Its massive trunk, which measured 52 feet (16m) in girth in 1769, has fragmented into separate stumps, thanks to souvenir-hunting in the 19th century. There's no Visitor Centre and not much on the information boards, making it surprisingly quiet when we visited.

OPEN   All year round.

AMENITIES   P

293 SEE THE GREATEST SCOTTISH VISTA AT THE QUEEN'S VIEW VISITOR CENTRE

Off the B8019, Tay Forest District, Strathtummel by Pitlochry, Perthshire PH16 5NR (© 01796 473123, www.forestry.gov.uk).

Perched high above Loch Tummel and about 100 metres up a short hill from the Visitor Centre, an incredible vantage point (avoided by big tour buses) gives a spectacular view up the spine of Scotland all the way to the mountains around Glencoe. Named after Robert the Bruce's wife Isabella, this spot was popularised by Queen Victoria when she visited Loch Tummel in 1866. There are steep drops without railings so if your children are small, curious and have the sense of balance of a three-legged chair, be careful. You can get a decent cup of tea in the outside café by the Visitor Centre.

OPEN   Visitor Centre end Mar–mid-Nov 10am–6pm.

AMENITIES

㉙ SEE JUPITER AT THE PAISLEY MUSEUM & COATS OBSERVATORY

High Street, Paisley, Renfrewshire PA1 2BA (📞 **0141 889 2013**).

★

Stare at Jupiter and Mars through a 12-ft (3.7m) Grubb telescope, look out for shooting stars and, somewhat bizarrely, see the country's most prestigious collection of Victorian shawls. The Observatory holds guided star-gazing sessions every Tuesday and Thursday night from 6:30pm–9pm between October and March, although if the weather is poor and the dome cannot be opened, there are free Planetarium shows about the solar system instead. There's an education room, where film from the Hubble telescope can be seen, and talks are often given about astronomical subjects. The Paisley Museum is worth visiting to see its nationally acclaimed ceramics collection, the three or four art exhibitions staged each year, and the stash of Victorian shawls (see box at left) from 1805–1870. Dan the resident weaver demonstrates his paisley-weaving skills on a loom if you're there between Tuesday and Friday.

> ### Wrap It Up
>
> The paisley pattern – a recurring droplet-shaped vegetable motif – was devised in India but became associated with Paisley after the Scottish town started mass-producing shawls made in this style. They became hugely popular from the 1840s onwards when Queen Victoria bought some to wear at state functions to give the ailing town a PR boost. Nobody is really sure who is to blame for transferring this pattern to the tie, although I have grave suspicions about Rick Astley.

OPEN   Tues–Sat 10am–5pm; Sun 2pm–5pm.

AMENITIES

⓶⁹⁵ GO DOLPHIN-SPOTTING

Chanonry Point, Fortrose, Ross-shire IV11 (www.undiscoveredscotland.co.uk).

★ ♚ ☺

This spit of land on the east coast extends into the Moray Firth and is purportedly the best dolphin-watching spot in Europe. Although we saw nothing more than some broken water in the middle distance and a couple of Ecoventure boats, on a good clear day you can apparently spot a pod of 130 bottle-nosed dolphins and occasionally seals, porpoises and minke whales. They come here for the salmon that follow the tides up-river and are seen throughout the year. The beach, in the shadow of Chanonry lighthouse, has a small patch of sand for children to build castles on while you stand sentinel on the water's edge debating whether each ripple in the water is the dolphin fin that means you can get back in the car and drive off because you're very cold. Do take binoculars and also a flask of hot tea to keep out the biting wind. To find Chanonry Point drive to the end of the village of Fortrose and follow the golf club signs. The best time to come is the two hours before low tide and at the changing of the tides.

OPEN   All year round.

AMENITIES   ⛱ ♭

⓶⁹⁶ CURE YOUR RASH AT THE MUNLOCHY CLOOTIE WELL

Near Munlochy, Ross-shire IV8 (www.undiscoverdscotland.co.uk/munlochy).

☺

Now this is not everyone's cup of tea, but if you are a reasonably ghoulish person, are in the area and fancy scaring yourself so witless you don't sleep for three nights, we suggest you visit this pre-Christian magical spring on the south side of the Black Isle along the A832. A few miles after Cromarty and near Munlochy, you'll spot what looks like an outdoor laundry operation by the roadside. Reminiscent of something from a scary episode of *Wire in the Blood*, this clootie well is a natural spring hidden among trees with branches draped in rotting clothing. Superstition has it that if a sick person leaves a piece of clothing (a clootie) next to this magical spring, the illness will abate as the clothing decays. Needless to say my fearful wife, crossing herself furiously like a superstitious bog-woman, refused to get out of the car. I left a £15 driving glove hanging over one of the branches in the hope of curing an itch at the back of my knees.

OPEN   All year round.

AMENITIES   ♟

㉗ VISIT ROB ROY'S GRAVE

Balquhidder Church, Balquhidder, Stirlingshire FK19 8PA.

The churchyard of this tumbledown 17th-century church is where the legendary cattle-rustler, outlaw and Jacobite rebel Rob Roy is buried. Glamorised by Daniel Defoe (1723), Sir Walter Scott (1818) and in two Hollywood movies, Rob Roy lies beneath a headstone reading 'MacGregor despite them'. Also buried here is the wife of the David Icke of his day, the Reverend Robert Kirk (see box, p. 243), who was, if his story is to be believed (and yes we do believe it – every word of it), spirited away to a fairy kingdom upon his death. Kirk himself was once the reverend here.

OPEN   All year round.

AMENITIES   ♟

㉘ GO UFO SPOTTING

Bonnybridge, Stirlingshire FK4 (www.spookystuff.co.uk).

☺

If the truth is out there about aliens, then the best place to go looking for it is Bonnybridge. This small town is the world's hotspot for UFO sightings, with 300 reported annually and over half of its 6,500 residents allegedly having seen one. Twinned with Roswell in New Mexico, USA, where an alien spaceship is said to have crashed in Area 51 in 1947, the town is part of the mysterious Falkirk Triangle covering an area between Stirling and Edinburgh dubbed 'the alien landing strip'. It all started in 1992 when James Walker noticed strange lights in the sky. At first he thought they were stars but was startled when they moved to assume a triangle shape. Since then, UFO sightings have been coming in thick and fast. Local politician Billy Buchanan even wrote to the Prime Minister and the Ministry of Defence demanding that the sightings be investigated. Some sightings have been filmed

Kirk & Dagger

Minister of Balquhidder until 1685, the Reverend Robert Kirk was the first man to translate the Bible into Gaelic before he became convinced that fairies were real and he had been chosen to interpret their thoughts. By 1690 Kirk was writing *The Secret Commonwealth of the Elves, Fauns and Fairies*, claiming that the 'wee folk' communicated through whistling, wore plaid and stole milk from cows. The fairies must have resented these revelations because in May 1692 he was killed by a heart attack while his wife was pregnant. After his funeral, Kirk materialised before the minister's first cousin, saying he had been taken by the fairies. To return him to the land of the living, the local laird must attend Kirk's son's baptism and throw a knife across the room when Kirk appeared. The ceremony duly took place and near the end the Rev duly strode into the room but the laird was so stunned he didn't hurl the knife. Kirk disappeared and was not seen again. His fairy manuscript is now preserved at Edinburgh University after it was rediscovered in 1815; its claims so delighted Sir Walter Scott that he made his headquarters at Kirk's old home at Aberfoyle when he came to the Trossachs.

and range from orange lights to blue-white lights and even a flying saucer landing on moorland. Alien abductions have also been reported. Theories about the sightings range from the number of military bases in the area to the local councillor stoking up hysteria to attract tourism. There is currently talk of building a UFO Information Centre to boost tourism.

❷❾❾ TEST THE WHISPERING WALLS OF THE HAMILTON MAUSOLEUM

Strathclyde Country Park, Hamilton, South Lanarkshire ML3 6BJ (✆ **01698 328232**, www.southlanarkshire.gov.uk).

The interior of the last resting place of the family of the Dukes of Hamilton has the longest-lasting echo of any building in the world (five seconds), a phenomenon dramatically demonstrated by our daughter shouting, 'Charlie wet his pants his pants his pants his pants his pants', very loudly during our free tour. Built in the grounds of the now-demolished Hamilton Palace, the mausoleum's high stone vault is responsible for the acoustic, which also gives rise to the whispering walls, where two people stand at opposite ends of one of the curved interior walls, facing into the wall, and hold a whispered conversation. Normally there's a charge of £1.15 per adult and £0.70 per child for pre-booked tours of the 123-ft (37.5m) high mausoleum, although on the second weekend in September it's free, thanks to the South Lanarkshire Doors Open Season. Book tours via Lowpark Museum on the number above. Following your visit, access is free to nearby Chatelherault Country Park, full of walks, cycle routes and a children's play-park.

OPEN   Tours Wed, Sat, Sun at 2pm. Pre-booking is essential. Call ahead as times vary.

AMENITIES   P

⑨ EXPERIENCE EVIL MALEVOLENCE ON SANDWOOD BAY

Near Blairmore, Sutherland IV27 4RT (Durness Tourist Information Centre ℰ **01971 511259**, www.undiscoveredscotland.co.uk).

With its famous Am Buachaille sea-stack, this beautiful pink sandy stretch on the north-west tip of Scotland is the UK's remotest beach and possibly the only one with a resident ghost – a bearded sailor washed up during the Spanish Armada, who wanders forlornly in ragged breeches looking for his lost ship. South of Cape Wrath, it takes two hours to walk four miles (6.5km) down to the beach through forbidding moorland near the hamlet of Blairmore – follow the well-trodden path leading from the gravel car park in Blairmore. In the two hours we were here, we saw one surfer braving the North Atlantic waves but generally speaking you'll be alone with the ghost and the ruined cottage that overlooks Sandwood Loch. 'Ravishing' mermaids have been spotted on the rocks here over the years but there were none when we visited. To keep the children amused make sand-castles and then persuade them to look for the buried treasure from

Spanish galleons lying beneath the sand. But be warned – leave before daylight dies, as sinister sensations of being watched by evil spirits have been reported here. At least that's what we told the children when they were dragging their feet on the long walk back to the car.

OPEN   All year round.

INDEX